ELIZABETH GASKELL
A PORTRAIT IN LETTERS

I you don't send me those Dorkings by some of the Gaskells! Ughughe ughughe.

Nature intended me for a gypsey - bachelor; that I am sure of. Not an old maid for they are particular & fidgety, and tidy, and punctual. — but a gypsey - bachelor. I get up early. I breakfast with a book in my hand. I go out and feed all the animals, especially Tommy who is getting fatter than ever: and Fairy, who has had her eye bitten out, poor little mortal, and lives in a state of perpetual wink. I have set 2 hens on 2.4 eggs this morning, at which I am very proud. I go out and plant cabbages, — Cincinnatus did something to turnips, didn't he, Mr Fox? but mine are cabbages. Some great man dibbled about them, I think. Well! I am like that great man! 2 feet apart is the right distance. Then the post comes, and I have to write to every body; and feel like an ass between a great number of bundles of hay, with so many invitations, here there, & every where.

A typical specimen of Elizabeth Gaskell's dashing handwriting from a letter to her young artist friend, Eliza Fox, daughter of the journalist and M.P., W. J. Fox. (Three-quarters original size.)

Elizabeth Gaskell

A portrait in letters

J. A. V. CHAPPLE

assisted by JOHN GEOFFREY SHARPS

MANCHESTER UNIVERSITY PRESS

Text of letters © MANCHESTER UNIVERSITY PRESS
Other material © J. A. V. CHAPPLE 1980

First published by MANCHESTER UNIVERSITY PRESS
Oxford Road, Manchester M13 9PL

British Library cataloguing in publication data

Chapple, John Alfred Victor
Elizabeth Gaskell.
1.   Gaskell, Elizabeth Cleghorn – Correspondence
2.   Novelists, English – 19th century –
Correspondence
I.   Sharps, John Geoffrey
823'.8   PR4711.A4

ISBN 0–7190–0799–2

Printed in Great Britain by
WILLMER BROTHERS LIMITED, ROCK FERRY, MERSEYSIDE

CONTENTS

LIST OF ILLUSTRATIONS

ACKNOWLEDGEMENTS ARE DUE to the following: Newcastle upon Tyne Literary and Philosophical Society for 5; Manchester Central Public Library for 6, 7, 11 and 12; Sophia Smith Collection, Smith College for 15; John Rylands University Library Manchester for 16.

Numbers 1, 2, 3 and 4 were taken from Mrs E. H. Chadwick, *Mrs Gaskell* (new edition 1913); numbers 8, 9 and 10 from *A History of the Family of Holland,* ed. W. F. Irvine; frontispiece and 13 from manuscripts in the possession of J. G. Sharps and J. A. V. Chapple respectively.

TO KATHLEEN BOLTON

INTRODUCTION

ELIZABETH GASKELL (née Stevenson) was almost forty before she made any impression upon the reading public. She was born in Chelsea on 29 September 1810; she did not publish her first book, *Mary Barton*, until 1848. This had a considerable impact and was followed by a stream of novels and stories. Of these only *Cranford* was anything like as popular as the fiction of her more famous contemporaries – Dickens, Thackeray, Trollope and George Eliot. Together with a distinguished biography of her friend Charlotte Brontë, it was the basis of her reputation in the twentieth century. In recent years, however, there has been a dramatic reassessment of her literary stature. The interest of the early industrial novels is stressed, especially by those who are politically at odds with her; the turn to biography in mid-career is seen as a useful reinforcement of her powers of realistic portrayal; a tender story like *Cousin Phillis* is commended for the response it manifests to complex changes in society as well as for the artistic perfection of its form. The novel she had all but completed at the time of her sudden death on 12 November 1865, *Wives and Daughters*, receives perhaps the highest praise of all. 'It looks back to Jane Austen, the great writer of serious comedy, and forward to George Eliot, the great writer of witty tragedy, and seems to bridge the gap between them', declared Laurence Lerner in his introduction to the Penguin edition of 1969. Even allowing for the impetus of an epigram, the company a fine modern critic now intends her to keep is unmistakably superior.

We resist these claims or listen uneasily, half-convinced. So often her writing emerges without complication from the play between her character, her private circumstances and the wider society in which she lived. In almost everything she wrote we are aware of undigested prejudices and occasional failures of perception; we also glimpse, again and again, the shimmer of truth – her own truth without a doubt but permanent and universal in its value. To speak justly of her art we need to examine her life; and this happens to survive most remarkably of all in several hundred revealing letters. Some are formal, some are tired, some are dull. A glance at the cursive flow of her handwriting is enough to show that in the great majority she is her natural impulsive self, blessed with an animation that catches the tones of genuine conversation and runs easily into living speech:

To Parthenope Nightingale, 17 October 1854 (214)[1]

My dear Miss Nightingale,

You can't think how generous I feel myself in giving you a whole sheet of paper, when I have but two left; exclusive of foolscap, all ready paged. But I want to send you your fern, and I want to tell you that Mr Sam Gaskell *is* at No 2 St James Place, and will be glad at any time & in any way to give Miss Florence Nightingale any information in his power. *Also*, (as they tag banns of marriage on together without much connexion,) to say that I have never heard from the Glovers, to whom I wrote on the day I heard from Miss F. Nightingale; but then I desired them to consider with, & consult their medical man before they came to any decision. Don't let her think me ungrateful, because I don't bore her with a grateful letter before I can tell her what they settle to do. I went to see 'Widow' Littlewood on Saty. She was out, gone to Mrs Smedley's; but the daughter was in, with whom I sate some time. Then I went down to the river, *our* old walk; and coming back I gathered ever so many mushrooms, of which I generously made a present to Mrs Littlewood, whom I met in the meadow. She was so very much obliged to me for giving her what was not mine to give, that I felt ashamed of myself, and had to confess to Mr Nightingale. Sunday I meant to go to Church; but it rained and I did not, so my good intention went to pave the place where the thermometer stands high. Yesterday – Oh! how I wrote! and in the middle, to clear my brains which were becoming addled, I went with Soyer to the pig and Glass: made Mrs Radford's acquaintance; then went on and saw 'Jane', who was downstairs & considerably better, though obliged to give up nursing on one side, & feeding her baby on *sago*, which I disapproved of, rather to the old lady's annoyance. The old lady burst in (as a test of my right to judge of baby's food I believe) with 'Did I know *Lady Adeliga*?' Surname not given. And I think she looked upon me & my advice contemptuously when she heard I did not.

She was then staying at the Nightingale's home, Lea Hurst near Matlock, whilst the family were away. A few days later she again took time off from writing her novel *North and South* to send another letter to Florence's sister. It opens in a completely different vein:

To Parthenope Nightingale, 20 October 1854 (215)

All I can say is that the light *is* shining bright on the Cross this morning that I receive your letter, and that God, whose angel has led her hitherto, will have her in His holy keeping. I, not having my eyes dimmed with the anxieties of affection, *see* this as if it were a visible march to heaven; but I can understand how you tremble in the midst of all your thankfulness *for* her, and *in* her.

Like almost everybody else, she had been enormously impressed by the news that the Secretary at War had formally asked Florence Nightingale to take the first party of nurses to the hospital at Scutari. The *Times* correspondent had just revealed the horrors endured by the sick and wounded in the Crimean War; Florence's official appointment, sensational in its day, answered the mood of the nation. Yet within a page or so the crusade is forgotten, or left in its proper place, and there is another humorous touch. 'I went', she tells Parthenope, 'to Crich yesterday; & called on Mrs *Diarrhea* (for I don't know her other name,) who is much better, and sent her "love", & the "medecine [sic] did her a power of good".'

Given this kind of flexibility of mind and spirit it is not surprising to find that she is capable of criticising the living legend, however much she thrills at the thought of Florence's extraordinary activities:

To Emily Shaen (née Winkworth), 27 October 1854 (217)[2]
Speaking of the cholera in the Middlesex Hospital, she said, 'The prostitutes came in perpetually – poor creatures staggering off their beats! It took worse hold of them than of any. One poor girl, loathsomely filthy, came in, and was dead in four hours. I held her in my arms and I heard her saying something. I bent down to hear. "Pray God, that you may never be in the despair I am in at this time." I said, "Oh, my girl, are you not now more merciful than the God you think you are going to? Yet the real God is far more merciful than any human creature ever was, or can ever imagine." ' Then, again, I never heard such capital mimicry as she gave of a poor woman, who was brought in one night, when F. N. and a porter were the only people up – every other nurse worn out for the time. Three medical students came up, smoking cigars, and went away. F. N. undressed the woman, who was half tipsy but kept saying, 'You would not think it, ma'am, but a week ago I was in silks and satins; in silks and satins, ma'am, dancing at Woolwich. Yes! ma'am, for all I'm so dirty I am draped in silks and satins sometimes. Real French silks and satins.' This woman was a nurse earning her five guineas a week with nursing ladies. She got better. . . .
    That text always jarred against me, that 'Who is my mother and my brethren?' – and there is just that jar in F. N. to me. She has no friend –

she wants none. She stands perfectly alone, half-way between God and His creatures. She used to go a great deal among the villagers here, who dote upon her. One poor woman lost a boy seven years ago of white swelling in his knee, and F. N. went twice a day to dress it. The boy shrank from death; F. N. took an engraving from some Italian master, a figure of Christ as the Good Shepherd carrying a little lamb in His arms, and told the boy that so tenderly would Christ carry him, etc. The mother speaks of F. N. – did to me only yesterday – as of a heavenly angel. Yet the father of this dead child – the husband of this poor woman – died last 5th of September, and I was witness to the extreme difficulty with which Parthe induced Florence to go and see this childless widow *once* while she was here; and though the woman entreated her to come again she never did. She will not go among the villagers now because her heart and soul are absorbed by her hospital plans, . . .

A recently discovered portion of this same letter to Emily Shaen points a remarkable contrast :

And before I forget, I've got that poor Emma Gallagher (that girl I had in the summer) *cleaned* most thoroughly and decently clothed waiting for a place at our house. She is 16 but sharp and good for her age; I don't think she would do for London perhaps; but I should like her to have some nice place. She was starving at home.

Mrs Gaskell's admiration for her great contemporary was not unbounded, precisely because in her eyes Florence Nightingale could neglect individuals when intent upon larger solutions to social problems :

She and I had a grand quarrel one day. She is, I think, too much for institutions, sisterhoods and associations, and she said if she had influence enough not a mother should bring up a child herself; there should be crêches for the rich as well as the poor. If she had twenty children she would send them all to a crêche, seeing, of course, that it was a well-managed crêche. That exactly tells of what seems to me *the* want – but then this want of love for individuals becomes a *gift* and a very rare one, if one takes it in conjunction with her intense love for the *race*; her utter unselfishness in serving and ministering. I think I have told you all – even to impressions – but she is really so extraordinary a creature that impressions may be erroneous, and anything like a judgment of her must be

presumptuous, and what a letter I have written! Only if you are on the
sofa it won't tire you as it might do if you were busy. . . .

Your own grateful and affectionate Lily
My duty to Will, and dear love to Maggie, bless her.

Elizabeth Gaskell was a woman of acute sensibilities and usually shrewd intelligence, both of which find ample scope in these freely written letters. She
did her best to make them live upon the page; they are in consequence a mixture
of swift, intuitive felicities and rash judgments. There is always salt in her
utterances, sometimes plain error. But it is very clear that she constantly tried
to be just, to convey the totality of her responses to experience. She once wrote
that Charlotte Brontë's father was 'not dramatic enough in his perceptions to
see how miserable others might be in a life that to him was all-sufficient'. Her
own sympathetic thoughtfulness and care are exactly the opposite.

Nowadays, we are inclined to look for half-stated or implied attitudes in
letters written during the reign of Victoria, as well as explicit statements. It is,
for instance, fascinating to examine some of Elizabeth Gaskell's reactions to
the women's movement of her time. When in 1850 she was about to move to
a much larger house in Manchester ('while so many are wanting'), her conscience nagged. She tried to tell herself that it was her husband's business to
decide, 'and his feeling it right' ought to be her rule. 'And so it is', she continues, 'only that does not quite do' (69). Yet asked to take a stand against
what even Queen Victoria was prepared to call 'the yoke of a married woman',
she could not send an unqualified response:

To Eliza ('Tottie') Fox, 1 January 1856 (276)
My dearest Tottie,
    You ask for the petition back again without loss of time, so I send it
you although today certainly I shan't be able to write a long letter. I don't
think it is very definite, and *pointed*; or that it will do much good, – for
the Turnkey's objection (vide Little Dorrit) 'but if they wish to come over
her, how then can you legally tie it up' &c. will be a stronger difficulty
than they can legislate for; a husband can coax, wheedle, beat or tyran-
nize his wife out of something and no law whatever will help this that I
see. (Mr Gaskell begs Mr Fox to draw up a bill for the protection of
husbands against wives who will spend all their earnings) However our
sex is badly enough used and legislated *against*, there's no doubt of *that* –
so though I don't see the definite end proposed by these petitions I'll sign.

Her practical objections were valid enough, but there were almost certainly
other considerations at work. The founder of a committee to collect Petitions

for a Married Women's Property Bill was Barbara Leigh Smith, a pioneer advocate of rights for women. Writing of her in a later letter, Mrs Gaskell noted that she was 'illegitimate-cousin of Hilary Carter, F Nightingale, – & nas their nature in her'. Then she added, significantly: 'She is – I think in consequence of her birth, a strong fighter against the established opinions of the world, – which always goes against my – what shall I call it? – *taste* – (that is not the word,) but I can't help admiring her noble bravery, and respecting – while I don't personally *like* her' (461). For once the thoughts are as contorted as the expression, a sure sign that there was a strong emotional undertow. Elizabeth Gaskell was struggling to define her own, more complex view of a woman's role in life; unsuccessfully here, but at least in an attempt to be true to her whole self.

She undoubtedly lacked hard-edged radicalism; she did learn to give more rein to her basic feminism. When in 1850 she and Charlotte Brontë met that most masterful of Victorian males, Sir James Kay-Shuttleworth, her language was caustic but still inhibited:

To Eliza Fox, 27 August 1850 (79)
> She and I had much of our day to ourselves, with the exception of some lectures on art, and 'bringing ourselves down to a lower level,' and 'the beauty of expediency,' from that eminently practical man Sir James, who has never indulged in the exercise of any talent which could not bring him a tangible and speedy return. However he was very kind; and really took trouble in giving us, Miss Brontë especially, good advice; which she received with calm resignation.

She could not bring herself to wield the same verbal cutlass as Charlotte Brontë, who hacked without restraint in her account of the visit:

> Sir James was all the while as kind and friendly as he could be . . . The substratum of his character is hard as flint. To authors as a class (the imaginative portion of them) he has a natural antipathy. Their virtues give him no pleasure – their faults are wormwood and gall in his soul: he perpetually threatens a visit to Haworth – may this be averted!

Sir James was patronising two women whose sense of their own identity as successful authors was by then of some years' standing. Yet as guests and also, one is sure, as women, they were forced to behave submissively.

In later years Elizabeth's attitude hardened, though she never attained the mutinous bluntness of Charlotte Brontë. After Charlotte's death she wrote to their publisher about Sir James's part in her research for the *Life* in relatively severe terms:

To George Smith, 25 July 1856 (297)
I have had a very successful visit to Haworth. – I went from Gawthrop, accompanied by Sir J P. K Shuttleworth, to whom it is evident that both Mr Brontë & Mr Nicholls look up. – & who is not prevented by the fear of giving pain from asking in a peremptory manner for whatever he thinks desirable. He was extremely kind in forwarding all my objects; and coolly took actual possession of many things while Mr Nicholls was saying he could not possibly part with them. . . . Sir J. P K S. coolly introduced the subject of the portrait, as if he had known nothing of Mr Nicholls' reluctance, asked Mr Brontë's leave to have it photographed, whh was readily granted with a reference to Mr Nicholls for an ultimate decision, so then Sir James said 'Oh! I know Mr Nicholls will grant it – and we will trust to Mrs Gaskell to send over a photographer from Manchester, for I dare say he would not like to part with the portrait, – ' & he so completely took it for granted that Mr Nicholls had no time to object. But I can not feel quite comfortable in absolutely wresting things from him by mere force of words.

When Sir James, despite his natural antipathy to imaginative literature, actually produced a very reasonable novel himself and wanted to get it published, Elizabeth Gaskell bubbled over:

To George Smith, 5 April 1860 (462)
Mrs Smith is very very charming & kind and sweet & pretty, – and you are a bright warm genial witty man – but – I (privately) don't believe that Sir J. P. K. Shuttleworth seeks your acquaintance & society for any of these reasons, simple & pure – (he has generally a double set of motives for all his actions –) but he has a novel, – partly read to Mrs Nicholls the last time she was at Gawthrop, – partly to me, – *wholly* to many of his friends – a novel of Lancashire society, whh is at present in MS & which he wants you to publish I have no doubt. He is too vain a man to care to encounter a direct refusal of this story, – & will sound you on the subject I have no doubt before long. He is a clever painstaking man, and has really laboured hard to make this novel a good picture of country Lancashire society – manufacturers touching on the domains of squires of strong character & old family &c – but sooner or later, take my word for it, you or Mrs Smith will hear this subject gently touched upon. Marianne [Mrs Gaskell's

daughter] begs you will watch his left eye, & provide him with Savoy biscuits.

Her fun characterises Sir James, who was not without good qualities, far more effectively than simple denigration could. She was also capable of maintaining a precarious but real balance of attitudes; her growing sense of feminine independence never became total or unrestrained.

In the epic age of social progress for women, she was fully aware that some had talents they must not hide and powers to work for others that should not be denied. This is clearly affirmed in the sixteenth chapter of her *Life of Charlotte Brontë*,[3] but the same truth emerges just as authentically in her letters:

To Emily Shaen, 27 October 1854 (217)
   Well! I vow I won't write letters; but it is no use, and I must answer you. You *have* done me so much good, dearest Nem; more than anyone else in my life – (that I'm aware of) except my own darling Aunt Lumb and Miss Mitchell. I always feel raised higher when I'm near you, *held up* in a calmer and better atmosphere than my usual anxious, poor, impatient one. One person may act on some and not on others – it's no cause for despair because, darling, you can't work on everybody; very few *can* – only such people as F. N. . . . I'll enclose you two pieces of Mr S. Gaskell to show how *he's* carried off his feet. When I *told* him of Miss F. N. before he saw her, he called her my 'enthusiastic young lady' and irritated me by speaking very contemptuously of her; as well-meaning, etc. Now here's his first piece and his second piece, and *you need not return 'em.*

We can feel her triumphant delight. Her favourite brother-in-law, to whom she could speak more openly than to her own husband[4] and who was infinitely more congenial than Sir James Kay-Shuttleworth, had been forced to recognise transcendent power in a woman – even though in another context that woman was not above criticism, as we have seen. We remember one of her jokes against – or with? – Miss Jenkyns in *Cranford*: she 'would have despised the modern idea of women being equal to men. Equal, indeed! she knew they were superior'. She inevitably goes on to mention the all too predictable fact that Florence Nightingale's father thought she had 'quite a man's mind', without contradicting it in any way; but her intuitions were obscurely telling her that there would have to be changes in attitude as well as in law.

Reading these letters of Elizabeth Gaskell we discover that in this, as in many other respects, new social values were gradually evolving. The correspondence reveals what we now rather grandly call 'the emergent consciousness of the age', often implicitly and accidentally. She was more responsive to various forces for change and more in tune with the actual movement of history than she can always have realised as she penned these lively pages to friends and relations. No reader of her fiction will be at all surprised to find how sensitive she was to the complex movement of the human spirit in time and place: it is one of her major themes. But to this movement her letters are more informal and, on occasions, far more subtle witnesses.

With the exception of some recently discovered letters, the texts below have been quoted from *The Letters of Mrs Gaskell*, edited by J. A. V. Chapple and Arthur Pollard (Manchester University Press 1966, Harvard University Press 1967). For this selection we have deleted purely scholarly details and accepted the great majority of the main edition's conjectural dates, though it is worth bearing in mind that Elizabeth Gaskell only rarely gave a complete date. We have made a few slight changes for ease in reading, but in general the texts are faithful representations of the original letters with their characteristic mis-spellings, slips and errors.

The notes at the end are as brief as possible, indicating sources of new or unusual information in this context. Robert L. Selig has provided an annotated bibliography of standard secondary works, *Elizabeth Gaskell: a Reference Guide* (G. K. Hall & Co., Boston, Mass. 1977). J. G. Sharps gives full references in his *Mrs. Gaskell's Observation and Invention: a Study of Her Non-Biographic Works* (Linden Press 1970) for most matters treated in the commentary below. More recently W. Gérin has published a biography (Clarendon Press 1976) and A. Easson a study of the life and works of Elizabeth Gaskell (Routledge & Kegan Paul 1979). We also draw attention in particular to the sadly neglected *Letters and Memorials of Catherine Winkworth*, edited by Susanna Winkworth and Margaret J. Shaen (2 vols. privately circulated, Clifton 1883–6), an essential source for which the later condensation, M. J. Shaen's *Memorials of Two Sisters*, is not an adequate substitute.

ACKNOWLEDGEMENTS

We thank Mrs Trevor Jones, Mrs Gaskell's descendant in the direct line, for permission to publish her letters and the many private and institutional owners of them for allowing access to their texts when the *Letters of Mrs Gaskell* was being prepared. We are also indebted to the following holders of hitherto unpublished letters and documents:

Bibliothèque de l'Institut de France
Brontë Parsonage Museum, Haworth
Brotherton Collection, Leeds University Library
Church of the Divine Unity, Newcastle upon Tyne
Houghton Library, Harvard University
Keele University Library (with acknowledgements to Messrs Josiah
    Wedgwood & Sons Ltd, Barlaston, Stoke-on-Trent)
Newcastle upon Tyne Literary and Philosophical Society
Pierpont Morgan Library, New York
Principal Registry, Somerset House
Rutgers University Library, New Brunswick
Saint Helen's Record Office, Worcester
Sophia Smith Collection (Women's History Archive), Smith College,
    Northampton, Mass.
Symington Collection, Leeds City Archives Department

We are grateful for a variety of help from the following:
B. J. Barnes, A. S. Bell, Susan L. Boone, H. Cahoon, G. A. Carter, J. M. Collinson, E. J. Raymond Cook, Mrs G. Cowper, B. G. Cox, Anne H. Ehrenpreis, Naomi Evetts, Mrs A. C. Farr, Mrs K. Foster, Dr E. G. Franz, Dr I. H. C. Fraser, S. Gill, Ruth Green, J. Haslem, Mme L. Hautecoeur, Miss M. Henderson, Rev. A. M. Hill, Mrs C. Holland, J. S. Holland, E. Holland-Martin, H. Horton, Professor J. C. Ireson, Mrs E. Kemp, V. Klinkenborg, O. Knowles, Rev. A. J. Long, A. Marshall, D. I. Masson, Miss G. Matheson, R. C. Meadows, Mrs H. M. Nicholson, R. Ormond, C. Parish, Professor C. Pickford, Mme M.-L. Prévost, Dr F. W. Ratcliffe, Catherine Reilly, D. Rogers, A. J. Shelston, C. D. W. Sheppard, B. S. Smith, F. B. Stitt, Mrs S. Stonehouse, J. Treuherz, E. Watkins, M. D. Wheeler, Bill Williams.

To Professor Arthur Pollard, who has most generously allowed us to use the fruits of his labours in the original edition, we owe a very particular debt of gratitude. J. A. V. Chapple must also thank his colleagues and the University of Hull for a most valuable period of study leave during the year 1979.

CHAPTER ONE

Early influences

It is curious how much the spirit in which
she wrote varies according to the correspondent whom she was addressing
(Elizabeth Gaskell on Charlotte Brontë,
Letter 274)

ELIZABETH GASKELL'S MOTHER died in October 1811, only thirteen
months after the birth of her daughter:

To George Hope, 13 February 1849 (614)
I will not let an hour pass, my dear sir, without acknowledging your kindness in sending me my dear mother's letters, the only relics of her that I
have, and of more value to me than I can express, for I have so often
longed for some little thing that had once been hers or been touched by
her. I think no one but one so unfortunate as to be early motherless can
enter into the craving one has after the lost mother. . . . It never entered
my head to imagine you wished to see me for any other reason than as the
daughter of old friends. You cannot think how it gratified one to be
sought out for their sakes, – a gratification I should certainly have been
very far from feeling if I had for a moment suspected you of coming from
mere curiosity. I have been brought up away from all those who knew my
parents, and therefore those who come to me with a remembrance of them
as an introduction seem to have a holy claim on my regard.

Her father, William Stevenson, who was leading a busy and fairly successful
life in London, kept his twelve-year-old son John with him in Chelsea but sent

his baby daughter to be brought up by a sister of his dead wife in the little Cheshire town of Knutsford. Here she found abundant compensation for her loss: her aunt Hannah turned out to be a true second mother, she was in the heartland of her own mother's extensive family, the Hollands, and her imagination was given perhaps its strongest impulse:

To William and Mary Howitt, May 1838 (8)

Near the little, clean, kindly country town, where, as I said before, I was brought up there was an old house with a moat within a park called Old Tabley, formerly the dwelling-place of Sir Peter Leycester, the historian of Cheshire, and accounted a very fine specimen of the Elizabethan style. It is beautifully kept by its owner, who lives at a new house built about half a mile off, the velvet lawn up to the deep windows being mown and rolled most regularly, and the large laurels and the magnificent beeches trimmed with most excellent care. Here on summer mornings did we often come, a merry young party, on donkey, pony, or even in a cart with sacks swung across – each with our favourite book, some with sketch-books, and one or two baskets filled with eatables. Here we rambled, lounged and medi- tated: some stretched on the grass in indolent repose, half reading, half musing with a posy of musk-roses from the old-fashioned trim garden behind the house, lulled by the ripple of the waters against the grassy lawn; some in the old crazy boats, that would do nothing but float on the glassy water, singing, for one or two were of a most musical family and warbled like birds: 'Through the greenwood, through the greenwood,' or 'A boat, a boat unto the ferry,' or some such old catch or glee. And when the meal was spread beneath a beech tree of no ordinary size (did you ever notice the peculiar turf under beech shade?) one of us would mount up a ladder to the belfry of the old chapel and toll the bell to call the wanderers home. Then if it rained, what merry-making in the old hall. It was galleried, with oak settles and old armour hung up, and a painted window from ceiling to floor. The strange sound our voices had in that unfrequented stone hall! The last time I was there during the fall of rain from one of those heavy clouds which add to a summer day's beauty, when every drop of rain is sun-tinged and falls merrily amongst the leaves, one or two of Shakespeare's ballads: 'Blow, blow thou winter wind,' and 'Hark, hark the lark at Heaven's gate sings,' &c. were sung by the musical sisters in the gallery above, and by two other musical sisters (Mary and Ellen Needham from Lenton near Nottingham) standing in the hall below.

Back in London, however, her father had married again, a Miss Thomson, and within a few years two children were born. Elizabeth never really joined this new family, though a letter of 1820 from her brother John[1] indicates that she made quite lengthy visits: 'My mother has been proposing that if you can manage to come up this Summer, she will ask your cousin Isabella to come up to meet you, and my father will take you down in the Autumn'. It sounds cosy, but compared with the love she always expressed for the 'dearest of aunts' who was bringing her up the few references to her step-family are very cursory. 'I am longing to hear all about the Thomsons', she wrote in 1833; 'my little miss of a $\frac{1}{2}$ sister is to be married this Christmas – only 17 this 8th of December' (3). In 1855 she told a cousin she was going to see a step-mother and step-sister she had not clapped eyes on for twenty-five years or more (254) and a few months later she writes incidentally to a friend from Dunoon, Argyleshire, 'I am staying here with my unknown half sister . . .' (267a). The connection must have been broken about the time of her father's death in 1829, yet even before this she had felt emotionally starved:

To Mary Howitt, no date (616)
Long ago I lived in Chelsea occasionally with my father and stepmother, and *very, very* unhappy I used to be; and if it had not been for the beautiful, grand river, which was an inexplicable comfort to me, and a family of the name of Kennett, I think my child's heart would have broken. The sole remaining member of the family, Fanny Kennett, is now probably an old lady; the last thing I heard of her was her being dreadfully shocked that I had married a *Unitarian* minister.

Two letters from her brother John provide some context for these obscure early connections:

To Elizabeth Stevenson, 30 July 1828
They are all here except Papa going down to Scotland where they intend to remain till the end of September – They leave on Tuesday the 5th of next month and go by Berwick in order to leave Elisabeth – so Papa will have seven weeks of it to himself –
    The Kennetts are hardly yet recovered – they are really terribly boisterous – the colonel who is a very quiet man does not much seem to admire it – he continues to be in high favour with all who have seen him.

15 August 1828
There is some talk too of an attachment between Louisa Kennett and Mr. Miller the surgeon – I pity him if he gets her, that is if he is not pre-

pared beforehand to yield up the management of every thing to her and make himself a cypher in his own house.

The Colonel is not yet gone to France; he does not take either of his sisters with him which I am rather surprised at and which they are much disappointed at – perhaps he is afraid of their exposing him by being so noisy – Sophia Slade talks of writing to you – when she will I can hardly say.

These London links may be fragile, but for a future writer they were of considerable importance. The last paragraph of the 15 August letter is noteworthy:

I have just got the final answer from Smith and Elder – they are extremely sorry to decline taking my book &c &c. but dare say Longman would take – as a sort of douceur for thus disappointing me, they enclosed a friendships offering and a book on the present state of slavery in the West Indies – to end my hopes of being an author. . . . And now my dearest Elisabeth farewell – Should we never meet again, accept my very best wishes for your wellfare through life and may every blessing attend you – , With love to all enquiring

Believe me to be
Your ever affectionate brother
Jno. Stevenson.

John Stevenson failed as a writer, perhaps because the major bankruptcy of Constable and Ballantyne in 1826 had made the publishing world very cautious indeed. There was still hope for his young sister, because one day the firm of Smith, Elder would be taken in hand by a human dynamo, George Smith, who was to become one of the most successful publishers of the century and open entirely new markets for writers like her.[2] During these impressionable teenage years she was being 'brought up by old uncles & aunts, who had all old books, and very few new ones' (434). But John could offer more recent ones – *Paul and Virginia* and *The Exiles of Siberia*, for instance. He had now decided to leave England for good and remain in India, but we can see from his letters just what he has been to Elizabeth. He sent her parodies of verse and prose styles, gave vivid descriptions of life on board ship and in exotic foreign lands, begged her to write long letters full of news from Knutsford and praised her efforts to keep a journal:

To Elizabeth Stevenson, 30 July 1828
You have really made out a very pretty story of Captain Barton – it would almost make the foundation of a novel – it was indeed a narrow escape of

Kitty's and must have given her a tremendous fright – though I have heard and read many stories of them, I never saw a quicksand and hardly believed them to be so dangerous . . .

Nor can we now doubt her father's influence. Whatever his responsibilities to his new family may have entailed, his one extant letter to Elizabeth proves his concern for this side of his daughter's development:

To Elizabeth Stevenson, 2 July 1827

3, Beaufort Row

. . . I am glad to learn by your letter to your Mother that you are busy working for yourself: you must however, work a large portion of the day, if you have little or no time to read – as you have now been at Knutsford above a month. I hope you are again applying to your Latin and Italian; Let me know, when you write, in what manner you spend your day – I mean, so far as work or study is concerned.

I send the last No. of the Literary Gazette, which contains a review of Scott's Life of Napoleon, or rather long extracts from it. It was to have been published on Saturday – but I believe is not actually out yet. The Literary Gazette also contains a review of Moore's Epicurean – but I can hardly judge from what they say, what sort of a work it is. I dare say, very gaudy. I suspect from the style, the review is written by Miss Langden. . . .

If you should go into Wales, I expect you will keep a regular journal of what you see and remember. . . .

Your affectionate Father,
W. Stevenson.

A prolific and miscellaneous author on technical subjects himself, he was beginning to write important articles on political economy in the 1820s.[3]

Sadly, this varied and stimulating literary ambience was soon to collapse, leaving almost no record:

To John Blackwood, 5 March 1859 (415)

My father was one of the earliest contributors to Blackwood's Magazine; & some Mr Blackwood was for auld acquaintance sake extremely kind in assisting in the education of a half-brother of mine, since dead. And the first time I ever saw anything of mine in print was in Blackwood's Mag.

There are no other references to her father and brother in the correspondence, though the *Manchester Guardian* of 18 February 1914 provides a last footnote:

it records the sale of a copy of Thomas Gray's works presented to Elizabeth by her father.[4]

What she seems to have forgotten or repressed in later life glints through her fiction and, more obliquely still, through her letters. Their stylistic *tours de force* are a kind of acknowledgement of her family inheritance. Simple parody may not be too remarkable:

To Eliza Gaskell, 17 July 1838 (9)
> Now for a grand Johnsonian sentence which I beg you will read aloud to elevate me in the Dimockian[5] eyes. He who can wander by the melodious waters of the Menai and partake of the finny tribes that gambol in the translucent current, and can disport himself at pleasure in the lunar-governed tide; the man who can do this, I say, and return to the home of his progenitors neither more rotund, with the careless felicity of such a mode of existence, nor more attenuated from the excess of laudable excitement, deserves not to be classed with the human species, but to take his station among the moluscar tribes – Find out my meaning if you can, for I can't . . .

There is no mistaking the careless power of description displayed in an early letter written from the home of her Holland grandparents just outside Knutsford, a haunt of her girlhood and always thought to be the original of the idyllic Hope Farm in *Cousin Phillis*:

To Eliza Gaskell, 12 May 1836 (4)

> Sandlebridge

> My dearest Lizzy,
> I wish I could paint my present situation to you. Fancy me sitting in an old fashioned parlour, 'doors & windows opened wide', with casement window opening into a sunny court all filled with flowers which scent the air with their fragrance – in the very depth of the country – 5 miles from the least approach to a town – the song of birds, the hum of insects the lowing of cattle the only sounds – and such pretty fields & woods all round – Here are Baby, Betsy, Mama, & Bessy Holland – and indeed at this present moment here is Sue, who has ridden over, to bring us news of the civilized world – in the shape of letters &c &c. One from Aunt Lumb enclosing yours, & so full of gratitude about the rasberry wine, & so overflowing with thanks to you and your mother, that I fear there is little chance of my coming in for any of it. I shall try & put an *affront* into her head I can assure you, but I fear she will 'swallow' the affront. She begs her

6

kind regards to your mother, & that I will say how *very* kind she thought it of her, & how much she shall enjoy getting tipsy – It *was* very kind of you to think of it, & you are a nice creature, & every body has so liked you, & I do so wish you were here to revel in flowers, & such thorough country. We are up with the birds, and sitting out on the old flag steps in the very middle of fragrance – 'far from the busy hum of men', but *not* far from the busy hum of bees. Here is a sort of little standard library kept – Spenser, Shakspeare, Wordsworth, & a few foreign books, & we sit & read & dream our time away – except at meals when we *don't* dream over cream that your spoon stands upright in, & such sweet (not sentimental but literal) oven-cakes, and fresh butter.

Baby is at the very tip-top of bliss; & gives a happy prospect of what she will be at your Aunt Holbrook. There are chickens, & little childish pigs, & cows & calves & horses, & *baby horses*, & fish in the pond, & ducks in the lane, & the mill & the smithy, & sheep & baby-sheep, & flowers – oh! you would laugh to see her going about, with a great big nosegay in each hand, & wanting to be *bathed* in the golden bushes of wall-flowers – she is absolutely fatter since she came here, & is I'm sure stronger. I suspect I'm writing a queer medley, for I have had a walk in the heat, & my hand trembles & I think my brain trembles too – I ramble so. I was so sorry to miss you, and for James going when there was no need whatever for you to go. I rode above 18 miles that day, & lunched at Mr Davenport's at Capesthorne – such a beautiful place, not the house which is rather shabby; but the views from the Park – The next day Wm and I had a ride, Mr Deane mounting & accompanying us both – nearly to Bowden. Saturday & Monday I rode again, & came here on Tuesday, having my choice, between coming here, & another 18 mile ride with Mr Deane – but I longed to see the old familiar place. The house & walls are over-run with roses, honeysuckles & vines – not quite in flower, *but all but* – Betsy is quite in her element, and teaches baby to call the pigs, & grunt just like any old sow.

So it runs on, for pages more. The facility is as breathtaking as the lack of discipline. Whatever the weather, her hand and brain would tremble; her verve and high spirits always chafed at constraint. Throughout her life she was at cuffs with simple order, even though she seems to have spent no less than five years, 1821–6, at a school run by the redoubtable Misses Byerley. A fragment of a letter, probably written by Miss Jane Margaret Byerley, leaves us certain that their influence was exerted with lucid force:

To Elizabeth Stevenson, 14 June 1826

Avonbank
Stratford-upon-Avon

My dear Elizabeth,

I have been obliged to defer sending your books, because this is really a busy week and few minutes in it can be devoted to writing. We were sorry to find you were safely landed in Knutsford without taking Stratford in your way; we were led to expect you from Miss Master who desired us to keep the books till you arrived, and we should have been most happy to have seen you once more an inmate here, and to have known you in the new character of visitor. We have been highly favoured by our old pupils this half year – in the first place Emma came to us while her husband was at the Warwick Assizes, Jane Pickard and Sophy were here at the same time, and it was delightful to see this dear trio once more united and enjoying very naturally the *talking over* of past days. Sophy stayed with us many weeks which you may guess was no trifling pleasure to most of the inhabitants of this house if not to me. I am proud to say she gives promise of being an honor to our sex; she is a noble minded intelligent ingenuous creature, and in fact she is everything I wish her to be and all that I fondly hoped she would be, when I used to study her youthful mind, and narrowly watch her opening dispositions: at seventeen the character is *nearly* formed [Elizabeth Stevenson was fifteen then], and I am thankful to say that Sophia's principles and religious feelings are such that I could almost depend upon her acting conscientiously in any situation or assailed by any temptations; she has been introduced in the gay world of Cheltenham and she has left the place sick of its miscalled pleasures, and with as simple a taste as when she entered it; and we found that in this quiet place she was never dull and enjoyed truly a rural walk and more even than the gaiest ball or rout: such is your friend Sophy and I think you will be interested by this long account of her: it was curious to compare her with her dear friend Jane Pickard; the latter left us at the end of a week, and tho' she behaved in a very pleasing manner and is a lovely interesting looking girl we felt that we were parting with one who would go well through the world and ever act with remarkable and unusual decorum and propriety, but who would not be regretted like the warm hearted enthusiastic Sophy: they are both beautiful and elegant and fondly attached, and it will be interesting to mark their progress thro' life.

The Byerley sisters obviously provided firm, fond discipline during school years and perhaps thereafter. A fragmentary letter to a Mrs Montagu, written some twenty years after Elizabeth left, asks if she sees 'anything of dear Miss

Jane. When I was very ill of the measles last spring', it continues, 'I received a letter from her, which was mislaid, and consequently, when I recovered I was unable to write, not knowing her address' (20). She had been set a pattern of behaviour that was controlled as well as 'warm hearted enthusiastic', designed to make a 'noble minded intelligent ingenuous creature'. In many ways she was, though the combination of qualities was not an easy one to maintain. She can hover near the 'sort of very second-rate sweet sentimental affectation' (9) for which she herself criticises one of her old schoolfellows :

To Mary Howitt, 18 August 1838 (12)
I am very glad indeed Mr Howitt thinks of going to Clopton; and one of my reasons for wishing to write soon is that I may beg him thoroughly to explore the neighbourhood (that of Stratford-on-Avon). As a school-girl I could not see much, but I heard of many places that I longed to know more about; and yet I can only give you glimpses of what those places were. I know there was a mysterious old farmhouse near Clifford, which had been the family mansion of the Grevilles, and where Sir Fulke Greville, the servant of Queen Elizabeth, the counsellor of King James, and the friend of Sir Philip Sidney, was born and bred. A visit to this spot would not come inappropriately after Mr Howitt's visit to Penshurst.

Then there is an old curious seat of the Marquis of Northampton, who married Miss Clephane, Sir W. Scott's friend, Compton Winyates, near Edgehill, and someway connected with the history of the battle. Shottery, too, where Ann Hathaway (she hath a way) lived, is only a mile from Stratford. Charlecote, of course, is worthy of a visit, though it was not out of that park that Shakespeare stole the deer. I am giving but vague directions, but I am unwilling to leave even in thought the haunts of such happy days as my schooldays were.

And now to my country customs, by which I earn the privilege of again writing to you. Though a Londoner by birth, I was early motherless, and was taken when only a year old to my dear *adopted native* town, Knuts-ford, and some of the customs I shall mention are peculiar to the district around that little market town.

One of the customs, on any occasion of rejoicing, of strewing the ground before the houses of those who sympathise in the gladness with common red sand, and then taking a funnel filled with white sand, and sprinkling a pattern of flowers upon the red ground. This is always done for a wedding, and often accompanied by some verse of rural composition. When I was married, nearly all the houses in the town were sanded, and these were the two favourite verses :

'Long may they live,
Happy may they be,
Blest with content,
And from misfortune free.

Long may they live
Happy may they be,
And blest with a numerous
Pro-ge-ny.' . . .

About Knutsford we have Christmas carols, such a pretty custom, calling one from dreamland to almost as mystic a state of mind; half awake and half asleep, blending reality so strangely with the fading visions; and children's voices too in the dead of the night with their old words of bygone times! . . .

Many poetical beliefs are vanishing with the passing generation. A shooting star is unlucky to see. I have so far a belief in this that I always have a chill in my heart when I see one, for I have often noticed them when watching over a sick-bed and very, very anxious. The dog-rose, that pretty libertine of the hedges with the floating sprays wooing the summer air, its delicate hue and its faint perfume, is unlucky. Never form any plan while sitting near one, for it will never answer.

I was once saying to an old, blind countrywoman how much I admired the foxglove. She looked mysteriously solemn as she told me they were not like other flowers; they had 'knowledge' in them! Of course I inquired more particularly, and then she told me that the foxglove knows when a spirit passes by and always bows the head. Is not this poetical! and of the regal foxglove with its tapering crimson bells. I have respected the flower ever since.

Moreover, I know a man who has seen the Fairies and tells the story in the prettiest possible way. And if you were on Alderley Edge, the hill between Cheshire and Derbyshire, could not I point out to you the very entrance to the cave where King Arthur and his knights lie sleeping in their golden armour till the day when England's peril shall summon them to her rescue.

To go back in rather a random manner to old halls and family traditions. I have had very delicate health since I married, and have not been able to ramble about much, so I do *not* know Haughton Tower. I wish I did. I like your expression of 'an unwritten tragedy.' It quite answers to the sadness which fills my heart as I look on some of those deserted old halls. Do they not remind you of Tennyson's 'Deserted House' – 'Life and thought are gone away,' &c.

> Close the door, the shutters close,
>> Or through the windows we shall see
>> The nakedness and vacancy
> Of the dark deserted house.

Some kinds of sentiment have real justification. John Stevenson's feeling that he would never see his sister again had proved shockingly true, for he disappeared abroad. Within a few months, too, William Stevenson was dead, leaving a very small estate, and his widow went off to live in Scotland towards the end of 1829. 'She will have much to contend with in her new mode of life', wrote Miss Jane Byerley on 4 November 1829, but it is clear from this same letter that Elizabeth had been kept in England amongst her Holland relations. Addressed to Miss E. Stevenson at Mrs Hannah Lumb's in Knutsford, it also refers to a visit Elizabeth had made to Dumbleton in the Vale of Evesham, where a rich cousin, Edward Holland, owned extensive property – 'you describe a most happy kind of life, such as realizes ones ideas of felicity in the country', wrote Miss Byerley with decorous enthusiasm. That Elizabeth stayed about this time with Edward's father, Swinton Holland, in Park Lane, as all biographers report, is impossible, for Swinton had died over a year before.[6] It is likely, however, that she went to stay at 25 Lower Brook Street, Mayfair, with her cousin Henry Holland, a vastly successful doctor, who always figured as 'the fashionable young man in the vortex of London Society' in the memories of Miss Mary and Miss Lucy Holland of Knutsford.

Other visits were less grand. Exceptional charity, plain living and high thinking were the notes of the Reverend William Turner, Unitarian Minister at Newcastle upon Tyne and yet another connection by marriage (in two distinct ways). Then a vigorous man in his late sixties, he had been involved in every cultural and philanthropic enterprise in the town, the first sight of which – 'sky darkened by smoke from the steam-engines and the coal dust burned at the pit-head to get rid of it' – used to dismay visitors, but which soon impressed them with the vigour of its institutions, fine Assembly Rooms and 'magnificent building' just erected for the Literary and Philosophical Society William Turner had helped to found.[7] It was presumably from the modest house where he lived with his unmarried daughter Ann that Elizabeth wrote perhaps the earliest letter known:[8]

To Anne Burnett, c. 1830

Thursday Eveng

I can not tell you how much I felt gratified, my dear *Anne* on my return this evening from Bensham by your very kind note, and the accompanying book which I have long wished to see. I hope I shall never require any thing to remind me of any of my kind Newcastle friends, or of the many pleasant hours I have spent here, but as a token of your regard, you may be sure I shall always value it exceedingly. Like you I very much regret our having seen so little of each other, but that little has left so very pleasant an impression that I sincerely hope should I ever come to Newcastle again, I shall have more opportunity of enjoying your society. I am sure you may always depend upon my very cordial regard, and affectionate wishes for your welfare, and happiness –

Pray thank Mrs Burnett, and your sisters for their kind wishes, and remembrances. I am looking forward with great pleasure to reading your most acceptable present when settled for the Summer at Woodside, where I hope to join my Aunt the day after tomorrow. I shall often hear all about you from Anne Turner, & should you ever feel inclined to write to me, I will prove how welcome your letters will be by a speedy answer. With very kind regards to Mrs Burnett, and your sisters,

Believe me to remain
Your sincere & affectionate Friend
Elizabeth C. Stevenson

This is far too demure to be at all typical, but comes appropriately enough from the cheerfully good 'Dissenting Minister's Household' on which a graphic chapter in *Ruth* is based. When Elizabeth Stevenson came to Newcastle Mr Turner was receiving recognition for a lifetime of effort. The Literary and Philosophical Society had ordered his portrait to be painted and, on 21 December 1831, nearly a hundred people sat down to a dinner in the Assembly Rooms to mark his fiftieth year in Newcastle.[9] But by this time one of the worst attacks of Asiatic cholera in Britain had struck the town, its 'chares' or narrow lanes proving perfect breeding grounds for what was then a terrifying and unpredictable disease. It is said that Ann Turner and Elizabeth were sent to Edinburgh for safety's sake, though cholera reached the Scottish capital's crowded tenements early in 1832.[10] Very little that is definite has been discovered so far about this period in Elizabeth Gaskell's life. We must fall back upon the splendid evocation of a pinched life in mean Edinburgh lodgings, stiffly proper walks in the streets and visits to a friendly but brilliant salon found in the frame story of the much later *Round the Sofa* (1859). Some of it may well be autobiographical.

She always remained attached to Mr Turner, whose family gently combined to put some restraint upon his constant inclination to give all his money away.[11] Fashionable and superior relations like the dashing Henry Holland would flash by: 'Dr Holland *has* been at Moscow since you saw him', she once wrote to her daughter, '& *is* at Knutsford on his way to Algeria' (133). Now and again he would pause long enough to give the kind of advice one might expect from a Physician in Ordinary to Queen Victoria :

To Richard Bentley, 29 September 1853 (167a)
I don't know if I spell the word rightly, but viratria is the essential part of aconite; and though a new & very expensive drug, it is well known to all good chemists, who pronounce it, as I have written it. It was recommended to me by my cousin Sir Henry Holland, a physician of some repute. It was rubbed on *for* me; for I was convulsed with pain – a small (pins' head) quantity was put on flannel; and the rubbing was continued until a sting-ing pain was produced in the skin; a bad pain enough of it's kind. The next day the tic made an effort to return at the usual time; the rubbing was repeated (on the temple to which the nerve shot with keen agony,) the tic went away, & I have never had it since. I have named it to two sufferers, – in both the tic has disappeared; but one had to rub oftener than I had.

Her connection with the learned, unworldly William Turner seems much closer. He baptised her daughter Margaret Emily (Meta) on 28 September 1837. When he finally retired in the early 1840s, he came to live near his married daughter Mary in Manchester, eventually lodging with one of Eliza-beth Gaskell's oldest friends, the teacher Rosa Mitchell, who used to keep a boarding house for students at Manchester New College.[12] 'After tea to Miss Mitchell's', she wrote in 1851, 'to read to old Mr Turner which I mean to try & do very often both for his sake & Miss Mitchell's; as it sets her at liberty. I was well tired at night' (91b). William Turner's daughter Mary had in fact married the reverend John Gooch Robberds, senior minister at Manchester's famous Cross Street Chapel where the junior minister from 1828 was the Reverend William Gaskell. The whole context of Unitarian charity and practical affection is beautifully illustrated by one letter in particular :

To an unknown correspondent, 9 February 1856 (280)
Dear Sir
In a letter which my husband received from you, dated September 23 1853, you very kindly expressed your willingness to contribute 5£ annually towards the sum (50£) which we hoped to raise each year for Miss Mitchell. May I be allowed to remind you that your subscription for 1856 is due? When the arrangements were all made Miss Mitchell's state of health was such (owing to a heart complaint,) that the doctor attending her desired that every cause for anxiety that could be removed, might be obviated; and accordingly, in compliance with the advice of my cousin Miss Holland & Mrs Sam Greg I told her of the sum which some friends

of hers hoped to raise annually; I was almost afraid to see the tearful emotion of gratitude which succeeded; and she begged me earnestly to express her thanks to those, whose names she guessed, although we had agreed that they should be withheld from her.

Mr Gaskell thought it better to place the whole matter at once on a business footing, & to pay her 12£–10s, quarterly; which he has done. And I do believe if you could all know how much you have done to smooth away a very natural care & anxiety from the last years of as good and as Christian a woman as ever was, you would be very much touched & gratified. Her health is better, though it can never be strong. She lives in a small house where her only lodgers are old Mr Turner (aged 94,) and his companion Miss Howarth. When Mr Turner dies the sum she receives with him will cease of course, and unless she can meet with another lodger, paying equally well, her only dependence will be on the 50£. I told her plainly out the wish which we all felt, that no one else should benefit by our contributions; and she very seriously promised that our desire on this head should be attended to. She keeps one servant; does all the cooking herself; I am sure, Sir, you will excuse this long letter. I thought you ought to know all the particulars I could give you of our dear old friend.

It was probably at the house of Mr and Mrs Robberds that Elizabeth met William Gaskell, some time in 1831. Born near Warrington, he was about five years older and a graduate of the unfashionable Glasgow University – and as such 'unsettled for commercial pursuits', we learn from *North and South*! He had trained for the ministry at Manchester New College when it was for a time in York. The engagement was a short one:

To Eliza Gaskell, 20 March 1832 (1)
You ought indeed, my dearest Eliza, to consider it a great proof of my love, that I can even meditate writing to you on William's last evening (See how impudent I've grown) but my conscience would reproach me for ever and a day if I let him go without my portion of thanks for your kind letter. He may finish his half at Ardwick, and as I shan't be there to see, he may say what scandal he likes of us all, and give me as bad a character as he chooses. N.B. I have been behaving very well, so don't believe a word to the contrary.

He has not seen half, no nor a quarter so much as I wished of my darling Aunt Lumb. I scarcely like to think of the cause now she is so much better, but the very morning after he came, she broke a small blood-vessel which alarmed us all very much indeed, and has confined her to bed ever since. William has, however, seen her several times, and though not nearly enough, yet I hope knows her a little bit. And you can't think what rude speeches she makes to me. To give you a slight specimen – 'Why Elizabeth how could this man ever take a fancy to such a little giddy thoughtless thing as you' and many other equally pretty speeches.

And he's seen and properly admired his traveling companion from Leeds. But oh dear! I shall miss him sadly tomorrow, and I'm sure you will be very sorry for the reason when you hear it. He had a letter this morning from Mrs Robberds begging him to come home against Thursday morning to old Mrs Robberds funeral. She was not very well when we left, and on Monday her son was called up early in the morning – and before he could get to Mrs Alcock's she was dead. I could not say a word on such an occasion to urge your brother's staying, and I must look forward to the *28th of March 1832* when he has promised to come back again. Pray give my warmest thanks to your sister, for her kind addition to your letter – and do you, dearest, pray write again to me, and that right speedily – tell me anything that interests you – and oh! don't forget how to fight with pillows and 'farm yard noises' when Edward heard you laughing so plainly. I can't write a word more now, seeing I have 150 things to say to this disagreeable brother of yours – so believe me

Your every loving crony
E. C. Stevenson

This is the first of many long, lively letters to William's young sister, by far the most important of the early correspondents. Eliza could not possibly have realised then that one day Elizabeth Gaskell would be offering her odd *bundles* of old letters to amuse her in her ninth confinement, 'blest with a numerous Pro-ge-ny'. Her brother was about to marry an epistolary phenomenon, who was every bit as interested in receiving long and frequent letters as in writing them herself.

CHAPTER TWO

Marriage

Nonsense precipitate, like running Lead
That slip'd thro' Cracks and Zig-zags of the Head
(Pope, *Dunciad*, 1743, I. 123–4)

ON 30 AUGUST 1832 Elizabeth Cleghorn Stevenson married William Gaskell
at Knutsford, given away by one of her uncles, Dr Peter Holland, with her
cousins Susan and Catherine as her bridesmaids. The wedding trip was into
Wales, first to the little resort of Aber and then on to Plas Penrhyn, Portmadoc,
home of another uncle, Samuel Holland. From this favourite spot she added
her own scudding postscript to her husband's soberly enthusiastic letter :

To Eliza Gaskell, 16 September 1832 (2)
My dearest Eliza,
    That most wicked brother of yours & husband of mine, has left me such
a wee wee bit of time to write all *my* news, & thanks having taken such a
time to *his* eloquence that poor I must write helter-skelter. And first and
foremost thanks upon thanks from the very bottom of my long heart, for yr
letter which was *so* welcome, as we had been longing for news from *our
home*. It was very nice of you writing to *me*, your new *sister* too. Kate had
sent us a long long letter a few days before – and among other things made
us laugh exceedingly with telling us one *report* of which I dare say neither
you nor Sam were aware. Pray ask him with my love whether he knew that
Sue put his shoulder out of joint by pulling him to her at the altar, and
that so much force was required on *Susan*'s part, because Kate was pulling
so at his other arm. Since hearing this Wm & I have felt rather anxious to
hear of his health. As you justly conjecture I *have* a *great* deal of trouble,

in managing this obstreperous brother of yours, though I dare say he will try and persuade you the trouble is all on his side. I find he has been telling you I look very well, so I think that is a pretty broad hint that I am to tell you he is looking *remarkably* well which he really is. Mountain seems to agree with us & our appetites admirably. You would be astonished to see our appetites, the dragon of Wantley, 'who churches ate of a Sunday, Whole dishes of people were to him, but a dish of Salmagunde' was really a delicate appetite compared to ours. If you hear of the principality of Wales being swallowed up by an earthquake, for earthquake read Revd Wm Gaskell – How very good you are to be staying at home by yourself while   here's post

Your most affectionate Sister
E. C. Gaskell

Places always affected Elizabeth Gaskell. The memory of this trip lasted long, revived by later Welsh holidays and merging into even earlier ones, drawn upon for stories like 'The Well of Pen-Morfa' but especially for some of the most memorable scenes in *Ruth* :

To Eliza Gaskell, 17 July 1838 (9)
My very dearest Lizzy,
    Here's a sheet of paper for you! I only hope it may come to you on a wet day. I shall put down every thing; not knowing whether you will care to hear it, or not, but I have not much time, and I must write straight forward whatever comes into my head. (In the first place I do thoroughly sympathize with you, leaving a large merry party in a house, – and I can quite fancy the sort of looks you send to the mountains, the other side of which look *towards* if not *to* a place where you have been very happy.) Beaumaris itself I remembered as a pretty watering place, as watering places go; but not wild or grand or anything in that line; and it is rather tantalizing to see mountains without being able to get at them, and it is a very long round by the Bridge. Still I wish you could get to see Aber, (5 miles from Bangor on the Conway road & right opposite you by sea, only you can't get at it, coz of the shore being so bad) where Wm and I spent a fortnight of our wedding journey – and where I spent a very happy month with 17 aunts, cousins and such like, once before . . .
    I wish you would go to Priestholme or Puffin's Island – It is such a singular place & to a botanist (*like you* Ma'am) would be a great treat – Many ships returning from Foreign ports – used to make offerings at the monastery there, – and cast out their ballast, which often contained curious

seeds which took root – The old monastery is in ruins – but there is a telegraph station; the man who kept it years & years ago in my youth, had fought in the Victory with Nelson – the Puffins too are queer uncanny looking animals. I *long* to be in those wild places again, with the fresh sea breeze round me, so thoroughly exhilarating. How does Mr Dimock like Beaumaris? What a pleasant change to Ann after hot horrible smoky wicked Babylon the Great – only I wish you were in a wilder more Welshy place. I cannot help *feeling* the *feelings* for you. I know [how] you must be *feeling* at the last happy six weeks over & gone, with the uncertainty when such another may come again.

She writes with Romantic intensity, but wedding trip over, she had to go to live in smoky Manchester, in a house on the corner of Dover Street on the southern edge of the city. She went from wild Wales to a Broadwood piano, plants in saucers and properly earthed-up celery in the garden:

To William Turner, 6 October 1832[1]

No 1 Dover Street   Oxford Road.
Saturday Morning
... I have been so completely in a 'whirl' these two days that I feel as though I could hardly arrange my thoughts enough to give you an account of the few plans we have formed with regard to our future proceedings. Mr Gaskell has promised as soon as the *formal* bridal calls are made, to go with me and introduce me to most of the families under his care, as their minister's wife, and one who intends to try to be their useful friend. My dear colleague too has promised her assistance and advice with regard to my duties. I like my new home very much indeed – for Manchester it is very countrified, and is very cheerful and comfortable in every part. I was detained by a sore throat on the road, or else we had intended being at home last week; as it was, and we had dipped into another week, we staid a few days longer in my old home, and saw Aunt Lumb's almost daily improvement in health, spirits, and strength. She promises to come and pay us a visit very soon, and I enjoy the idea of receiving her in a house of my own, and where I can in some measure provide for her comforts, as she has so often done for mine.

I have just received on the part of Mr Gaskell & myself, a very handsome fish-slice and a very kind note from Mr James Turner. ...

And ever believe me to remain
My dear Mr Turner's very affectionate & grateful
E. C. Gaskell

It was her own home at last, to which she fully committed her formidable energies while always cherishing her various forms of escape.

After the disappointment of a still-born child, a girl was born on 12 September 1834 and baptised Marianne – always called 'MA' or 'Minnie'. Manchester and motherhood, however, did not cut out literature and the charms of country life:

To Eliza Gaskell, 12 May 1836 (4)

Sandlebridge

I have brought Coleridge with me, & am *doing* him & Wordsworth – *fit place for the latter*! I sat in a shady corner of a field gay with bright spring flowers – daisies, primroses, wild anenomes, & the 'lesser celandine,' & with lambs all around me – and the air so full of sweet sounds, & wrote my first chapr of W. yesterday in pencil – & today I'm going to finish him – and my heart feels so full of him I only don't know how to express my fullness without being too diffuse. If you were here, I think your advice, & listening, would do me so much good – but I have to do it all by myself alone, crunching up my paper, & scuttering my pencil away, when any one comes near. I have done all my *composition* of Ld B – , & done Crabbe outright since you left & got up Dryden & Pope – so now I'm all clear & straight before me. I shall dearly like seeing your book but I fear it will vex me by giving more beautiful quotations of people I can't go back to – but I want to see how many moderns he has done &c – If I don't get much writing done here, I get a great many thoughts on the subject – for one can't think any thing but poetry & happiness. . . .

Bessy & I have our German novel here, but I shy it rather being very anxious to get on with my poets – I think I shall go home (to M[ancheste]r) next Saturday week – or I may stay over the next week, as it will be M[ancheste]r Race-week which I hate – Sue sends 'very big thanks' for the song, and is so shocked at the length of the song but thinks it very pretty – It is *11* just, & Sue thinks we are so *late dining*; she has 'no idea of such fashionable hours *here*'. To comfort her I can tell her here is a capital skull come in, since she stuck her head through the window. Baby is gone into the wood to see the merry little Brook. Can you fancy us – Bessy is persuading Sue to stay – and offering her clothes – and Sue thinks if she does stay she must follow Bessy's Welsh example & turn her riding habit into a night-gown. Fancy the *comfort* of it this hot weather. Oh! that Life would make a stand-still in this happy place? Uncle Holland saw Baby yesterday & took word home (Sue says that she looks better already). Now mind you write again, & none of your nimini-pimini notes, but a sensible nonsensical crossed letter as *I do*.

Life never stands still. A second daughter, christened Margaret Emily but always called Meta, was born on 5 February 1837. Then came a sad blow. Hannah Lumb, 'dearest of aunts', was stricken with a painful paralysis that Dr Peter Holland could only treat by leeches and 'an anodyne draught' (5). After much suffering she died on 1 May 1837, leaving Elizabeth an income of £80 a year. This legacy may well have been welcome, since by middle-class standards of the time they were not too well off. Their rent was £32 a year. William had his stipend as a minister, perhaps some income from a family business and, later, private pupils. It may be significant that his name does not appear on the list of donors to an association set up in 1836 to fight legal attempts to deprive Unitarians of their chapels and endowments, when his fellow ministers in Manchester subscribed and so too did relations like Holbrook and Samuel Gaskell.[2] In 1838 Elizabeth Gaskell could exclaim, 'How I wish my dear husband and I could afford to ramble about the country this summer, the sun is shining so brightly. But we are not the richest of the rich (my husband is a Unitarian minister), and, moreover, I have two little girls to watch over' (8). Nevertheless, she managed to get about:

To Eliza Gaskell, 17 July 1838 (9)
Then I saw *the* Coronation gaieties in Knutsford which I enjoyed because I knew every body. – And the next morng I left by Ruffley with my children twain. That was on Friday – Monday we drank tea with the Miss Marslands, and went to see a night blowing Cereus at Dukinfield Darbishire's. Such a flower – a splendid white flower with a golden glory round it. Tuesday went to see the Collins in their new house – Mrs C – as large as life. Wednesday had an invitation to a Christening where we had never been before – at a Mr Bradford's an American, who married a Miss Taylor sister of that pretty Mrs W. Holland you saw here once on a call – both very nice looking people. So we set off earlyish 4 o'clock say & called on Sam on the way whom we found not looking well certainly though he said he was better than he had been. About six we arrived at a large handsome house far away on the left of Pendleton toll bar. Ushered in with much astonishment, heard scuttering away to dress – and found that the Christening had been in the morning, and that we were dreadfully too early. However when Mr & Mrs Bradford were dressed – (she in a *beautiful* worked white muslin over white satin, white satin shoes, brussels lace, & flowers in her hair looking so very pretty,) I in the very gown I am now sitting in, great thick shoes, & Wm in boots & without gloves) they came in & very agreeable he was & very lovely she. He is a great friend of Bryant the poet, so W. & he had some pleasant confabulation – about 8 o'clock full dessed people began pouring in, and we went into a large

dancing room – windows open, hot-house plants, muslin curtains &c, & there we danced till supper at 12, & such a supper! I suppose the Bradfords are very rich, – for wine & grapes, & pines, & such cakes my mouth waters at the thought, & ducks & green peas, & new potatoes & asparagus & chickens without end, & savoury pies, & all sort of beautiful confectionery – and we wended our way home by day*light* – ½ past 3 when we got home walking to be sure. You would have enjoyed it – waltzing, galloppes, &c &c – Mrs W. Holland looked so well, & on dit is going to be married again to a Mr Bischoff a german. . . .

They were so taken with the Bradfords that they called their last child Julia Bradford in 1846, but the name vanishes from the correspondence after 1847.[3]

Sunday to chapel in the morning two walks in the afternoon – Oh Rivington is such a very pretty place, & so thoroughly country. Yesterday morning I sketched & Wm came; in the afternoon we both rode on horseback up & down the country – then a walk after tea. This morning we were off at half past 8 for Bolton, home per rail road – found your letter, & refusals to every one of our invites to meet the Bradfords, so we are in a comfortable dilemma as to who will come to meet them at so short a notice. Carvers & Marsdens we ought to have & we shall have a respectablish supper – but too short an invitation, & too cardplaying, too old, – Worthingtons, – too young, wd come but what must we do with 'em when we have got 'em – Not room enough for dancing, – and people get tired of bagatelle else we have got the Mason's bagatelle board – So what *are* we to do – Well! that job will be jobbed before you get this letter.

Next Tuesday W, I, & MA, go to Mrs Alcocks of Gatley for a day or two. I forgot to say Mrs Green had put off her coming which is just the most provoking thing in the world, as I had engaged a girl from Knutsford who is here to stay over this week to help in all the extra work, & meant to get all sorts of things in. – Baby *really* walks alone now & is getting a sweet little thing – MA's cough is much better thank you. This Rivington air has done wonders; and made me so strong & so hungry. Good air for ever! Hurrah! I wonder if we ever can hit upon the same excursion at the same time. I should so like to be at Beaumaris with you. Wm is with Dr Bernstein or I would ask him your propriety questions. Oh! who *must* we ask to meet the Bradfords – hang 'em. You have been a precious sister in the writing line, and Mrs Purse is not at all displeased with you. Did you see Mr Brown? did you think my memory sketch of the house like? We staid rather longer at Knutsford in the sweet thought that perhaps Aunt Ab might do what she once talked of – ask us to keep house for her while she went to Weston Point; but I thought she repented & cooled in her invite and Susan said we should be more prudent to go, for Aunt Ab would be sure to find fault with every thing we did in her absence, and we shd only get into scrapes. *Perhaps* in August we go to Rowsley Wm I & Susan – I don't go if Sue does not. W. preaches at Buxton on the 17th. My love to Ann & ask her how the Queen was when she last saw her? How's John – The Masons are in Paris. Alcocks & Asplands in Scotland, – 'Dance Merryman dance Out of Scotland into France.'

The Gaskells might not have been able to afford to ramble very far, but they could certainly explore the environs of Manchester. It is, she wrote to the Howitts, 'a great manufacturing town, but when spring days first come and the bursting leaves and sweet earthy smells tell me that 'Somer is ycomen in,'' I feel a stirring instinct and long to be off into the deep grassy solitudes of the country, just like a bird wakens up from its content at the change of the seasons and tends its way to some well-known but till then forgotten land' (8). The rural myth is powerful and recurrent; she is a true contemporary of John Clare. At Sandlebridge she had been unable to 'think any thing but poetry & happiness'; now she is delighted to hear that the Howitts are going to bring out a book 'describing some of these solemnly poetical places'. She actually sent them a prose description of the history and hauntings of old Clopton Hall in Warwickshire, which was printed in his *Visits to Remarkable Places* in 1840 as the contribution of 'a fair lady'. It is all charmingly old-fashioned, almost as backward-looking as another early literary enterprise of the Gaskells. In this, however, content and new setting are infinitely more important than the form they chose:

To Mary Howitt, 18 August 1838 (12)
My husband has lately been giving four lectures to the very poorest of the weavers in the very poorest district of Manchester, Miles Platting, on 'The Poets and Poetry of Humble Life.' You cannot think how well they have been attended, or how interested people have seemed. And the day before yesterday two deputations of respectable-looking men waited on him to ask him to repeat those lectures in two different parts of the town. He is going on with four more in the winter, and meanwhile we are *picking up* all the 'Poets of Humble Life' we can think of.

As for the Poetry of Humble Life, that, even in a town, is met with on every hand. We have such a district, and we constantly meet with examples of the beautiful truth in that passage of 'The Cumberland Beggar:'

'Man is dear to man; the poorest poor
Long for some moments in a weary life
When they can know and feel that they have been,
Themselves, the fathers and the dealers out
Of some small blessings; have been kind to such
As needed kindness, for this simple cause,
That we have all of us a human heart.'

In short, the beauty and poetry of many of the common things and daily events of life in its humblest aspect does not seem to me sufficiently appreciated.

We once thought of *trying* to write sketches among the poor, *rather* in the manner of Crabbe (now don't think this presumptuous), but in a more seeing-beauty spirit; and one – the only one – was published in *Blackwood*, January 1837.[4] But I suppose we spoke of our plan near a dog-rose, for it never went any further.

Manchester Unitarians were noted for both culture and philanthropy, but it is not altogether certain that poetical sketches and lectures were the first literary requirement of 'an agglomeration the most extraordinary, the most interesting, and in some respects, the most monstrous, which the progress of society has presented', where 'chemistry is held in honour; but literature and the arts are a dead letter'. Of course Leon Faucher was only an intelligent Frenchman, and the 'Member of the Manchester Athenaeum' who annotated his *Manchester in 1844*[5] was at pains to point out that the manufacturing districts were 'emphatically reading communities', but in this instance Elizabeth Gaskell has given her own verdict:

To John Blackwood, 9 March 1859 (417)
My article was a poem on a character whom I subsequently introduced into 'Mary Barton'; and I remember it began

> In childhood days I do remember me
> Of a dark house behind an old elm tree
> By gloomy streets surrounded &c &c

It was worth very little; but I was very much pleased, and very proud to see it in print. I sent some articles, in prose, afterwards to Blackwood, – but they were, as I now feel, both poor & exaggerated in tone; & they were never inserted.

However rural and poetic her basic sensibility, her form was to be the novel. Popular authors, a friend of hers wrote[6] about this time, 'do not speak to men luxuriating at ease, so much as to men occupied in labour or living in scenes of constant excitement'.

Her sense of humour in any case was much too strong to let her be 'solemnly poetical' for long, as we see from the comical roulades of information poured out for her young sister-in-law:

To Eliza Gaskell, 17 July (9), 7 August (10), 17 August (11) 1838
William is going to give a course of lectures on the poets & poetry of humble life at the Mechanic's Institute (or Institution?) at Miles Platting – a new subject, & if W had taken time to it he would have done it capitally – as it is I fear his usual fault of procrastination will prevent him doing justice to it. Mrs J J. Tayler has got an impromptu baby at Blackpool; – went there and lo & behold a little girl unexpectedly made her appearance, & clothes have had to be sent in such a hurry. Bathing places do so much good. Susan & Mary went to Blackpool last year, but did not derive the same benefit. Mr J J Tayler came home from London on Saturday hoping to find wife & children at home but had to post off to Blackpool leaving Father Abraham to preach, & on Sunday morning Mrs J J T presented him with the little lady – So ends Mrs J J Tayler's *'delicate state of health, arising from some internal complaint,'* as Mr Ransom called it.

In the eveng to a stupid dinner at the Darbishires. Horners, Alcock & Jas Turners. Wm went off to finish his lectures in the shape of one on Burns. He was famously clapped bless him, though for want of you to plague he plagues me. I say it is a godsend for me to have something to write about. Today Nasmyths & Gaskells.

I went to tea to the Miss Marslands uninvited – Sunday to chapel as usual, walked back as *un*usual – consequently rather tired. Sam came in the evening as true as he always is, bless him. I asked him to come and see Anne thinking she would come on Monday as Chas half promised for her. But she never turned up all Monday – and in the eveng Mrs Robberds came, and Sam came but no Anne was there – I felt very poorly too – But Wm read his 2 first lectures on Poetry &c aloud which people seemed very much to like & I lay on the sofa & enjoyed myself in listening. . . . He has had 2 deputations today to ask him to repeat his lectures – one from the Teachers of the Sunday School & Senior Scholars – the other from the Salford Mechanic's institution. Neither of them pay, whilk is a pity – but *if* the Manchester M. Institution come – shan't they pay for all. In the mean time we look gracious & affable as a new made Queen, and are 'most happy' &c.

These are family names (Sam and Anne Gaskell, Charles Holland) and those of Manchester Unitarians (Tayler, Darbishire, Alcock, James Turner, Marsland, Robberds). Her feelings are complex: pride, impatience, amusement, *joie de vivre*, boredom, lassitude, pleasure – she seems almost too vivid and aware for her circle. But she chose it freely and would never desert it.

She would later dismay friends and members of her husband's middle-class congregation (with his support) by writing social-problem novels of urban life, joining those mid-century authors who stirred the conscience and transformed the consciousness of the nation. She would in many ways remain provincial, domestic even, but one of her major themes was to be the 'shock city' of the age, Manchester, as it went through the first great crisis of industrial capitalism in the history of the world. The Gaskells belonged to what a modern historian has called the forgotten middle class;[7] not in the economic front line, to be sure, but in touch with poor weavers as well as rich manufacturers; able, expert and professional. William was a teacher besides being a minister. His wife could be inhibited by his accuracy and precision: 'When I had finished my last letter Willm looked at it, and said it was "*slip-shod*" – and seemed to wish me not to send it' (13), she confessed to his sister once, but she found him immensely helpful when preparing material for the press and correcting proofs. He was something of an author himself. He wrote many hymns for the Reverend J. R. Beard's *Collection of Hymns* in 1837, and published his own *Temperance Rhymes* anonymously in 1839, a kind of literary welfare work that drew a letter of praise from Wordsworth. For the Victorians, writing could easily become a branch of philanthropy.

A letter of 12 June 1841 to that lively American Unitarian, the Reverend John Pierpont,[8] reveals that William Gaskell's habit of taking holidays apart from his family began fairly early in the marriage: he had been abroad for ten weeks with a friend in autumn 1839. But his wife obviously missed him when he was away and did not hesitate to encourage his sister to get married:

To Eliza Gaskell, 19 August 1838 (13)
> Better to suffer a little poverty than to have the *wearing* anxiety of an engagement, for certainly one if not both of the parties suffer. . . . As to your mother – finish yourself first, and then wonder if your mother would consent. An you love me don't have it in the winter – Fancy slip, slop, splash splash to the chapel, or going in pattens to the carriage – and red noses and blue cheeks, and a great red swelled finger to wriggle out of the glove, and present for the ring. William said the other night I had not said half enough to you about coming here – he says your mother promised him, and he does not know who has a claim upon you at this particular time if we have not. You only came over for the *gaiety* of the Bazaar. *Now*

come and see if you could enjoy a *quiet* visit with us – we saw nothing of you.

Eliza did marry Charles Holland, yet another cousin of Elizabeth Gaskell, and received a letter of welcome to her new home that ended, 'It is a *silly piece* of *bride-like affectation* my dear, not to sign yourself by your proper name. . . . So goodbye my dear Mrs Elizabeth Holland . . .' Then comes a postscript: 'Dear Lizzie I've only just time to send my love to you & Charles & Anne, which Lily in her hurry has forgetten – W.G.' (14). Called 'Lily' at home and by her close friends, Mrs William Gaskell always insisted upon using her own first name and not her husband's.

By far the most interesting early letter about her relationship with him was to his sister Anne, who had by now married a William Robson, a prominent Unitarian, and postmaster in Warrington until 1861 when he retired 'on a handsome and well earned pension' : [9]

To Anne Robson, 23 December 1840 (16)[10]

Wednesday Evening.   9 o'clock

My dearest Nancy,

I am sitting all alone, and not feeling over & above well; and it would be such a comfort to have you here to open my mind to – but that not being among the possibilities, I am going to write you a long private letter; unburdening my mind a bit. And yet it is nothing, so don't prepare yourself for any wonderful mystery. In the first place I got yr letter today and thank you very much for it – I will send for the eggs on Saty. I am so glad to say MA is better; – she has jelly & strengthening medicine each twice a day, & is to have broth & eggs whenever she can particularly fancy them, and seems much less languid – though still I fear she is not strong. – I once did think of offering myself and her for a week or so, to Sam as visitors, for I have such faith in him; & have fancied that *if* there were any *latent* disease in her (which sometimes haunts me fearing that there is some return of her old baby complaint in the head) *he* could detect it, and would take such interest in her, & know so well how to prescribe for her. We have Mr Partington of course & he was very encouraging this morning and she certainly *is* better – but one can't help having 'Mother's fears'; and Wm, I dare say kindly, won't allow me ever to talk to him about anxieties, while it would be SUCH A RELIEF often. So don't allude too much to what I've been saying in your answer. William is at a minister's meeting to-night, – and tomorrow dines with a world of professors and college people at Mark Philips – and the next day Xmas day it has been a sort of long promise that we all should spend at the Bradford's – by all, I mean

Wm, myself, two children & Elizth and all stop all night – Yesterday this plan seemed quite given up – today Mr Partington seemed to think the little change might do MA good, – so it's *on* again – if all goes on well.

I have of course had MA more with me during this delicacy of hers, and I am more and more anxious about her – not exactly her health; but I see hers is a peculiar character – *very* dependent on those around her – almost as much so as Meta is *in*dependent & in this point I look to Meta to strengthen her. But I am more & more convinced that love & sympathy are very *very* much required by MA. The want of them would make MA an unhappy character, probably sullen & deceitful – while the sunshine of love & tenderness would do everything for her. She is very conscientious, and very tender-hearted – Now Anne, will you remember this? It is difficult to have the right trust in God almost, when thinking about one's children – and you know I have no sister or near relation whom I could entreat to watch over any peculiarity in their disposition. Now you know that dear William feeling most kindly towards his children, is yet most reserved in *expressions* of either affection or sympathy – & in case of my death, we all know the probability of widowers marrying again, – would you promise, dearest Anne to remember MA's peculiarity of character, and as much as circumstances would permit, watch over her & cherish her. The feeling, the conviction that you were aware of my wishes and would act upon them would be *such* a comfort to me. Meta is remarkably independent, & will strengthen MA, if she is spared. Now don't go & fancy I am low-spirited &c &c. As for death I have I think remarkably little constitutional dread of it – I often fear I do not look forward to it with sufficient awe, considering the futurity which *must* follow – and I do often pray for trust in God, complete trust in him – with regard to what becomes of my children. Still let me open my heart sometimes to you dear Anne, with reliance on your sympathy and secrecy. And now I won't write any more about feelings but try & give you some news . . .

The product of a mood of depression perhaps; even so, the few letters to Anne Robson that survive are important for the intimacy of their revelations about the marriage relationship and family matters in general. One may suspect that as the years went by Elizabeth Gaskell tended to strengthen and develop her Holland connections rather than the Gaskell ones. The case of Holbrook Gaskell Junior seems most striking. A successful and cultivated man, collector of books, fine china and English art, he is not mentioned in the correspondence after 1838, though he did not die until 1909.[11] The letters to Eliza Holland, William Gaskell's other sister, seem to stop in 1859 and there are hints that the friendship eventually lapsed (414, 506a). But to the end of her life Elizabeth

Gaskell kept up her confidences with Anne Robson, an 'ever affectionate sister' telling what appears to be the simple truth without a sign of reticence or embarrassment. We hear the unforced voice in which she told her last, everyday story, *Wives and Daughters*.

CHAPTER THREE

Contrasts
of the forties

Let there be meadows and mountains, but
there must also be streets, alleys, work-
shops, and jails, to complete the scenery of
the poetry of poverty.
(W. J. Fox, 'The Poor and Their
Poetry', 1832[1])

ONE OF THE WORLD'S GREATEST calico printers, William Gaskell's friend
Edmund Potter, proudly maintained that his manufacturing district near Manchester had scarcely a resident 'living on independent means – leading a strictly
idle life'.[2] But, as Elizabeth Gaskell had written to her hesitating sister-in-law,
'Remember in trade there always are ups & downs, and you must make up your
mind to times of anxiety' (11). During the years 1841–2 unemployment and
economic depression coincided with political strife and agitation.[3] On 2 June
1841 Anti-Corn Law Leaguers, their Irish allies and Chartists fought a pitched
battle in Stevenson Square:

To John Pierpont, 12 June 1841
  We are feeling as indeed all English people *must* do, that we are at a great
  crisis, and that there is a great struggle going on in the matter of the Corn
  Laws. Perhaps it may have been decided before this reaches you; if not
  peacefully decided, at least by agitation and distress which it is most painful to think of. The manufacturing classes around us are in very great

trouble, and if it were winter the lower classes would find it almost un-
bearable; as it is the early warmth of the season has been a great blessing.
I send you a few temperance tracts which were especially recommended to
me by the revd F. Howorth, who, since you were here has married a cousin
of mine, and is very much interested in the Temperance Cause.

In these years of distress, 'to prolong their sad existence, the infants were
wrapped up like parcels, in pieces of calico'. Committees of relief distributed
clothing and bedding, the ministers of various denominations 'distributed
themselves in the different quarters of the town' and sent 'town missionaries'
into the slum dwellings. Soup was given out daily at six in the morning to
people who had waited for hours. Meanwhile, the Anti-Corn Law Leaguers
intensified their efforts. Prominent Manchester Unitarians were amongst
leaders of the League. Holbrook Gaskell, Charles Holland, Edward Holland,
the Reverend J. G. Robberds and the Reverend J. R. Beard were involved.
William Gaskell was not, at least in any obvious way. Some years later his wife
reminded his daughter that 'speechmaking, public-meetings and such noisy
obtrusive ways of "doing good" are his dislike, as you know, but oh! he is so
good really in his own quiet way, beginning at home and working outwards
without noise or hubbub'. She agreed: 'I am more & more convinced *be* good,
& *doing* good comes naturally, & need not be fussed and spoken about' (123).
   Summer was coming, distress was declining, and William's month of absence
was at hand. They decided to leave the two children with a faithful servant and
an aunt and spend July abroad, away from Manchester altogether. They
journeyed through old Flemish towns, admiring in a Ruskinian way the 'practical poetry' of the architecture, to the Rhine at Cologne – 'which smells of the
bones of the 3,000 virgins'! (15) She evidently escaped the traditional
Rheinschwärmerei of English tourists, preferring Heidelberg on the Neckar.
Her friends the Howitts had gone to live there for a while and also Manchester
had a large German colony active in the textile trade, many of whom the
Gaskells knew; Souchays and Beneckes were related to Schuncks and Schwabes.[4]
They stayed in Heidelberg with a sister of Grace Schwabe, a 'Frau von Pick-
ford', widow of William Pickford:

To Eliza Holland (née Gaskell), August 1841 (15)
   Mrs Pickford is a widow with 3 daughters at home. Emma 29, very good
   & very plain, – sensible unselfish & the refuge of the whole family in any
   dilemma, Thekla 19, *very* lovely, and one of the most elegant people I
   ever saw, and Matilda sixteen – fine looking with pale red hair – the two
   youngest very full of fun, and all very ladylike. The house is out of
   Heidelberg, with a splendid view from the windows, gardens & fountains

on each side, and most tiring walk up the wooded hill behind from which you have splendid views (don't be tired of '*splendid views*', I can't help it there were so many.) We got there the first evening at tea-time unexpected as to the day, though they were aware of our coming. Mrs P. told us they were all planning to go with Mrs & Miss Howitt to a festival at the Wolf's brunnen about 2 miles off – would we like to go. To be sure we were up to anything – and hardly staid to enquire what & where but flew to put on our things and on returning to the drawing room found Mrs & Miss H & every body ready. . . .

At Heidelberg they moved in a society more aristocratic and elegant than any they can have come across before, even at the Bradfords :

Mme Schlosser & Mme Nies are sisters – very wealthy – live in Frankfurt in the winter in grand old mansions one of which belonged to Charles Vth and in summer live near Heidelberg. – Mme Nies is a protestant-matter of fact person living in a new country-house, full of new elegances, with the most beautiful new paintings up & down – she is a widow. Mme Schlosser is a strict Catholic, lives in a house 450 years old, which till lately was a convent, has a picture-gallery filled with the oldest productions of art Van Eycks, Albert Durers &c. – She is a highly accomplished woman – has made some very fine published translations from the Spanish dramatists & is in correspondence with many foreign literati. Wordsworth has lately been staying there – James the novelist Mrs Jamieson &c. She is cousin of Goethe. – Her ball was not 'zu ehren Herrn, und Frauen Gaskell', but Mme Nies was. Notwithstanding this, I preferred Mme Schlosser's. We first went to call & present our letters – and were then taken over the old conventual house & grounds – terrace below terrace – walks trellised with vines – and farther away, a wilderness of wood, rock & waterfall – the house with noble old oak furniture polished floors, a library with 40,000 vols – room within room & recess beyond recess, with the fine painted glass arch windows throwing a 'dim religious' light over all. The chapel is magnificent though small, and in every nook – on the wide staircase, along the galleries were orange trees, & oleanders in tubs, – in full flower. – Mme Schlossers had the house full of company as it always is during summer, and a gay party were assembled on the terraces where footmen were handing them coffee in a very al-fresco style. . . . So to the ball one lovely evening about 7 we went, and on alighting found ourselves in the middle of 180 gay people who were promenading about on the terraces. Fancy the picturesqueness of this, with the setting sun lighting up the noble views in the background. No one had hat, bonnet or shawl on. I must first tell you of the etiquette about dress. No one under 40 in summer wears anything but muslin, white of course in general – Artificial flowers too are quite out of the question, yet if you mean to dance, flowers in your hair is the signal, so every German girl knows how to weave the prettiest natural garlands – Mine was geranium – Thekla wove it, – but the prevalent & fashionable flower was the intensely scarlet pomegranate blossom with its deep green leaves – Matilda had ivy & looked like a Bacchante. Orange blossom & myrtle are never worn except the former by a betrothed, the latter by a bride. . . .

I had a glorious share of dancing every dance till I was worn out & when the end of the evening came I had danced every dance but one, the great mistake of the eveng. William said I was sadly tired & very dizzy, when a very ugly man asked me to dance – I told him I was too much tired when lo & behold he turned out to be Wolfgang von Goethe, grandson to the illustrious Wolfgang – and Wm said I shd have danced with the *name* – numbers of illustrious names were in the room.

A casual exclamation in this same letter is worth noting:

Sometimes some of the students when we had music dancing & all manner of games; sometimes the Howitts – when we all told the most frightening & wild stories we had ever heard, – some *such* fearful ones – all true – then we drank tea out at the Howitts, – looking over all the portfolios of splendid engravings, casts &c they had collected – (My word! authorship brings them in a pretty penny) . . .

One day Charles Dickens will teach her the full force of *that* realisation. She will come to rely upon the extra income she could gain from telling her stories in print.

Light years away, in Manchester, agitation continued.[5] The Anti-Corn Law League had the brilliant idea of staging a conference in August 1841 for ministers of religion. The Reverend J. R. Beard, Unitarian minister at New Bridge Street, was a member of the Committee, but William Gaskell does not seem to have been involved in any way. Later in the year Richard Cobden's wife led the ladies of Manchester in sending a Memorial to the Queen and in the organisation of a Grand Bazaar in the Theatre Royal. The *Manchester Times* devoted many closely printed columns to these activities but amongst the hundreds of names, which include Mrs Beard, Mrs Robberds and Mrs Tayler (the wives of Manchester's senior Unitarian ministers), Mrs Holbrook Gaskell and even Mrs Charles Holland, Elizabeth Gaskell's name is absent. Husband and wife stood aloof, perhaps on principle, like James Martineau.[6]

In August 1842 there was a major strike. Gangs of youths roamed the suburbs begging, but even a girl could deal with them, Susanna Winkworth discovered, provided she had a good stock of coppers, some bread and a determination to give *civilly*.[7] The Gaskells opened their shutters each morning and did the same, but domestic affairs must have taken precedence. A daughter, baptised Florence Emily, was born on 7 October and they also moved to a new house. It was 'a mile and a half from the *very* middle of Manchester; the last house countrywards of an interminably long street, the other end of which touches the town, while we look into fields from some of our windows' (48). In the summer of 1843 the family went to Silverdale, a favourite holiday spot on the shores of Morecambe Bay. Then, on 23 October 1844, a son was born:

To Eliza Holland, Summer 1845 (16a)

Sunday morning

Willie asleep everyone else out. . . . I am so busy & so happy. My laddie is grunting so I must make haste. . . . I have Florence & Willie in my room which is also nursery, call Hearn at six, $\frac{1}{2}$ p 6 she is dressed, comes in, dresses Flora, gives her breakfast the first; $\frac{1}{2}$ p. 7 I get up, 8 Flora goes down to her sisters & Daddy, & Hearn to her breakfast. While I in my dressing gown dress Willie. $\frac{1}{2}$ p. 8 I go to breakfast with parlour people, Florence being with us & Willie (ought to be) in his cot; Hearn makes beds etc in nursery only. 9 she takes F. & I read chapter & have prayers first with household & then with children, $\frac{1}{2}$ p. 9 Florence & Willie come in drawing room for an hour while bedroom & nursery windows are open; $\frac{1}{2}$ p. 10 go in kitchen, cellars & order dinner. Write letters; $\frac{1}{4}$ p. 11 put on things; $\frac{1}{2}$ p. 11 take Florence out. 1 come in, nurse W. & get ready for dinner; $\frac{1}{4}$ p. 1 dinner; $\frac{1}{2}$ p. 2 children, two little ones, come down during servants' dinner half hour open windows upstairs; 3 p.m. go up again & I have two hours to kick my heels in (to be elegant & explicit). 5 Marianne & Meta from lessons & Florence from upstairs & Papa when he can comes in drawing room to 'Lilly a hornpipe', i.e. dance while Mama plays, & make all the noise they can. Daddy reads, writes or does what she likes in dining room. $\frac{1}{2}$ p. 5 Margaret (nursemaid) brings Florence's supper, which Marianne gives her, being answerable for slops, dirty pinafores & untidy misbehaviours while Meta goes up stairs to get ready & fold up Willie's basket of clothes while he is undressed (this by way of feminine & family duties). Meta is so neat & so knowing, only, handles wet napkins very gingerly. 6 I carry Florence upstairs, nurse Willie; while she is tubbed & put to bed. $\frac{1}{2}$ past 6 I come down dressed leaving (hitherto) both asleep & Will & Meta dressed (between 6 and $\frac{1}{2}$ p.) & Miss F. with tea quite ready. After tea read to M. A. & Meta till bedtime while they sew, knit or worsted work. From 8 till 10 gape. We are so desperately punctual that now you may know what we are doing every hour.

They all seem snug and safe within the fortress of the Victorian home, though there is an odd note later in the letter when she mentions a visit Marianne and Meta were going to make to their aunt at Liscard Vale, Wallasey: '*Please* (though not likely at all) don't let them ever come in contact with Martineau children. You need not ask why but please *don't*.' Can she possibly mean the children of James Martineau, Unitarian minister in Liverpool, just across the Mersey? He was a colleague of William Gaskell at Manchester New College, coming over regularly to give his lectures. He had seven children, all carefully taught on his own high principles, and had recently moved to a new house in a healthy location. But nobody with children could feel totally secure then. She probably knew that his nine-year-old son Herbert had been stricken with a mysterious disease early in 1845.[8] If so, her mother's care was in vain. Her own children caught scarlet fever whilst they were on holiday in Wales that summer and little Willie did not recover. He died in Portmadoc on 10 August, some months before Herbert Martineau. 'That wound will never heal on earth', she wrote a few years later to a friend she began corresponding with about this time,[9] Anne Shaen, 'although hardly any one knows how it has changed me. I wish you had seen my little fellow, dearest dear Annie. I can give you no idea what a darling he was – so affectionate and *reasonable* a baby I never saw' (25a).

A fourth daughter, Julia Bradford, was born on 3 September the following year, 1846, and simple family life resumed:

To Marianne and Meta Gaskell, April 1847 (17a)
Flossy says I am to give her love & Papa has made her two kites. The first went up into some trees where it stuck but the last is still to be seen & flown when the wind bears. She & Papa are very happy together flying it sometimes. I ask Flossy what message I am to send & she says 'Sunday and Monday' so you may make head or tail out of that as you can, for I can't interpret. 'I got grapes yesterday & to-day did you?' 'Monday and Tuesday'. Oh! nonsense Flossy, I shan't write any more so I am your very affectionate mother

E. C. Gaskell.

A long, contorted letter to her aunt, Fanny Holland, however, declared the cost. The children's nanny, a Miss Fergusson, is leaving for another situation because she cannot manage the girls:

To Fanny Holland, 9 March 1847
I disapprove and see more and more the bad effects of her mode of treatment; and yet I, my own self, scarcely dare to look forwards to the time when she will no longer be our inmate, and my dear household friend, and sometimes I can not keep down the feeling which I yet know to be morbid, that it is ungrateful to ever part with one who was *so tender* to my poor darling boy, and that makes me most miserable. However I do try to look stedfastly to the *right* for my children; and I am comforted by Miss F's *own* right understanding of my different feelings, and own agreement of judgment with mine, as to her not managing the girls well.

After Willie's death she began writing in real earnest, encouraged by her husband. She started a rural tale : it did not answer her deepest needs. She then began a story set in Manchester 'a town so full of striking contrasts' (39) that she could not ignore them :

To Mrs Samuel Greg (draft), Early 1849 (42)
I can remember now that the prevailing thought in my mind at the time when the tale was silently forming itself and impressing me with the force of a reality, was the seeming injustice of the inequalities of fortune. Now, if they occasionally appeared unjust to the more fortunate, they must bewilder an ignorant man full of rude, illogical thought, and full also of sympathy for suffering which appealed to him through his senses. I fancied I saw how all this might lead to a course of action which might appear right for a time to the bewildered mind of such a one, but that this course of action, violating the eternal laws of God, would bring with it its own punishment of an avenging conscience far more difficult to bear than any worldly privation. Such thoughts I now believe, on looking back, to have been the origin of the book. 'John Barton' was the original title of the book. Round the character of John Barton all the others formed themselves; he was my hero, *the* person with whom all my sympathies went, with whom I tried to identify myself at the time, because I believed from personal observation that such men were not uncommon, and would well reward such sympathy and love as should throw light down upon their groping search after the causes of suffering, and the reason why suffering is sent, and what they can do to lighten it. . . .
There are many such whose lives are tragic poems which cannot take formal language. The tale was formed, and the greater part of the first volume was written when I was obliged to lie down constantly on the sofa, and when I took refuge in the invention to exclude the memory of painful scenes which would force themselves upon my remembrance. It is no

wonder then that the whole book seems to be written in the minor key; indeed, the very design seems to me to require this treatment. I acknowledge the fault of there being too heavy a shadow over the book; but I doubt if the story could have been deeply realized without these shadows. The cause of the fault must be looked for in the design; and yet the design was one worthy to be brought into consideration. Perhaps after all it may be true that I, in my state of feelings at that time, was not fitted to introduce the glimpses of light and happiness which might have relieved the gloom.

Susanna Winkworth used to meet 'violent Chartists, always railing' when walking around her Districts in Ancoats and London Road.[10] Elizabeth Gaskell's experience for the District Provident Society was no different, though on one occasion there was a stunning addition when the head of a poor family she was visiting took her arm in a tight grasp and said with tears in his eyes, 'Ay, ma'am, but have ye ever seen a child clemmed to death?'

She ignored the explanations of political economy, the 'dismal science' of the time, so powerfully criticised by her father a generation before. James Martineau used to give a popular course in it at Cross Street Chapel. His eloquent, compassionate sermon on 'Ireland and Her Famine', preached about the time *Mary Barton* was sent to the publisher in early 1847, shows that his sympathies ran with hers, but his reserved austerity may have been out of key. Some years later, admittedly whilst on holiday, she expressed a wish to avoid the Martineaus: 'I like to range about ad libitum, & sit out looking at views &c; not talking sense by the yard' (163). Her response to another of Manchester New College's lecturers, Francis Newman, brother of the future Cardinal, is strikingly different:

To Eliza Fox, November 1849 (52), 25 November 1849 (53)
We first knew Mr Newman from his coming here to be a professor at the Manchester College – and the face and voice at first sight told 'He had been with Christ'. I never during a 6 years pretty intimate acquaintance heard or saw anything which took off that first conviction. Oh dear! I long for the days back again when he came dropping in in the dusk and lost no time in pouring out what his heart was full of, (that's the secret of eloquence) whether it was a derivation of a word, a joke or a burst of indignation or a holy thought. I can't go into his life just now, it's too interesting to be compressed . . .

You have heard Mr Newman speak 'I guess.' His voice and pronunciation are perfect; I do like that rich melodious accent which Oxford men have, though it is called 'bumptious', but Mr Newman's self is not bumptious. He dresses so shabbily you would not see his full beauty, – he used to wear detestable bottle green coats, wh. never show off a man. Mrs Newman is a Plymouth Brother which is a sort of community-of-goods-and-equality-of-rank-on-religious-principles association and *very* calvinistic.

Eccentric as he was, he then insisted that the value of faith must be measured by 'the *intensity* with which the grand ideas of GOD and duty and holiness are realized'. This, despite the fact that he was not a Unitarian, sounds much more like Elizabeth Gaskell:

To Miss Lamont, 5 January 1849 (39)
Some people here are very angry and say the book will do harm; and for a time I have been shaken and sorry; but I have such firm faith that the earnest expression of any one's feeling can only do good in the long run, – that God will cause the errors to be temporary, the truth to be eternal, that I try not to mind too much what people say either in blame or praise. I had a letter from Carlyle, and when I am over-filled with thoughts arising from this book, I put it all aside, (or *try* to put it aside,) and think of his last sentence – 'May you live long to write good books, or *do silently good actions which in my sight is far more indispensable.*'

To judge by the letters that have survived, his influence did not last – by 1852 Mrs Gaskell sounds just as interested in John Henry Newman, though the two brothers had taken diametrically opposite paths in matters of belief. Indirectly, however, we know that as late as 1863 her husband would talk about Francis Newman in a way that was '*admiring* almost to enthusiasm, which you know is saying much in Mr Gaskell's case'. It was, William thought, 'impossible to estimate the good that was done by such a *character* as his, however one might disagree with special views'.[11]

Mary Barton did not find a publisher easily. Whilst she was waiting, three of her stories appeared in the short-lived *Howitt's Journal*, together with an account of the lectures given in Manchester by the New England sage, Ralph Waldo Emerson. Eventually *Mary Barton* was accepted by Chapman and Hall on the recommendation of John Forster, who was to become a great friend and literary adviser, but publication was delayed for months on end. William Howitt acted as her agent, and at the end of 1847 she went on a visit with her husband to his house at Clapton. Authorship, they found, was still bringing in a pretty penny:

To Marianne and Meta Gaskell, December 1847 (18)

Aunt Anne can describe the house having been here, but I don't think she can describe the room we had, – such a blazing fire – such a crimson carpet – such an easy chair – such white dimity curtains – such a pretty vase of winter flowers before the looking glass. Then we came down into an equally comfortable dining-room, where was a dinner-tea to which we did ample justice I can assure you. Then Mr & Mrs & Miss & Master Howitt, and we went on talking till 12 o'clock. What do you think of *that*? And now I am sitting writing in such a pretty dining room, looking into a garden with a rockery, and a green-house, & all sorts of pretty plants, arbutus, and ever-greens – There are so many pretty casts here that you would like so much to see. The Isis out of a flower that Selina Winkworth copied is on the stair-case – And a Venus picking up a shell, that is so beautiful – I wish you could see it. We dine here today, & then go on to Crix, & shall be there about six; Tell Aunt Anne to send a message *by the electric telegraph*, if you are both drowned, or burnt, &c – My best love to her & Grandmama; to you two darlings – write very soon to yr very affectionate

E C Gaskell

They then went to an even finer house, the home of the Shaens at Crix, near Chelmsford:

To Marianne and Meta Gaskell, December 1847 (19)

The next morning you may be sure we were curious enough to see what sort of a place it was we had got to for it was dark when we came here. Our window looked out upon a lawn with beautiful ever greens and beyond that only separated by a wire fence, a large parklike field with sheep in it and beyond that woods. . . . You should have seen the sirloin of beef (more than 40 lb.) we had at the bottom of the table and *2 turkeys* at the top yesterday – but then we were 10 in the parlour and 32 in the servants hall. I never saw such an immense piece of beef, as I have been telling Flossy she might have hidden herself behind it. Last night we had talking, laughing and singing (Oh! I forgot! yesterday for a walk I went to the farm and round the kitchen garden and saw all the peach trees – but no peaches alas! !) Today Mr Shaen has been reading a sermon to us . . .

The 'two nations' of rich and poor exclude the huge servant class of those days, provided of course that they had good employers.

Back in Manchester again, she began to press her publisher:

To Edward Chapman, 13 April 1848 (24)
Dear Sir,

Allow me to remind you of the promise you kindly made of letting me know what decision you came to, with regard to the publication of my novel.

I fear from your delay in writing, you have thought it desirable to defer the appearance of my work until a volume of a different character has appeared; and I must confess this will be a disappointment to me; as both from Mr Howitt's report of the agreement you came to with him on my behalf, and from your own statement to me, I believed there was no doubt it would have been published by this time. However I am, (above every other consideration,) desirous that it should be *read*; and if you think there would be a better chance of a large circulation by deferring it's appearance, of course I defer to your superior knowledge, only repeating my own belief that the tale would bear directly upon the present circumstances.

Just a few days before this letter the Chartists had called off their great march on the Houses of Parliament. Historically speaking, the way was now open for a gradual transition to a new order of society without violence or revolution :

To Mary Ewart, Late 1848 (36)
I can only say I wanted to represent the subject in the light in which some of the workmen certainly consider to be *true*, not that I dare to say it is the abstract absolute truth.

That some of the men do view the subject in the way I have tried to represent, I have personal evidence; and I think somewhere in the first volume you may find a sentence stating that my intention was simply to represent the view many of the work-people take. But independently of any explicit statement of my intention, I do think that we must all ac-knowledge that there are duties connected with the manufacturing system not fully understood as yet, and evils existing in relation to it which may be remedied in some degree, although we as yet do not see how; but surely there is no harm in directing the attention to the existence of such evils. No one can feel more deeply than I how *wicked* it is to do anything to excite class against class; and the sin has been most unconscious if I have done so.

Mary Barton had been published anonymously in October 1848. She had caught the tide as it was turning.

Great manufacturers like Edmund Potter and Samuel Greg were satisfied; the old radical weaver Samuel Bamford assured her that she had drawn a 'fearfully true' and 'mournfully beautiful' picture – he was a devotee of Tennyson. Others saw emotionalism and error rather than truth and compassion:

To Edward Chapman, 1 January 1849 (37)
> Half the masters here are bitterly angry with me – half (and the best half) are buying it to give to their work-people's libraries. One party say it shall be well abused in the British Quarterly, the other say it shall be praised in the Westminster; I had no idea it would have proved such a fire brand; meanwhile no one seems to see my idea of a tragic poem; so I, in reality, mourn over my failure. – Mr Carlyle's letter remains my real true gain.

She sounds depressed here, but during this period we can see that she is making a successful effort to pick up the threads of life again after the death of her little son. 'Read "Jane Eyre", it is an uncommon book', she orders Anne Shaen. 'I don't know if I like or dislike it. I take the opposite side to the person I am talking with always in order to hear some convincing arguments to clear up my opinions. Tell me what Crix thinks – everybody's opinions' (25a). She binds her husband's pupils to her with hoops of charm and charity, especially Catherine Winkworth, who was ill at Southport when *Mary Barton* was published. If she was not actually running over to see her, thin and unwell as she was herself at the time, she was dashing off letters that hum with confident, nervous vitality. Mrs Gaskell could never have recommended herself to the more strait-laced members of her husband's congregation – 'the men with faces like a meat-axe; the women most palpably without bustles', as Jane Carlyle once unkindly described some Liverpool Unitarians:[12]

To Catherine Winkworth, 2, 11, 29 November 1848 (29, 30, 32)
> Oh dear! I envy you the *Times*; – it's very unprincipled and all that, but the most satisfactory newspaper going. Now is not that sentence unbecoming in a minister's wife? I never can ascertain what I am in politics; and veer about from extreme Right, – no, I don't think I ever go as far as the extreme Left. . . .
>
> Do call me Lily, and never mind respect to your elders. *Ils sont passés ces beaux jours là*, when old people were looked upon as people who could do no wrong; and were to have all outward and inward respect paid to them; so let me for one of the body, have affection instead of respect. I wish I had five sisters, who were bound to love me by their parents' marriage certificate; but as I have not, I mean to take you for sisters and daughters at once. . . . By the way, Emily was curious to know the name of the person

who wrote 'Mary Barton' (a book she saw at Plas Penrhyn), and I am happy in being able to satisfy her Eve-like craving. Marianne Darbishire told me it was ascertained to be the production of a Mrs Wheeler, a clergyman's wife, who once upon a time was a Miss Stone, and wrote a book called 'The Cotton-Lord'. Marianne gave me many proofs which I don't think worth repeating, but I think were quite convincing.

I have had a busy week arranging lessons and children's winter things; both of which are now satisfactorily in progress. I am writing while I am eating my lunch, which must be an excuse for my letter if it has more of the body than the mind in it. There is three-quarters of a pig awaiting me in the kitchen; and work of all kinds in the nursery; and the girls should go out before callers 'come down like a wolf on the fold'. . . . The Darbishires' house is in a most upside-down state; not an atom of furniture in either of the drawing-rooms, and we are to go there to a very large party (according to Mrs D.) on Wednesday next. I suppose we are to sit in white-washers' pails, and on steps of ladders, which will be original. . . .

I don't hear anything of the Schwabes; nor who is lion now in the interregnum between Mr A. J. Scott and Jenny Lind, who is coming to them again in December for two Concerts for the Infirmary; one in the Concert Hall, supported by the Liedertafel, price £1 1s. (*one guinea*, my dear!), the other in the Free Trade Hall, supported by the Madrigal Society. Chevalier Neukomm has been couched, and can see to a certain degree, but has great pain in his eyes. . . . The weather here is the perfection of dreariness; grey black fog close to the house; clinging to everything and penetrating to one's very soul. . . .

I had the Sunday School girls here last Sunday, and Susanna came to help me, and I thought we went off gloriously, only – (everything has its *only*) – in repeating our subjects of conversation, I named an accidental five minutes conversation with one or two of the girls about Sir Walter Scott's novels (*apropos* of a picture of Queen Elizabeth, *via* 'Kenilworth', &c.) and Mrs J. J. Tayler is shocked at such a subject of conversation on a *Sunday*, – so there I am in a scrape, – well! it can't be helped, I am myself and nobody else, and can't be bound by another's rules. The Darbishires are coming tonight with 'Zoe' [the novelist Geraldine Jewsbury], Dr Hodgson, Mr Green (shan't we be intellectual, that's all?) and a few others. I wish myself well thro' it.

It is hard to credit that she had thought she was dying in the previous spring, even if she had been in real danger for a day or two according to her husband, but her temperament was volatile as well as earnest. The strong friendships she was making with younger women were an obvious release – something that will become very evident in the many letters she was to write to Eliza Fox, 'a bright, black-eyed, intelligent, merry girl' who had, most unusually in those days, begun to study art as a profession at Sass's school in London. Moreover, *Mary Barton* turned out to be a runaway success. 'Not the least agreeable part of yr letter', she wrote rather simply to Edward Chapman, 'is that in which you speak of the book "being a source of profit to the publisher"' (38). The £100 she received for the entire copyright, later supplemented by an unexpected £100, must have been very gratifying. It was a trivial sum beside the thousands of pounds an alert professional author like Dickens had shown it was possible to achieve, but not out of the way for an author like her. Nor does she seem at this stage in her life to rely upon such earnings. Indeed, the death of aunt Abigail Holland in 1848 released more of aunt Lumb's legacy, and it is said that William Gaskell inherited £500 per annum from Holbrook Gaskell, though this is doubtful.[13] They certainly had money to invest:

To Edward Holland, 13 January 1849 (39a)
> Your proposal about the Cath. Dock Shares seems to both my husband & me a very kind & advantageous one; & we gladly consent to having the £1500 so invested put into the general fund at its present value; and in the division to form part of the moiety which is to be invested for me – to be considered as an investment already made in my behalf in short. I don't know if I have expressed myself sufficiently clearly to shew you that I fully sanction what you propose; but I *do*.
>
> My poor Mary Barton is stirring up all sorts of angry feelings against me in Manchester; but those best acquainted with the way of thinking & feeling among the poor acknowledge its *truth*; which is the acknowledgment I most of all desire, because evils being once recognized are half way on towards their remedy. I am ever dear Edward
>
> > Your affectionate cousin
> > E. C. Gaskell.

It does look rather complacent. Her conscience clear, her spirits rising, her situation comfortable, she seems to be resting on her laurels. She can now sit back and take a benevolent interest in Chapman's next literary-cum-philanthropic venture:

To Edward Chapman, 9 March 1849 (41)
> Thank you for the two copies of Mary B, safely received through Simms and Dinham yesterday. I am not thinking of writing any thing else; le jeu

ne vaut pas la chandelle. And I have nothing else to say. I shall be amused to read the manufacturing novel you tell me is forth-coming; I suppose the writer's name is a secret, but I wish her every success. It is a large subject, & I think it ought to be written upon.

Charlotte Brontë's *Shirley* was published by Chapman and Hall on 26 October 1849; and to Elizabeth Gaskell, as to a famous person, the author sent a copy. 'Currer Bell (aha! what will you give me for a secret?)', Elizabeth crowed to Catherine Winkworth, 'She's a she – that I will tell you – who has sent me "Shirley" ' (57). For the past sixteen years Mrs Gaskell had been a Mancunian, only visiting friends and relations elsewhere, going away from the city – but on holiday. Heidelberg in 1841 had opened windows on a much wider life, but personal and social traumas of the forties must have almost wiped the experience from her mind. With the success of *Mary Barton* comes a qualitative change. Her spirits are high and she feels confidence in her powers. Life is to be lived to the full. 'The people here,' wrote Geraldine Jewsbury to Jane Carlyle, 'are beginning mildly to be pained for Mr. "Mary Barton". And one lady said to me the other day, "I don't think authoresses ought ever to marry," and then proceeded to eulogise Mr Gaskell.' This may be yet another contrast – Susanna Winkworth regretted that he was left 'so little time and opportunity for original work of his own, especially in history and criticism' – but at least Manchester will always remain Elizabeth Gaskell's centre. She will never give up the roles of provincial minister's wife and mother, hostess and housekeeper, though the circles of her experience widen. Her correspondents multiply and change; her travels increase and extend. She seems quintessentially Victorian now in her love for infinitely ramifying detail, in her desire to swallow down people, places and life-styles. Her letters, always informal, approach telegraphese as she strives to record everything she does and discovers. She immerses herself in the doings of others, sympathises with everyone. Whatever she is doing, it is not resting on her laurels . . . collapsing, sometimes.

CHAPTER FOUR

Home in Manchester

> I am screaming out loud all the time I
> write and so is my brother which takes off
> my attention rather, and I hope will excuse
> mistakes
> (Fanny Squeers to Ralph Nickleby)

MRS GASKELL'S REMARK to Edward Chapman that she was not thinking
of writing anything else was hardly serious. The twin impulses of benevolence
and a simple urge to write could not be denied. In 1848 the indefatigable
Travers Madge came to Manchester as 'Home Visitor' for the Lower Moseley
Street Sunday Schools, which looked after fifteen hundred children and young
people. He began a *Sunday School Penny Magazine* and of course Elizabeth
Gaskell sent stories; 'far more may be done by the loving heart than by mere
money-giving', she wrote in one of them. Mary Howitt acted as as intermediary
for an American magazine, which printed a descriptive piece on 'The Last
Generation in England'. By the time Jane Loudon, editor of *The Ladies'
Companion*, had persuaded Mrs Gaskell to write 'Mr. Harrison's Confessions'
(1851) – also set in a small town scarcely removed from a village – the rich
seam leading to *Cranford* was being mined. The first sketch of this, one of the
most popular works of the century, appeared in *Household Words* on 13
December 1851. It was by no means the only, or even the first, piece she con-
tributed to the new periodical, conducted by Charles Dickens himself. 'There
is no living English writer whose aid I would desire to enlist in preference to

the authoress of Mary Barton (a book that most profoundly affected and impressed me)', he wrote in terms pitched far higher than those he used to that
other Manchester authoress, Geraldine Jewsbury. The result of this letter was
her serial story 'Lizzie Leigh'. Dickens was to receive much more from her – a
Welsh tale, a Lancashire story, an article on 'Disappearances', a ghost story,
'Cumberland Sheep-Shearers', 'Traits and Stories of the Huguenots' and so on
– all within the next few years, including a complete novel, *North and South*.
Edward Chapman wanted a Christmas story, 'recommending benevolence,
charity, etc.' in 1850. 'However I could not write about virtues to order,' she
sighed, 'so it is simply a little country love-story ...' (81). Chapman also published *Ruth*, her protest against the double standard in sexual morality, in 1853.

Had she wished she could have made a career in literature alone. Her anon-
ymity did not last long and her 'finely-cut mobile features' were seen everywhere when she visited London in the spring of 1849 following *Mary Barton*'s
success. She had breakfast with the cultivated old 'patriarch poet' Samuel
Rogers, dinner with Dickens and dinner with John Forster. She called upon
Carlyle to hear an hour's 'spouting'. She was entertained by Richard Monckton
Milnes, who knew everybody: 'There were the House of Lords there, Miss
Holland says; but independently of the Lords, there was Guizot, and Whewell,
and Archdeacon Hare ...' (45a). But after all the lionisation back to Man-
chester she went:

To Eliza Fox 29 May 1849 (48), Early November 1849 (51)
Mr Gaskell meeting me; (I wonder what yr notion of him is, – he *is* 6 feet
tall, thin hair inclined to grey as far as outward man goes, does that accord
with clairvoyance?) ... The four girls rushed upon me, and almost
smothered me; (the second is Margaret, always called Meta) and to the
best of my recollection, we all six husband wife and children four,
talked at once, upon different subjects, incessantly till bed-time for the
younger ones; when the elder two had a little peace, and did really talk.
The next day my husband left home on business; and Susanna Winkworth
came to spend the day; my ancles ached with talking at the end of the day;
its a *true* and not a figurative expression; they did ache, and I had (not)
walked a step only talked. The next day I fairly settled down to home life,
lessons till 12 – lunch walk, etc; and so we've gone on ever since. The
Winkworths are at Alderley; (18 miles off) for the summer which is a
great loss to me; Selina came over yesterday, and we had a charming long
piece of enjoyment of each other; and abuse of Emily for never writing.
... I do think our home *is* very bright.

I always feel very full of something to the exclusion of almost everything else; and just now houses haunt me. . . . Are you prepared for a garret, rather like Campbell's rainbow, 'a happy spirit to delight mid way twixt earth and heaven;' with *no* fireplace, only a great cistern, which however we lock up for fear of our friends committing suicide. Are you prepared for a cold clammy atmosphere, a town with no grace or beauty in it, a house full of cold draughts, and mysterious puffs of icy air? Are you prepared for four girls in and out continually, interrupting the most interesting conversation with enquiries respecting lessons work, etc: — If these delights thy mind can move, come live with me and be my love. I like the house very much, though I acknowledge we have out grown it; you shall have a bottle of hot water in bed, and blankets ad libitum, and we keep glorious fires. The girls *are* very nice ones though I say it that should not say it, and I do think that you will like them all in their separate ways, so please write soon and fix your time for coming.

My dear Eliza I am your affectionate
E. C. Gaskell.

The house in Upper Rumford Street was rather small, but it was a fascinating place to visit. Susanna Winkworth once found its mistress 'overwhelmed with household cares and literary business' to the point of exhaustion, wanting advice about writing for a newspaper and letters taken off her hands. The following day, Sunday, she 'needed real nursing and let me make tea and give orders, and Mr. G. carry her upstairs. . . . Monday, did not get home from District till 6.30, then scampered off to nurse Lily, whom to my astonishment I found sitting in her silk gown in drawing-room, and Mrs. Wedgwood come on a visit, and Darbishires coming to meet her'.[1] 'Tottie' Fox especially had, by late 1849, become as close a friend of Elizabeth Gaskell as the Winkworth sisters, despite her upbringing as the daughter of a Unitarian minister who had been forced to withdraw because of his radical views on divorce and unconventional *ménage*. It was a tolerant family as well as a lively one.

With William Gaskell's many professional commitments increasing year by year, and all his wife's flourishing social involvements, they had to think of moving again. It was not easy:

To Eliza Fox, 26 November 1849 (55)
We are going to the Ss. on Friday to go and call on the Bishop and Mrs Lee, who took the decided step of calling upon us, (Units) the other day. Don't congratulate us too soon my dear! The house is as far off as ever. The nurseries were not healthy in the otherwise perfect house at Cheetham Hill, windows looked into a dry well in the middle of the house; so that's thrown up sky-high, and we're still hovering and quavering and waver-

ing. . . . Next week, Monday I go to Mrs Davenports Capesthorne – a place and person for an artist to be in – old hall, galleries, old paintings, &c. and such a *dama* of a lady to grace them: you would long to sketch her, it and them perpetually, and would be hiding up a corner with yr little sketch-book.

And even when they had found a house, she could not be content to grace it without a second thought:

To Eliza Fox, April 1850 (69)
And we've got a house. Yes! we *really* have. And if I had neither conscience nor prudence I should be delighted, for it certainly *is* a beauty. It is not very far from here, in Plymouth Grove – do you remember our plodding out *that* last Saty in snow to go and see houses? and looking at 2, one inhabited by a Jewish Mrs Abram *and* old clothes. Well, its nearly opposite to the *first* we looked at (*not* the old clothes one) I shall make Meta draw you a plan. You *must* come and see us in it, dearest Tottie, and try and make me see 'the wrong the better cause,' and that it is right to spend so much ourselves on *so* purely selfish a thing as a house is, while so many are wanting – thats the haunting thought to me; at least to one of my 'Mes,' for I have a great number, and that's the plague. One of my mes is, I do believe, a true Christian – (only people call her socialist and communist), another of my mes is a wife and mother, and highly delighted at the delight of everyone else in the house, Meta and William most especially who are in full extasy. Now that's my 'social' self I suppose. Then again I've another self with a full taste for beauty and convenience whh is pleased on its own account. How am I to reconcile all these warring members? I try to drown myself (my *first* self,) by saying it's Wm who is to decide on all these things, and his feeling it right ought to be my rule, And so it is – only that does not quite do.

Who else could she consult? James Martineau had just advised a fellow-minister to extend and improve his parsonage rather than give his money away, for as a general principle 'it is plainly better that the recipient should give labour for what he gets, than give nothing'.[2] On the other hand, Travers Madge was deliberately living in poverty. 'Well!', she decided in this letter, 'I must try and make the house give as much pleasure to others as I can and make it as little a selfish thing as I can. My dear! its 150 a year, and I dare say we shall be ruined; and I've already asked after the ventilation of the new Borough Gaol . . .' But she is plainly uneasy still:

William has just been pleased to observe that it is not often I make such a 'sensible' friendship as the one with you, which I rather resent; for I am sure all my friends *are* sensible. Emily Winkworth is I think the very essence of good sense. Yes that discovery of one's exact work in the world is the puzzle: I never meant to say it was not. I long (weakly) for the old times where right and wrong did not seem such complicated matters; and I am sometimes coward enough to wish that we were back in the darkness where obedience was the only seen duty of women. Only even then I don't believe William would ever have *commanded* me.

Her husband's position in the community must have been a powerful argument. A sense of this, as well as his wife's irony and independence, comes from her account of the return call upon the Bishop of Manchester:

To Eliza Fox, 26 April 1850 (70)

As luck would have it it was a visitation or a something-ation, and upwards of 20 clergymen were there. Such fun! we were tumbled into the drawing room to them; arch-deacons and all (Florence stay'd in the carriage). Mrs Lee is a little timid woman – *I* should make a better Bishop's wife if the Unitarians ever come uppermost in my day: and she thinks me 'satirical' and is afraid of me Mrs Schwabe says. So you may imagine the mal aproposness of the whole affair. Mr Stowell was there and all the cursing Evangelicals. Luckily we know Canon Clifton and one or two of the better sort, so we talked pretty well till the Bishop came in. I thought I would watch him and see how he took the affair; if he skirted Unitarianism as a subject, as he generally talks about it to William, but no! he pounced on the subject at once; and it was funny to watch the clergymen of the Evangelical set who looked as if a bombshell was going off amongst them. . . .

She is being defensive, but on one matter her self-confidence was absolute:

Well! when the call was ended the Bishop took us into his library and that brings me to the picture. Over the door being an exquisitely painted picture of a dead child perhaps Baby's age, – deathly livid, and with the most woeful expression of pain on its little wan face, – it looked too deeply stamped to be lost even in Heaven. He made us look at it and then told me the history. It was painted by some friend or pupil of Maclises and was so true to the life that an anatomist of that sort of thing on seeing it said 'that child has lost its life by an accident which has produced intense pain' – and it was true, – it had been the child of the people with whom the artist lived, and had been *burnt*, had lingered 2 days in the greatest agony, poor darling – and then died! I would not send my child to be educated by the man who could hang up such a picture as that for an object of contemplation; for it was not the quiet lovely expression of angelic rest, but the look of despairing agony. Not all his kind pleasant tattle with Florence set him right with me. He's got something wrong with his heart.

The basis for her confidence had been displayed in the first part of the letter:

Do come to us soon! I want to get associations about that house; *here* there is the precious perfume lingering of my darling's short presence in this life – I wish I were with him in that 'light, where we shall all see light,' for I am often sorely puzzled here – but however I must not waste my strength or my time about the never ending sorrow; but which hallows this house. I think that is one evil of this bustling life that one has never time calmly and bravely to face a great grief, and to view it on every side as to bring the harmony out of it. – Well! I meant to write a merry letter. . . .

Do you know I believe the garden will be a great delight in our new house. Clay soil it *will* be, and there is no help for it, but it will be gay and bright with common flowers; and is quite shut in, – and one may get out without bonnet, which is a blessing, I always want my head cool, and stray about in the odd five minutes. You should see Baby and Florence! their delight is most pretty to see every day they go there; and every new flower (plant) that peeps up is a treasure. Hearn is back and the idea and thought about the removal comforts her for her mother's death in a gentle natural kind of way.

Life and bitter experience had at length brought her to a state of balance. Both she and her servant Ann Hearn, who was to be their friend and companion for life, looked forward with delight as well as back with sorrow.

Despite a summer at Silverdale in 1850, her health was still precarious; 'spinal irritation' (81) had been diagnosed and she told a new friend that she had been forced to leave Manchester to spend 'two months, (usually so damp in Manchester,) in a warmer and drier place'. She writes from The Cliff, near Warwick:

To Lady Kay-Shuttleworth, 12 November 1850 (83)
Before very long I shall be obliged to go up to London for a few days, for we have determined to place my eldest girl at school there for a year;

and I want to see for myself the various school-mistresses that have been recommended to us . . . Both Mr Gaskell and I are very anxious about the school to which we send our dear girl. She has hitherto been brought up at home entirely, but my husband thinks she has some faults of mental indolence which may be cured by associating with other girls for a year or so; and we want to obtain good music and singing lessons for her, because her only talent seems to be for music, and we want her to view this gift rightly and use it well.

More intimately, to Tottie Fox, she hinted at an entanglement:

To Eliza Fox, Late 1850 (85)
Wm is almost as grateful as I am about your thought for MA – but says exactly what I thought he would, – viz that he should not like her to be without me for so long a time *just now*, when we want to examine into the real state of her feelings – (not much touched I fancy,) – and besides you know Wm's anxiety about his girls, and I believe he is afraid of her going to London for the first time without me to take care of her. *We* are very much obliged to you and Mr Fox, dearest Tottie, and if you'll offer *me* $\frac{1}{2}$ your bed for a few nights in about 3 weeks or a month I won't despise it. We are very much taken with your opinion of Mr Lalors.

Rather more than Marianne's feelings and her mother's 'spinal irritation' may have been involved, for Catherine Winkworth told her sister in February 1851 that the Gaskells were thinking of leaving Manchester altogether.[3] In the event they stayed and Marianne was sent off to school in Hampstead, to the brusque but kind and efficient Mrs Lalor, wife of the editor of the Unitarian *Inquirer*. Home values were still powerfully enforced, even when it was a question of visiting the family of the Unitarian minister at Marylebone:

To Marianne Gaskell, 17 February 1851 (90)
Mrs Tagart is very kind in asking you; but I think I had rather *you did not go there*. If you go to one place there are many who would ask you, & with whom we are quite as intimate as with the Tagarts. Of course if you and Mrs Lalor have made an *engagement* for next Saturday, it is quite another thing, and it must be kept to *this once*; but not again, my dear girl; as I think you and I agreed before your going to school. I do not like the *tone* in the Tagart's family *at all*, though I feel all their kindness; now do not tell this last Item to any one, but remember I wish you *not* to visit anywhere, unless Mrs Lalor is kind enough to take you with her in the Easter holidays to any of her friends; perhaps you will give this as a message

from me to Mrs Lalor with my kind regards. I *particularly* wish this to be kept to. I know Mrs Lalor does not wish you to go; and I know (in your wise days) you did not wish to go; and I know I have a decided and explicit objection to it *anywhere*; and I make *no exception in favour* of the Tagarts. In case Mr and Mrs Austin come up with Annie I will write a note, requesting Mrs Lalor to allow you to see *them*; which perhaps she will allow. Miss Ewarts are going up to Mrs Henry Enfield's, sometime this spring, and if you go to one place, you must go to all; indeed there are *many* places I should prefer to Mrs Tagart's, as I dislike the rude quarrelsome tone there. Helen, Emily & Mrs Tagart are all very kind separately, but as a family there is something so decidedly wrong that I should indeed be grieved if you fell into their mode of thinking and speaking.

With Marianne away at school her mother's letters to her are stuffed with domestic detail:

To Marianne Gaskell, 31 March 1851 (92)
There were some capital words on Thursday, which Annie, Meta and Tottie got up. They acted in the outer lobby, under the gas; and we stood on the stair-case, in the inner hall, and the folding doors were thrown open. The first word was Author. Awe – a nun brought before the Inquisition. Tottie (nun) rushed in from the back stair-case door, was caught by Annie and the doors flew open, and displayed the three judges dressed in black with blk masks on (your 3 sisters.) Thor the Scandinavian god, – a piece of his life &c. Author a scene or tableau of Hogarth's Distressed Author, – Farewell & Breakfast were the two other words; but I won't go through them all. Mrs Davenport comes on the 14th. Baby has *had* a cold, Meta has a little but not enough to prevent her going to the lecture (Dr Carpenters). Papa is quite well again now; it was lumbago. The house the Austins have taken is in Chester Terrace (4 I *think*, near the gate nearest to Albany Street. Goodbye my darling. I have got a new silk gown, quaker-brown coloured, – Miss Daniels making it. If you want a new bonnet which I think you will, a white LINEN one, (like white *chip*) is both pretty and cheap. And have as little trimming put on as possible, but let that trimming be *good*.

Your affectionate Mother E C Gaskell

With a large house went a large garden, complete with gardener: 'We have got peas, Jerusalem Artichokes, cabbages, mignonette etc down, pinks, carnations, campions, canterbury bells & the hot bed is just "set agait" (vide Frank) for cutting for the borders etc.' (91a):

To Marianne Gaskell, 16 March 1851 (91b)

Yesterday I was very busy in the garden where I mean to be tomorrow too. Papa has bought a new frame at a sale, & we are going to have it for a cold frame to harden out the plants from the hot bed; & we are sowing Thunbergias & planting gladioli etc. for the greenhouse in which by the way a pair of robins are building a nest between two flower pots on the top shelf near the dining room window. Flossy & Baby enjoy watching them fly backwards & forwards with the dead leaves which they bring from out of doors. . . .

What must the little ones wear out of doors over their every day prints? Meta is going to have the Warburton's garden for her own; but at present it is very empty. Flossy continues very faithful to you. I have got the 'Guesses at Truth', & thank you for them darling. And Papa has given me a new writing case, a *little* larger & much better made than the old one, which is regularly defunct having come all to pieces all on a sudden. We have sown our first crop of peas. We are giving up beans as they did not answer; we have sown mustard, cress, radishes, lettuces, cauliflowers, mignonette, etc. Can you tell who wrote the Review of Miss Martineau's letters in the (this week's) Inquirer signed I. R. You have never given your reasons for being glad a Protectionist government has not come in : & both Papa & I want to know them; & to have them straight from yourself without your asking any one. Admire Flossy's envelope – it is one Ellen Green gave her which she thinks you will like.

It was becoming quite an elaborate enterprise :

To Eliza Fox, 17 November 1851 (108a)

Do you know I think we're going to keep a cow, and I'm sure we're going to keep a pig, because our pig stye is building and I find my proper vocation is farming; and Frank is gone poor fellow! and so going to live at Southport and we've got a new man James by name; and I've got a new cook instead of Mary, who is to be married 'by Master' in February and said new cook is coming in January, and her name is Isabella Postlethwaite of Legberthwaite in Tilburthwaite, you may guess her habitat from that; and we have got a Bessy instead of Maria, and a Margaret instead of Margaret, all changes against my will at the time, but improvements I think. . . . Our cow is such a pet. Half Alderney, quarter Ayrshire quarter Holderness. . . . We've got a mangle and we're washing at home, and we do it so beautifully.

The stye was built, the cow acquired, and they began to churn their own butter. The pigs flourished. They thought of getting a second cow because the butter answered so well. Uncle Robert Gaskell sent some rhubarb. Manchester rain fell and 'our pretty white ducks quack about with delight', she reported, though the poultry '*will* go up & down where they have no business to' (120). Once, incautiously, she told Marianne, 'All our new servants do very nicely. To be sure we are a very small family, and there is proportionably very little work to be done' (117). Within a few months she had to confess that the outside man was 'so drunken, poor fellow' that all the farmwork was thrown amongst the women – 'and I *carried the cow*, taking her under my care, & avoiding the pigs. Oh! it was such a commotion! past description, only very provoking & very funny at the time' (123).

William Gaskell, of course, had his comfortable study. His wife did her reading and writing wherever she could. Even though the house had two sitting rooms, they could be full of daughters, friends and visitors. This total immersion in domestic affairs must have taken her mind back to the arrangements and shifts and contrivances of her youth in Knutsford:

To Eliza Fox, December 1851 (110)
I've a deal to say more than mortal can get through in the $\frac{1}{4}$ of an hour I have before me, and now it's Sunday and I've the comfort of sitting down to write to you in a new gown, and blue ribbons all spick and span for Xmas – and cheap in the bargain, 'Elegant economy' as *we* say in Cranford – There now I dare say you think I've gone crazy but I'm not; but I've written a couple of tales about Cranford in Household Words, so you must allow me to quote from myself.

The family and its four or five servants may seem large to us, but they were living in Victorian times; as she wrote to Marianne, 'Your Aunt Lizzie and your Aunt Robert are both expecting babies before Xmas; & little cousins are pouring in upon the world' (134):

To Marianne Gaskell, 2 October 1852 (135)
Uncle Sam staid till Monday morning; taking us by surprize by going off suddenly to Liverpool (Liscard) on Sunday morning. He brought a good account of Aunt Lizzie & her 8. The old house looks only like a little piece by the side of the additions; which themselves are only the beginning of a very large new house. They have built a large drawing-room with a boudoir opening out of it, & six bedrooms above. [Here is inserted a rough plan of the house] I have left out a very handsome hall with flight of front stairs *between* old & new; the *old* front door forming now the door of communication between the two parts.

William Gaskell's sister was like Elizabeth Gaskell in manners and appearance, clever, energetic and animated. Her husband, Charles Holland, was also clever, 'a great traveller, a great quiz, and a great Radical'. But they had so many children that they found it quite impossible to keep up with social life in Liverpool and therefore moved across the Mersey to Cheshire, where they purchased the estate of Liscard Vale in 1844:[4]

To Eliza Holland, Christmastide 1852 (145)
Your house sounded as if it would be very pretty indeed from Sam's account in August. When do you expect your 9th? I thought it was to have come before Xmas! *And* I am wanting a waiter. Do you know of one? I wonder if odd bundles of old letters would amuse you in your confinement? I dare say you would not care for them; but you *might*. Last week – no the week before, Wm brought me Bernard Palissy, but it so happened I had not a moment of time for reading except one day, when I got very much interested in four or 5 chapters, & then the book had to go back. We are buying a new piano which is a grand event in the family, semi-grand Broadwood, – not come yet. And I am turned farmer, do you know? and particularly poultry farmer; & Wm will insist my bantams are neither so small nor so pretty as yours. What sort *are* yours.

In the intervals of rearing ten children, some of them educated by a future Professor of English Literature recommended by William Gaskell,[5] she managed to engage in writing and translation herself. Perhaps Elizabeth Gaskell would have done well to move into Cheshire too, but her books got written – at very irregular intervals and to the accompaniment of much well-meant advice:

To Eliza Fox, Early October 1852 (137)
Dr Davy's, Lesketh How, Near Ambleside.

Friday.

Well I'm here! *How* I came, I don't seem to know for of all the weary, killing wearing out bustles in this life that of the last week passed all belief. Thackeray's lectures, two dinners, one concert card party at home, killing a pig, *my* week at the school which took me into town from 9 till 12 every morning – company in the house, Isabella leaving, Wm too busy to be agreeable to my unfortunate visitors, (Mr and Mrs Wedgwood, Dot and Jane, their servant, Annie and Ellen Green, closely packed!) so I had to do double duty and talk æsthetically (I dare say) all the time I was thinking of pickle for pork, and with a Ruskian face and tongue I talked away with a heart like Martha's. And at last when Meta's and my cab came to take us to the station not before the house cleared, they smashed into Ruth in grand style. I have not much hope of her now this year, now I've been frightened off my nest again. Mr Chapman wrote a polite invitation to me to come and see the Duke's [Wellington's] funeral from his shop window (a sight I should dearly have liked,) *and*, also, that civility being furnished, informed me that Mr Forster had given him the MS. of Ruth and that the first 2 vols. *were printed*; all complete news to me! But I set to on the trumpet sound thereof, and was writing away vigorously at Ruth when the Wedgwoods, Etc. came: and I was sorry, *very* sorry to give it up my heart being so full of it, in a way which I can't bring back. That's *that* . . .

Money earned by writing must have been a useful addition to their income. Despite legacies, she could confess to her other sister-in-law, Nancy Robson, '*Our* house is proving rather too expensive for us, – MA's schooling taken into account; we aren't going to furnish drawing room, & mean to be, and are very œconomical because it seems such an addition to children's health & happiness to have plenty of room, & above all a garden to play in' (101). Other expenses, like charity, must have taken a proportion of their income: on the famous occasion when William received the £20 for 'Lizzie Leigh' he promised his wife some for her Refuge. But this was also a period in which standards of middle-class comfort continued to rise, however carefully they were achieved:

To Marianne Gaskell, Early March 1854 (185)
This won't be an elegant letter but I will write on any scrap of paper to set you at ease. I wish I could have afforded to let you go to Portsmouth but you see I can't. You may get those songs Papa says, as I told you yesterday. Your note this morning was *very* nice, darling. Remember Miss Chorley's hours, *after* 12 *before* 2 – The man came (M. Hallé's man Hinxman) to tune the piano yesterday – it was more than $\frac{1}{2}$ a note *flat*, besides being altogether out of tune – and he says it is all but ruined by being so shockingly tuned. It will take 4 tunings this next month, & cost *two guineas*, – something about the frame &c, – and so I must scrubble up money for that. *Pray* burn any letters. I am always afraid of writing much to you, you are so careless about letters.

The mid-Victorian home contained innumerable objects for use and for show. Personal adornments, too, were prolific, though Mrs Gaskell's taste seems to have been fairly restrained. She criticises a dance for being 'large, vulgar & overdressed' (175). She talks of trying to sell a cameo for a friend 'to some of our rich Manchesterians but, thank you, it is not "large" enough for them, & cutting & execution is nothing to size' (255). Yet she once wrote to Marianne with heavy emphasis, 'Be sure you take care of MY *cameo* brooch. I find you have got it; now I only lent it you and I value it extremely, and would not have it lost on any account'. Is it mere chance that she continues, 'We had some friends last Friday. Uncle Sam (who was only just arrived,) the Owens' professors, and appurtenances in the way of sisters & wives' (93)? Even in scenes of clerical life there is a hint of the materialism Dickens satirised in Mrs Merdle, who was just a splendid bosom on which her husband could display the signs of his wealth. It is no more than a hint, however:

To Marianne Gaskell, May 1851 (96)
  Your letter wanting a new gown came just before she left, so I have sent you my green merino one, which I have not worn since the beginning of winter, and which you may as well wear out. I have no time to spare Hearn for gown-making; it did very well while we were away and all the servants had comparatively little to do; but now I must have Miss Daniels for your gowns, and her charge is somewhere about 25s a dress. If you have any gowns made in London *have them well made*; I would rather put the expense into the make than the material; *form* is always higher than *colour* &c.

By such means the Plymouth Grove house was made 'as little a selfish thing' as possible:

To Anne Robson, Late January 1853 (148)
  I wanted to have got to see you before Ruth was published. I have taken leave of my '*respectable* friends' up & down the country; *you*, I don't call respectable, but you are surrounded by respectabilities, & I can't encounter their 'shock'. Meta goes to Miss Martineau on the 27th I take her to Liverpool. I wish, dearest Nancy, you would bring your boys & servant, & Mr. Robson and come and see us. Seeing you would be a great comfort and pleasure to me and I want you to see both my girls. Say you came next Saturday. *Friday Evg* we are engaged, and I shd grudge losing your company, or else Friday would be better. I have ½ a large bed (with Flossy or Hearn could share it with her, and your nurse could sleep with one of our servants,) and a small bedroom opening out of our large spare room, said spare room and all at your service. Do come on Saturday. Willie might have the little room out of yours; (doors left open) your nurse is provided

for – and the large spare room for you and Eddie and Mr Robson if he came, or we could arrange it differently at your pleasure only do come dearest Nancy and you would have a quiet little time with us and see your 4 nieces &c., &c., &c., &c., don't you see the charms of the place?

CHAPTER FIVE

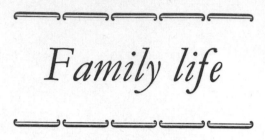

Family life

It really quite pained my eyes to walk out.
– Inside however all is very pleasing . . .
never any bustle & never any dawdling
('Snow' Wedgwood to her sister
Katherine, 3 November 1855[1])

WHEN MISS FERGUSSON LEFT IN 1847 because she could not manage the two little girls, the most elaborate arrangements were made for their education. One teacher for French, another for writing and arithmetic; their father for history and natural history; Emily Winkworth *'for the present* to teach Marianne music' and Rosa Mitchell to give Meta two half-hour music lessons a week; together with dancing lessons and visits to the School of Design:

To Fanny Holland, 9 March 1847
My part will be reduced to general superintendence & help-giving in the preparation of their lessons; we shall work together, & read some book aloud at nights. I shall give them dictation & grammar lessons, walk out with them (to be regular in *this* will be one great difficulty,) and make myself as much as possible their companion and friend.

It is easy to see why she was later shocked to hear that the Reverend Patrick Brontë had never taught his girls anything – 'only the servant taught them to read & write' (75), she was told.
Education was always important in the Gaskell family:

To Anne Robson, 1 September 1851 (101)

Now about the children. It is delightful to see what good it had done MA, sending her to school; & is a proof of how evil works out good. She is such a 'law unto herself' now, such a sense of duty, and *obeys* her sense. For instance she invariably gave the little ones 2 hours of patient steady teaching in the holidays. If there was to be any long excursion for the day she got up earlier, that was all; & *they* did too, influenced by her example. She also fixed on 9 o'clock for her own bed-time, & kept to it through all temptations. These are but small instances but you will understand their force. She grew strong, & fat, & ruddy in the holidays, & I could not find out any reason for the paleness &c on first coming home. She seemed well, had plenty and good food to eat; plenty of rest & exercise, and was evidently very happy at school, & with reason, for Meta (who staid one night with her while we were in London, & was strongly prejudiced against the school before going,) said every one was so kind, such good dinners, such a pretty garden, & a bathroom to every bed-room, all which things took my second little lady's fancy very much. I wish you could hear MA sing. It is something *really* fine; only at present she sings little but Italian & Latin Mass Music. It is so difficult to meet with *good* English songs; and then they all say so difficult to pronounce our close sounds clearly & well. Now to turn to Meta, who is a great darling in another way. MA looks at nothing from an intellectual point of view; & will never care for reading, – teaching music, & domestic activity, especially about children will be her forte.

Meta is untidy, dreamy, and absent; but so brim-full of I don't know what to call it, for it is something deeper, & less showy than talent. Music she is getting so fond of, which we never expected; and I'll tell you a remark of hers the other day, whh will explain a little of what I mean. She had a piece by Mendelsohn to learn called The Rivulet. When she was playing it to me she said towards the end 'Now Mama I transpose this into the minor key, for I think the rivulet is wandering away and lost in the distance, & then you know brooks have such a sad wailing sound'. Now it's a great deal of trouble to transpose a piece, but she had done it perfectly & played it so. Then her drawings are equally thoughtful & good. She has no lessons, for Miss Fox said lessons from any drawing master *here* would spoil her, but she reads on the principles of composition &c, & does so well. She is *quite* able to appreciate any book I am reading. Ruskin's Seven Lamps of Architecture for the last instance. She talks very little except to people she knows well; is inclined to be *over*-critical & fastidious with everybody & everything, so that I have to clutch up her drawings before she burns them, & she *would* be *angry* if she could read this note, praising her. Then she loses time terribly, – and *wants* MA's sense of duty, for she gets so absorbed in her own thoughts &c that she forgets everything. Florence has no talents under the sun; and is very nervous, & anxious; she will require so much strength to hold her up through life; everything is a terror to her; but Marianne at any rate is aware of this, and is a capital confidante for all Florence's anxieties; which are often on *other* people's behalf, not her own. Julia is witty, & wild, & clever and droll, the pet of the house; and I often admire Florence's utter absence of jealousy, & pride in Julia's doings & sayings.

Meta was the next to go away to school:

To Marianne Gaskell, 27 November 1852 (142)
Now I've a great piece of news for you. Meta is going to school, to Miss Martineau's on the 20th of Jany. It is all fixed suddenly on hearing that Miss M. had a vacancy, as I always felt that hers was the only school that would do for Meta, but until the sudden leaving of Rosa I had given up all thoughts of her going. She has been *so good* of late. Up early as soon after six as she cd, at her practising at 7 &c — . But Rosa doubted if you could teach the little ones if Meta were here, she said she occasioned such interruptions, & altogether it has been settled in a minute, & Miss Martineau seems very much pleased, for it seems she took a great fancy to Meta. I can tell you little more of the plan, except that it makes me busy about her clothes, & that she is to learn dancing, Italian, German, & music from Herman. And that she rather likes the idea, only wishes she could 'take all her family with her'. . . .

Miss Rachel Martineau kept an excellent boarding school at Liverpool, where her brother James taught some academic subjects and James Herrmann, leader of the Liverpool Concerts, took the music.[2] With Meta away, fresh and elaborate arrangements were needed at home:

To Marianne Gaskell, November 1852 (143)
About you, love, — we think you must have music lessons once a fortnight when you come home, but this we must talk over — and we are hesitating whether we ought not to have Mr Gunton for Flossy, — not that she plays well, but to save you that worry. However one can't fix everything in a minute. Yes! love, get those books if you like them. Only remember they must do *hard* & *correct* as well as interesting work — I mean such things as French verbs, & geography for Flossy; the dry bones of knowledge. *Oh! poor baby sobbed so because she had no letter from you this morning.* Do write to her next, although I want to hear a great deal.

The schemes must have had many defects but also some very unusual strengths. 'MA is at home, so good, never reads a word; but is patience sweetness etc: personified with the little ones' (151), Eliza Fox was told. She was also having music lessons with no less a man than Charles Hallé and was promised a very special tutorial on *Ruth*:

To Anne Robson, January 1853 (148)
   Of course it is a prohibited book in *this*, as in many other households; not a book for young people, unless read with someone older (I mean to read it with MA some quiet time or other;) but I have spoken out my mind in the best way I can, and I have no doubt that what was meant so earnestly *must* do some good, though perhaps not all the good, or not the *very* good I meant. I am in a quiver of pain about it. I can't tell you how much I need strength. I could have put out much more power, but that I wanted to keep it quiet in tone, lest by the slightest exaggeration, or over-strained sentiment I might weaken the force of what I had to say.

When *Ruth* was published Marianne was eighteen. One wonders how long she would have to wait before her mother broached a strong subject. The Gaskells' outdoor man James ('so drunken, poor fellow') had been replaced by Will Preston, member of a Lake District family that Mrs Gaskell was so fond of that she employed two of his sisters as well. When a third sister became a real-life fallen woman in London, she acted at once:

To Miss Hannah Kay, 7 March 1854 (182)
   My dear Miss Kay,
      I cannot tell you how much obliged to you I am for your note. It made me most completely share in your anxiety, for all the Prestons have been friends of ours ever since we first went to lodge there five years ago. We have *two* sisters and a brother of Eleanor's living here; the elder Margaret is our Cook. I thought a good deal about it before I spoke to her; and then, (never saying from whom it was that I heard, so your maid may be quite at ease,) I read her parts out of your letter; and I told her that I thought it was the duty of one of the family to go up and see Eleanor and *if possible* bring her down; indeed that it must be done, if she was to be saved from shame. I told Margaret that partly on account of her mother's failing health & partly for other reasons that I thought this devolved upon either her, or the brother, & that I advised her to go; as the brother is what they call 'an easy temper' easily persuaded, imposed upon or even intimidated by a person of passionate wilfulness as they represent Eleanor to be. Margaret cried sadly; said Eleanor never would be guided ... Margaret

has never been in London & her going even makes me a little anxious; as I fear this bad man.

To Miss Hannah Kay, 14 March 1854 (184)

I only write now to say that Margaret goes up tomorrow, Thursday, by the Parliamentary train, which stops at Kilburn I find; arriving there at 20 m. past 6. I told her yesterday through whom I had obtained my information, and she seemed very grateful to you. I also told her of your kind offer respecting Hird; and she shook her head, and said she should hardly dare to leave Eleanor. Only I think Eleanor sounds as if she would be busy in the day time, & as if Margaret's supervision wd be more needed in the evenings. Margaret seems to think such decided opposition as Miss Bramorll's now is, likely to do harm to one of Eleanor's temper; so I gave her every possible warning as to her own conduct to Eleanor. I feel very anxious on Margaret's account as well as Eleanor's. Her only friends to whom she can apply for advice &c, will be yourself, and Mr Joseph Kay; and I have also put up a little basket & asked her to take it to Mrs Shaen, a friend of mine, who was a Miss Winkworth and as such was known to Margaret formerly. She lives at 8 Bedford Row, and her husband is a solicitor, and agent for some protection Society which Mrs Shaen says makes him well acquainted with what snares to avoid in London &c.

All very serious and practical, but Elizabeth Gaskell could not resist making the best of the situation : 'I do hope that Margaret may manage to see a little of London. She has a friend who is maid to a Miss Stirling living [in] Knightsbridge . . .'

Not a word of all this appears in letters to Marianne, then staying in Hampstead. Her mother displays a very positive, and perhaps associated, solicitude : 'If Lady Holland asks you – and you can manage it – *not alone in a cab*, at night; *go*' (183). And then, very casually, at the end of another letter : 'Margaret in London, coming down on Thursday with Eleanor Preston – No news' (187). Of course Marianne *was* careless about burning letters, unlike Meta. Perhaps their education became fully liberal when they helped their mother prepare the *Life of Charlotte Brontë* in 1855 and 1856; some of the letters being copied then were 'too intimate for publication'.[3]

In the early summer of 1854 cholera raged in Manchester and the two youngest children were sent with Marianne to stay at Poulton, Meta being away on a visit :

To Marianne Gaskell, 14 May 1854 (193)

I am very sorry I did not reply yesterday, by return; but the bare *writing-*

time was not to be found, – callers all day long, which was doubly pro-voking as Emily Shaen was here for a solitary day, & I had to leave her (and my lunch) perpetually. But I really don't know how to fix. I should *like* to come to Poulton, but I don't see any *chance* of it till far on in next week. *If* your bedroom is *airy* enough you had better keep to it at present, & let me decide a little more first about things. Cousin Mary stops till Saturday; because Mr Harry Holland is coming down to Manchester about a 'reference-case' Friday & Saturday, & I have asked him to come & sleep here, so as to see as much of his Aunt as possible. And Arthur Darbishire has this morning written to ask if he may have a bed on Friday night, perhaps afterwards, as Mr & Mrs D – & Vernon are coming to Manchester – & there is fever in his York Place lodgings & he can't go there because the lady is not to be moved. Of course I have sent him word he can come & for as long as he likes : but *I* can't leave till he goes, even other things permitting, whh I don't think they would. . . .

No letters this morning from any of you absentees. Meta sounds very gay, does not she? I was so sorry to part from Emily last night. Oh! Mrs Ed. Potter called yesterday to ask Mrs Lalor's school for Polly. I recom-mended it, & I think she will go. Write soon there's a darling. Can you tell what the week's expenses have been – *about* I mean?

Yours very affectionately
E C Gaskell

I shall write to Flossy next. Love to all.

The absence produced a fascinating revelation of her moral and religious principles :

To Marianne Gaskell, May 1854 (198a), May–June 1854 (198b)
I *do* think Mr & Mrs Langshawe are charming and as you say he is so thoroughly good and true and kind, the source of his charmingness lies in his out and out goodness, and that in his quiet deep religion. I shan't for-get how that was brought to bear long ago on my shirking Miss Noble.

I have been thinking about Church. I quite agree with you in feeling more devotional in Church than in Chapel; and I wish our Puritan an-cestors had not left out so much that they might have kept in of the beautiful and impressive Church service. But I always *do* feel as if the Litany – the beginning of it I mean, – and one or two other parts did so completely go against my belief that it would be wrong to deaden my sense of it's serious error by hearing it too often. It seems to me so dis-tinctly to go against some of the clearest of our Saviour's words in which he so expressly tells us to pray to God alone. My own wish would be that you should go to Chapel in the morning, and to Church in the evening, when there is nothing except the Doxology to offend one's sense of *truth*. I am sure this would be *right* for me; although I am so fond of the Church service and prayers as a whole that I should feel tempted as you do. With our feelings and preference for the Church-service I think it is a temptation *not* to have a fixed belief; but I know it is wrong not to clear our minds as much as possible as to the nature of that God, and tender Saviour, whom we can not love properly unless we try and define them clearly to ourselves. Do you understand me my darling! I have often wished to talk to you about this. Then the one thing I *am* clear and sure about is this that Jesus Christ was not equal to His father; that, however divine a being he was *not* God; and that worship as God addressed to Him is therefore wrong in me; and that it is my duty to deny myself the gratification of constantly attending a service (like the morning service) in a part of which I thoroughly disagree, I like exceedingly going to afternoon service. But I must leave this subject now.

Pray don't take too long walks. I am afraid I never told you that I did not mind your reading Jane Eyre. . . .

I should be very glad if you could read the Psalms a little with the children on a Sunday. I want to go on with Joseph's history myself. I felt sorry I had said what I did just at *last* dearest, before you went; only it is true that I think there are some temptations to concealment etc. in your friendship with Mr Ewart which have always made me very uneasy; & do take care love against this. I wish you would write & speak openly to me; if not of your thoughts & feelings at all times at any rate of your wishes & troubles. But I must end. The 'worry' relates to the congregation & I must try & arrange matters without passing the 'worry' on to Papa; so I see no chance of leaving home at present though I long to accept the invitation renewed & *re*-renewed from E. Shaen.

To her youngest daughter, then seven years old, she displays another kind of instinctive delicacy:

To Julia Bradford Gaskell, May 1854 (199)
My dearest Julia,
    Do you know Fairy has been poorly, and has been to pay the doctor a visit, and has come home quite well, only very thin; and she was so pleased she came scampering upstairs. And do you know we are to have a kitten all the way from Paris, called Cranford; with very very long hair, and soft pretty eyes? I wonder if it will understand our English *Pussy*. I am getting

my lunch (or rather dinner) while I write. Ham sandwiches and beer if you wish to know; and it is 12 o'clock. Then I shall go and dress, and go with Mrs Shuttleworth to pay calls; and go to a School Committee at five o'clock, on my way back, and then come home to a *thick* tea. I wonder how your cold is, my darling? No one tells me, so I hope it is better. Tell Minnie I am going to try to trim a bonnet for myself. My *mourning* bonnet has gone to be lined with double tarlatane at Miss Ogden's; and then I am going to set to work. They have got down in their cleaning to the study, and a pretty piece of work they are making of it. All dust, and soot, and pother! The cow does give such good milk, and such a quantity of it, now she has gone out to grass. Flossy's cuckoo-red sits very well; and it is supposed the eldest Dorking wants to sit, so I am going to write to Mrs Edmund Potter for eggs.

Many years before, under the date 10 March 1835 in the diary she kept when Marianne was a baby, she spoke of works like Mme. Necker de Saussure's *Sur l'Education progressive* ('the nicest book I have read on the subject') and planned 'to act on principles *now* which can be carried on through the whole of her education'. In this apparently casual letter to a later child, 'witty, & wild, & clever and droll' (101), there may be more intelligence than we realise. Instincts can be very cultivated.

She could be just as sensitive towards her husband. Though her literary career soon became quite distinct, there was one very definite point of contact. He had given lectures on the Lancashire dialect, so much a feature of the dialogue of *Mary Barton*; his wife arranged to have them printed with the fifth edition, with Chapman striking off a few copies of the lectures alone. For these she had to pay herself. It was not the only occasion when she looked after his interests:

To John Forster, Early May 1854 (192)
I have worried Mr Gaskell, by assuring him he shall have no peace or comfort at home, into going away. He has fixed to go away next Monday, & looks better already with the prospects of a change, in which he now indulges himself. He will form no plans, but bachelorize off comfortably guided by the wind of his own daily will; but he faintly purposes to be in London, – & at the opening of the Crystal Palace. *You cannot think what a relief this is to me.* All last week I was *stupid* with anxiety, & the utter want of power to influence him. Now, if, as I said, we were not a full household till the 20th, and longer – (I could fly & I could run,) and I could write M. Hale, whh Mrs Shaen has put me into spirits by liking, much to my surprize; and she, trained in German criticism is a far severer

judge than you, – grunting & groaning when she does not like. She says
it is good – but out of proportion to the length of the planned story,
written or published – & so cramfull of possible interest that she thinks
another character would make it too much – she finds faults, but not disheartening ones, – only still I feel it to be flat & grey with no bright clear
foreground as yet – Oh dear! I can't get Mr Gaskell to look at it, & it is
no use writing much longer, – only I don't like showing it to you till I
have got in something more distinct & telling.

William Gaskell's senior colleague at Cross Street Chapel had just died and he
must have been too busy to look at the serial story she was in the midst of
writing, *North and South*, then called 'Margaret Hale'. She *sounds* a typical
Victorian wife – and certainly believed herself to be one, as we see from her
letter about Charlotte Brontë's husband-to-be, the Reverend Arthur Bell
Nicholls:

To John Forster, 23 April 1854 (191)
However, with all his bigotry & sternness it must be charming to be loved
with all the strength of his heart as she sounds to be. Mr Shaen accuses me
always of being 'too much of a woman' in always wanting to obey somebody – but I am sure that Miss Brontë could never have borne not to be
well-ruled & ordered – well! I think I have got into a 'fiasco' and I have
hardly any right to go on discussing what she could or she could not do –
but I mean that she would never have been happy but with an exacting,
rigid, law-giving, passionate man – only you see, I'm afraid one of his
laws will be to shut us out, & so I am making a sort of selfish moan over
it & have got out of temper I suppose with the very thing I have been wanting for her this six months past. . . .

I did so like your good long handsome note four or five days ago. I do
so thank you for all your kindness. There! there are 2 sentences with 'so'
in them not followed by 'as' as Mr Gaskell says they ought to be. I will
make one grammatical sentence, & have done.

I am *so* much obliged to you *as* to be incapable of expressing my obli-
gation but by saying that I am always

Yours most truly
E. C. Gaskell.

. . . Mr Gaskell is pleased about the lectures I am sure, though he does not
say anything, except pitying Mr Chapman. I will do my best to make
things smooth & rapid at this end.

Though there is always a suspicion that she was never any more submissive than she wanted to be, one of her most brilliant letters celebrates an escape from the chains of being a wife and mother:

To Eliza Fox, Summer 1854 (206)

IF you don't send me those Dorkings by some of the Gaskells! Ugh ugh ugh ugh.

Nature intended me for a gypsy-bachelor; that *I* am sure of. Not an old maid for they are particular & fidgetty, and tidy, and punctual, – but a gypsy-bachelor. I get up early. I breakfast with a book in my hand. I go out and feed all the animals, especially Tommy who is getting fatter than ever; and Fairy, who has had her eye bitten out, poor little mortal, and lives in a state of perpetual wink. I have set 2 hens on 27 eggs this morning, at the which I am very proud. I go out and plant cabbages, – Cincinnatus did something to turnips, didn't he, Mrs Fox? but mine are cabbages. Some great man dibbled about them, I think. Well! I am like that great man! 2 feet apart is the right distance. Then the post comes and I have to write to every body; and feel like an ass between a great number of bundles of hay, with so many invitations, here, there, & everywhere.

Margaret comes in to know what time I would like, & what I will have for, dinner; but that fixes me too much; so I despise dinners, and eat when & where I like, like Sancho Panza & the birds. Not the fish, for mackerel come up regularly every 4 hours to feed; I have been out a long day in Cardigan Bay, mackerel-fishing. Then I think of Poulton, & the sea, – and the children there – apropos of fish, d'ye see. And I long to be with them. Then on the other side come letters from Emily & Mr Gaskell, – Emily wanting me there, & Meta ditto. So between the two I go nowhere. But I have told every body I am going away, so they all think I am gone. And every morning in bed; I think I will go; and then I find too much to do, & the time slips by. I wonder where you *would* write, oh wretched woman, if I didn't –

Send me my Dorkings. Not if they're *above* 7s 6d a piece on any account. I am very poor; which eases my cares wonderfully, see somethingth satire of Juvenal. I don't know where the plate is. Nobody can find it, now Hearn (trusty guardian) is away. And I have 4 shillings in silver & some odd coppers. So I sleep with my windows wide open, listening to thrushes & defying burglars. We've got a thrush that sings in it's sleep, I'm sure. I bade farewell to a Capn Campbell, bound for the East, last week – he told me there would not [be] a soldier left in Manchester on Saturday last; whereupon somebody observed that we were on the verge of a precipice! I don't know what they meant; but don't be surprized if you hear of a rising of the weavers, headed by a modern Boadicea. I am thinking of fastening Will's scythe to *one* of the wheels of the poney carriage and defending my country if the Russians do land at Liverpool. – Your affectionate bachelor

E C Gaskell

She ends in splendid fantasy, but real life could not be long denied, especially when the Crimean War began to go badly:

To Eliza Fox, 24 December 1854 (222)
Oh what a shameful time it is since I've written to you! and what a shame of me not to write, for yr last letter was such a nice one, though its been stinging me with reproaches this two months past, but I believe I've been as nearly dazed and crazed with this c – , d – be h – to it, story as can be. I've been sick of writing, and everything connected with literature or improvement of the mind; to say nothing of deep hatred to my species about whom I was obliged to write as if I loved 'em. Moreover I have had to write so hard that I have spoilt my hand, and forgotten all my spelling. Seriously it has been a terrible weight on me and has made me have some of the most felling headaches I ever had in my life, so having growled my growl I'll go on to something else. We are all well that's the first unspeakable comfort. . . . Altogether everything looks very sad this Xmas. The war accounts make one's blood run cold at the rotting away of those noble glorious men. What *is* Mr Fox about to allow it?

North and South was finished eventually, but just as she was on the point of sending a copy of the book edition to Charlotte Brontë, news came of her death. There followed a year and a half of delicate negotiations and decisions, together with much frantic industry, to prepare a fitting memoir of her dead friend:

To Emily Shaen, 7 & 8 September 1856 (308)
I used to go up at Dumbleton & Boughton to my own room, directly after 9 o'clock breakfast; and came down to lunch at $\frac{1}{2}$ p 1, up again, & write without allowing any temptation to carry me off till 5 – or past; having just a run of a walk before 7 o'clock dinner. I got through an immense deal; but I found head & health suffering – I could not sleep for thinking of it. So at Broad-Leas (the Ewarts) I only wrote till lunch; and since then, not at all. I have been too busy since I came home. I enjoyed Broad Leas far the most of my visit, perhaps owing to my not having the sick wearied feeling of being over-worked; & Mr Gaskell being very jolly;

& delicious downs (Salisbury Plain), get at able in our afternoon drives great sweeps of green turf, like emerald billows stretching off into the blue sky miles & miles away, – with here & there a 'barrow' of some ancient Briton, & Wansdyke, & Silbury Hill, and the great circle of Avebury all to be seen, while the horses went noisily over the thick soft velvety grass high up over blue misty plains, and villages in nests of trees, & church spires which did not reach nearly up to where we were in our beautiful free air, & primitive world. . . .

It is now Monday morng – this letter has been written under all sorts of difficulties, & now I'm trenching on my precious Brontë time, – I got such a nice letter from my darling little Annie Shaen t'other day, – & a letter from Katie; that dear friend, – and I *should* like to answer both at length, only what *can* I do? The interruptions of home life are never ending; & I want to read &c with the girls.

The *Life of Charlotte Brontë* was published in March 1857 whilst she was away with Marianne and Meta on holiday in Italy. It raised a storm of protest. Her husband, himself enmeshed in complicated problems of his own as Chairman of the Committee of Trustees for Manchester New College at a critical time in its history, was forced by threats of legal action to issue a public retraction and apology on her behalf through William Shaen, their friend and solicitor. She came back on 28 May into this 'Hornet's nest'. She had felt it her 'duty' to tell 'painful truths'; now she was being asked to take out passages and prepare a revised edition.

To Ellen Nussey, 16 June 1857 (352)
I am writing as if I were in famous spirits, and I think I *am* so *angry* that I am almost merry in my bitterness, if you know that state of feeling; but I have cried more since I came home than I ever did in the same space of time before; and never needed kind words so much, – & no one gives me them. I *did so try* to *tell the truth*, & I believe *now* I hit as near the truth as any one *could* do. And I weighed every line with all my whole power & heart, so that every line should go to it's great purpose of making *her* known & valued, as one who had gone through such a terrible life with a brave & faithful heart.

Hysteria seems very close. After her experience with *Ruth*, can the public outcry have been so very affecting? In fact there was a third great problem.[4] Whilst in Italy a certain Captain Hill of the Indian Army Engineers, a widower with one child, had been their constant companion; they seem to have met him on the boat going out and may even travelled back as far as Paris in his company.

Within a few weeks of their return Meta had become engaged to him, but his 'furlough was almost immediately recalled' (363) because the Indian Mutiny had broken out. In early July Meta told Snow Wedgwood that she was 'sure she could not live through his absence', though Snow noted that she was writing, 'poor child, in a great state of agitation'.

Frantic preparations were made for an immediate marriage, only for them to be cancelled. In late July, 'utterly knocked up and ill' (362a), Mrs Gaskell went to stay with the motherly Mrs Preston in the Lake District. A friend who saw her on the day of her return reported that Meta's affair had driven the Brontë one quite out of her mind. It was not, apparently, the kind of marriage Meta had been expected to make and she had 'grown very stout – & not improved in beauty as is generally said to be the case you know with engaged young ladies'. It all sounds desperately unhappy, though a brave face is presented to the world. To the young American whose friendship they had just made in Italy Elizabeth Gaskell wrote that she and her husband would take Meta out to Alexandria in the winter of 1858 to get married. Then the couple would go to India:

To Charles Eliot Norton, 28 September 1857 (374)
There they remain until his time of service May 1862 entitles him to a retiring pension, of 200£ a year; when, if we or he can in any way obtain an appointment at home, – Manager of railways, inspector of railroads &c &c &c they would come home & live at home; and oh! no one knows how much I wish this may be done, – and, if possible, that we might have a *promise* of it before Meta goes; as a thing to look forward to. He left us on August 24th and Meta is very bright & cheerful, much less anxious, indeed, I think than any of us.

There was even a period of calm, or what used to pass for calm, at Plymouth Grove:

To Charles Eliot Norton, 7 December 1857 (384)
Plymouth Grove –
Monday, Decr   (1st Monday
in December at any rate, because Mr Gaskell has a dozen committees (be the same more or less,) to attend to, every first Monday in the month, and
he is going to them today.)
My dear Mr Norton,
    Your letter to Polly (Novr 24) is just come. Breakfast is still on the table; waiting for Mr Gaskell, who was very much tired last night, and so is late this morning. I am sitting at the round writing table in the dining-

room, – Marianne is mending me a pen, over the fire place, in order that the bits may drop into the fender; Meta is gone into the garden, to tell Joseph about perennials for next year (new pen – Thank you Polly,) the said Meta's last words being 'Dear good Mr Norton!' as she left the room, after hearing Polly read yr *note* – your *letter* to me came 10 days ago. – So here we all are, placed, ready to your imagination. Flossy & Julia have been spending Sunday with a Schoolfellow in the country four miles off, – and we have not seen them since Saturday. It is not exactly wintry weather here; – but a *grey* sky all over, with a line of watery pale light in the west, – no snow though. . . .

But I really am going to write a proper stately letter; full of news; only I have not any news, and have a very runaway kind of mind. Thank you for telling us about your library. It sounds very pretty & pleasant, – and the views out of the windows make me have a kind of a Heimweh, – as if I had seen them once, & yearned to see them again, – instead of dear old dull ugly smoky grim grey Manchester. And your views of Torcello – *where* DID *you get that Photograph*, & the other Venetian one; and why did not we get them? Oh! that exquisite dreamy Torcello Sunday, – that still, sunny, sleepy canal, – something like the Lady of Shalott, – tho' how, why, & wherefore I can't tell. If I had a library like yours, all undisturbed for hours, how I would write! Mrs Chapone's letters should be nothing to mine! I would outdo Rasselas in fiction. But you see every body comes to me perpetually. Now in this hour since breakfast I have had to decide on the following variety of important questions. Boiled beef – how long to boil? What perennials will do in Manchester smoke, & what colours our garden wants? Length of skirt for a gown? Salary of a nursery governess, & stipulations for a certain quantity of time to be left to herself. – Read letters on the state of Indian army – lent me by a very agreeable neighbour & return them, with a proper note, & as many wise remarks as would come in a hurry. Settle 20 questions of dress for the girls, who are going out for the day; & want to look nice & yet not spoil their gowns with the mud &c &c – See a lady about an MS story of hers, & give her disheartening but very good advice. Arrange about selling two poor cows for one good one, – see purchasers, & show myself up to cattle questions, keep, & prices, – and it's not $\frac{1}{2}$ past 10 yet! . . .

Then follows a long, racy account of a visit to Oxford, which ends:

Monday to the Bodleian, – lunch with Mr Jowett. Bodleian again. Mr Cox showing us illuminated MSS. To the Union, – trying to understand the meaning of the paintings, – & in a little measure understanding; to call on the Aclands & Wellesleys – to see the Museum, home. I saw so much, I have hardly yet arranged it in my mind. But I like dearly to call up pictures, – & thoughts suggested by so utterly different a life to Manchester. I believe I *am* Mediæval, – and *un* Manchester, and un American. I do like associations – they are like fragrance, which I value so in a flower. None of your American flowers smell sweetly (do they?) any more than your birds sing, – now I like a smelling and singing world. Yes I do. I can't help it. I like Kings & Queens, & nightingales and mignionettes & roses. There! . . .

But in the real world of Manchester, strain seems to lie just beneath the surface :

Now about Capt Hill. We (*i.e.*) Meta get very nice letters from him – always remembering – & several times remembering – to send nice little presents to Hearn. He is appointed to the command of his regiment of sappers & miners at Dowlaisheram where they are busily employed on Godavery Irrigation. Meta is very well. Marianne accuses her of two of the seven deadly sins, sloth & gluttony, for she sleeps like a top and is always hungry.

To Ellen Nussey, 30 December 1857 (385a)

Capt. Hill is appointed to the command of his Regiment Sappers and Miners, and is stationed at Dowlaisheram and getting 800 rupees (£80) a month, *besides* his military pay, so as far as money goes their affairs are prospering. Mr Gaskell never names his name! Marianne has turned round ever since *your* talk with her, dear Miss Nussey – for which thank you truly, and is as unselfish a sister, and generous sensible and prudent an adviser as need be.

It had been a very difficult year. 'If ever we are conscious of a breathing of the Godhead in man,' Harriet Martineau had written in her Unitarian days, 'it is in the sanctified presence, actual or ideal, of martyrs to truth'.[5] One is sure that Elizabeth Gaskell (who liked to end letters with a 'Yours truly') felt she belonged to that noble band, whatever the objections to the *Life of Charlotte Brontë*. In Meta's engagement, however, she found great anxiety rather than exaltation or even common joy. The situation in India was an obvious factor, especially when reports came of friends lost in the fighting, but something more personal was involved. That year, too, saw the Great Art Treasures Exhibition in Manchester. Plymouth Grove was full of guests and bustle. Their faithful servant Hearn 'had a good number of distressing events in her family,

& lost all her savings' (401). The Gaskell family don't seem to have lost all their savings, but they lived through a more than average number of stressful events. We notice a somewhat tougher, certainly much less naïve tone when she tells Norton about 'The Doom of the Griffiths' :

To Charles Eliot Norton, 7 December 1857 (384)

The story, per se, is an old rubbishy one, – begun when Marianne was a baby, – the only merit whereof is that it is founded on fact. But at Mr Sampson Lowe's earnest entreaty I promised it to Messrs Harpers more than a year ago; – and, of course I relied a little on payment; (though what that is to be, I have not a notion;) and when Mr Lowe, (whom I have found out in other things to be rather a 'tricky man',) took such care not to acknowledge the receipt of the story in London, *until* he had sent it off to America, – coupled with rumours of Messrs Harpers' insolvency, I became suspicious, and determined to outwit the sleek old gentleman, & have my tale back, if it could not be paid for. Very worldly, is it not? But really I had relied on the money; and this will be an expensive winter to us, for we are, thanks to you Americans, surrounded with poor people out of work, and are beating our wits to pieces to know how best to relieve their present wants, without injuring them permanently. So don't give me up as a mercenary tricky woman, though I acknowledge I *should* like to out-dodge Mr Sampson Lowe if ever our wits came in contact. Are you never as wicked as this? I am sure if I were a servant, & suspected and things locked up from me &c, I should not only be dishonest, but a very clever thief.

CHAPTER SIX

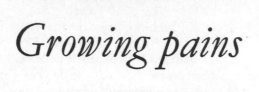

Growing pains

I do not like the plan in fashion formerly,
of *making* trials for young children; there
will naturally be some which the child
must bear, and the parent calmly witness . . .

(*My Diary*, 4 October 1835)

EARLY IN THE FOLLOWING YEAR, one publisher must have restored
Elizabeth Gaskell's faith in his kind. He had already paid her £800 for the
Life:

To George Smith, 17 March 1858 (387)
   I do not think I was ever more surprized than by the contents of your letter
   this morning. I had always felt that you had behaved to me most liberally
   in the first instance, and that in some respects, the book must have been a
   great source of annoyance and vexation to you; it was only the other day
   that I expressed my sense of your good & kind behaviour, under mortifi-
   cation & disappointment caused by me, to Mrs Clive; and now to receive
   a cheque for 200£! I am most sincerely & heartily obliged to you for it. As
   money it is very acceptable, just now, but I am even more touched by the
   kindness & liberality, which will always make me feel beholden to you.

But we notice a little wryly that 'The Doom of the Griffiths' actually appeared
in *Harper's New Monthly Magazine* and that before very long she was able to
tell her sister-in-law of further business with Sampson Low:

To Anne Robson, Early February 1859 (414)
  You will be seeing a book of mine advertized; but don't be diddled about it; it is only a REpublication of H W Stories; I have a rascally publisher this time (Sampson Low, who publishes Mrs Stowe's books,) & he is trying to pass it off as new. I sold the right of republication to him in a hurry to get 100£ to take Meta abroad out of the clatter of tongues consequent on her breaking off her engagement.

It is clear that Meta was very distressed and that her mother was determined to support her as much as ever she could:

To Charles Eliot Norton, 10 and 14 May 1858 (394)
  I believe it is certain that Meta will break off her engagement to Capt Hill. She has heard some things which have made her have a very different opinion of his character to what she had at first. These come from so good authority (in fact from his own sisters) that Meta's mind is quite made up, only she thought it right to write to him, and to ask if he could give any explanation. It does not seem to her *possible*; but you will see why, until his answer comes, she nor I feel justified in speaking of the engagement as definitively broken off. Nor shall we say more at any time, than that it *is* broken off. Those who wish or care to know the reasons must apply to him for them. Meta is *far* from well, – more from deep disappointment in character, I think than from wounded affection; for she says 'he is not in the least what she fancied he was'. All I do, is to wait to help her to bear much 'public-talking' – & possibly upbraiding from him; and to give her what strength & sympathy I can. I am sure she has done right, & with a pure & simple mind. It has been a most terrible anxiety to me. But the little loophole of blue sky, & sunny heavens is widening daily. Neither she nor I are well or strong, – we are each ordered 'tonics' & 'change of air & scene,' but we do not like to separate. Marianne's good sense & merry ways make us cheerful whenever she is with us. If I can muster up money (but you see I am very poor, what with doctor's bills, half-got Indian outfit, inability to write, for want of health –) I would try & persuade Mr Gaskell, to take us three abroad, after we come back from Silverdale, and leave us (when the children would be settled at school) for a few weeks somewhere, – Rhine, Avranches in Normandy – &c &c. But Mr Gaskell dreads foreign diet like poison. *He* is so much better you would not know him! My own belief is that he had some internal digestive complaint which had been coming on for years; came to a crisis last autumn, & he has been gaining flesh, colour, strength ever since.

At first she took her girls to Silverdale for six weeks. The 'charming primitive desert' (399) by Morecambe Bay could not have been far enough from the clatter of tongues, however, for off she went to Heidelberg with the three older girls early in September 1858. Marianne returned in October. The others went into lodgings for nine weeks with 'a friend of Meta's, an orphan young lady who joined us, Miss Jackson' (418). They did not come back till just before Christmas.

A long letter to Charles Norton, fast becoming one of her regular correspondents and taking the place of Eliza Fox, who went to Rome in autumn 1858 and married the artist F. L. Bridell,[1] seems to show that the family was once more on an even keel:

To Charles Eliot Norton, 9 March 1859 (418)

Yes! we have got our drawing-room chairs & sofas covered with a new chintz. Such a pretty one, little rosebuds & carnations on a white ground. All the other furniture stands where it did. By little bits we pick up little bits of prettiness (such as two Black Forest carved brackets at the fair at Heidelberg,) but you'll be happy to hear we are not rich enough to make many or grand changes. Indeed I don't think I should like to do it, even if one could. The house is to be painted and papered (passages & bedrooms) in May, but we shall rather adhere to the old colours. We mean to have prettier flowers than ever this year in the conservatory. We are always full of hope and of plans in the flower-line, just about this time of the year. But the east winds, & the smoke always come; only one cannot live without hoping. We have just the same servants. Elliot (waiter) often asks after you; and is very critical about the two photographs. – Yes! thank you, much, we got the second, and like it very much, but I don't think quite so well as the other because that was Roman.

The girls go on, right down well. Meta is turning out such a noble beautiful character – Her intellect and her soul, (or wherever is the part in which piety & virtue live) are keeping pace, as they should do – She works away at German & Greek – reads carefully many books, – with a fineness of perception & relish which delights me, – teaches patiently and tenderly at the Ragged school, – has poor old people whom she goes to see regularly, as a friend not as a benefactor, and is ever ready with household sympahty. She has gone back a year or two into her childhood, although professing to feel 'very old' at twenty two Febry 5th, and declining to be called a '*young* woman' saying she is 'middle aged.' Marianne is as practical and humourous as ever. Her quick decision always makes me feel as if she was a kind of 'elder *son*' rather than daughter. She is going to stay at the Bright's, next Tuesday. Flossy is gone to school! Yes, our pretty

Flossy, who stept into the gay world of Heidelberg, went out to two dances, and began to be a little belle, has had to don the chrysalis-shell, & go to school, at dear old Knutsford, – with some Miss Greens, (the daughters of the Unitarian Minister there,) who are like sisters to our elder girls. And Julia is sprouting up, almost as tall as Marianne. (I forgot to tell you that Meta reads with & teaches Elliot every night, & has a little orphan lad to teach French to, – among her multifarious duties. She is learning to *whip-a top* today in order to show some boys at the Ragged school.) Hearn went off yesterday into Devonshire (her native shire) for a long holiday of six weeks. Julia & I are going to see Flossy at Knutsford on Saty next, March 12. But that Saturday will be long past by the time you get this letter.

The same letter also contained the significant news that William Gaskell had been asked to go as minister to Essex Street Chapel in London. He had declined. Though his preaching had struck the young Henry Morley as 'intellectual', he had not been one of the four Unitarian ministers who ran the advanced *Prospective Review* during the 1840s (Thom and Martineau of Liverpool, Wicksteed of Leeds and Tayler of Manchester). He had stayed behind when Manchester New College had removed to London in 1853, becoming more and more embedded in local affairs and more and more attached to his study, 'out of which room by his own free will he would never stir' (418). He was 'liable to spasmodic asthma, for which, curiously enough,' his wife remarked with her tongue in her cheek, 'no air does so well as Manchester smoke' (439a). Even if he could be persuaded to go away, it was not, as we know, with his own family :

To William Wetmore and Emelyn Story, 23 June 1861 (490)
'*The* congregation' have given Mr Gaskell a holiday of *two* months (not very long after 33 year's faithful service,) and fifty pounds, to make 'a continental tour.' Now he does not particularly care for the 'Continent', yet is tied to go there; he cannot meet with a companion, (his own womankind wd any of them, be *thankful* to go with him, but he says he needs 'entire freedom from responsibility' which he could not have if he had the charge of any of us, and of our luggage, – (you need not say 'Impedimenta' Mr Story! I can hear you!) so that altogether he was very 'low' about where he was to go, and what he was to do, and his feeling of loneliness on the Continent, until Friday at dinner; when on our suggesting that he should make his way to you in your summer retreat his face brightened immensely, and all he said was 'Oh they would think I was intruding upon them! I have no right to force myself on people!' So I took all the blame,

promised, that if need were, you should hate *me* & not *him* for 'pushing himself in upon you', – and I sate down immediately to write the letter, ... Oh HOW I shall envy Mr Gaskell if he does reach you. I feel so sure you will like each other. He is very shy, but *very* merry when he is well, delights in puns & punning, is very fond of children, playing with them all the day long, not caring for them so much when they are grown up, *used* to speak Italian pretty well, but says he can't now, 6 foot high, grey hair & whiskers & otherwise very like Marianne in looks. You'll think him stiff till his shyness wears off, as I am sure it will.

They were 'like Adam and Eve in the weather glass' (79), she had once joked to Tottie Fox. While she is becoming a national figure, offered £1000 for the manuscript of her next novel, his life is largely bounded by Owens College, 'Herald Office, Chapel-room, – Home Mission – Boardroom' (542). He is a pillar of the Unitarian community in Manchester.

The household flourished at this time. Julia 'trots to Miss Mitchells day school every day; she is grown nearly as tall as Flossy and is very spirited and wilful, more like Meta in her naughty days than anything else' (421). She had 'crêpé hair' and 'ticklish b-w-ls'; Marianne was instructed to give her 'stewed rhubarb, and that sort of thing' (457). A new cook was needed. 'Of course I shall gladly allow her to go to Church', Mrs Gaskell wrote to her former mistress; 'all our servants go there, excepting a German maid, and one who is an Independent. (We have five women-servants, and an out-of-doors-man, or gardener.)' (468)

The house was robbed once:

To Marianne Gaskell, 26 May 1860 (471)
Luckily, they *only* took a round of beef, lying in salt, & all the towels & dirty clothes out of the wash-house, – the *back-door* must have been left open, (which annoys Papa,) & Lion did *not* bark, whh make the Police & all of us think it must have been some one in the habit of coming about the house – some of those horrid Dripping women I think, whom Sarah brought about the place. She had left (breakfast, & supper things unwashed) at 10 o'clock AM; so one can't suspect her. Such a good riddance! However though it is vexatious enough perhaps it may be a warning; as the servants were evidently terribly frightened – Mary & Hearn sitting up the greater part of the night, for they feared some one was in the house &c &c.

In this summer Meta was taken on a splendid Continental tour as companion to 'an oldish Miss Darwin (sister of Mr Chas Darwin) in quiet respectable luxury, stopping where they liked, – and sketching' (476). Marianne went

1 left Mrs Hannah Lumb, the widowed aunt who brought Elizabeth Gaskell up at Knutsford after the death of her mother.

Sandlebridge Farm, a few miles from Knutsford, was the home of Elizabeth Gaskell's Holland grandparents. In 1816 it passed to her cousin, the physician and traveller Sir Henry Holland.

2 below

3 *left* Elizabeth Gaskell's bust was executed at Edinburgh about 1830 by David Dunbar.

4 *right* The bust of Jane Byerley, Elizabeth Gaskell's teacher, was by 'Pepper, of Brighton' in 1858.

5 After the death of her father in 1829, Elizabeth Gaskell stayed with the Reverend William Turner, Unitarian minister at Newcastle upon Tyne.

6 The Unitarian chapel in Cross Street, Manchester was drawn by M. P. Calvert. Its congregation included many influential citizens.

7 An early photograph (1859) by James Mudd of the river Irwell, which ran through the heart of industrial Manchester.

8 left William Gaskell's sister Eliza, the most important of the early correspondents.

9 right Charles Holland, a cousin of Elizabeth Gaskell, who married Eliza.

10 Charles Holland purchased the estate of Liscard Vale, Wallasey, in 1844. He greatly enlarged the house, which looks over the river Mersey.

11 The Plymouth Grove drawing room as it was *c.* 1897 when the house was lived in by the two unmarried daughters, Meta and Julia Gaskell.

12 A favourite country holiday place, Silverdale. The Gaskells used to stay in 'a queer pretty crampy house' (Letter 394) called Lindeth Tower.

vii. *Harmony or Melody* ↗ style; depends much on: ear. Avoid an accumulation ↗ harsh consonants — repetitee + ↗: same sound ("Of r'c note delightte) — too much ↗: sibo ant (hissing) s — a needless recurrence ↗ open vow (i.e. vowels ending one word & beginning : next).

Of course, a literary taste must ⊢ cultivated by a fa- miliarity ε: best models ↗ excellence in vb; There 2 a cl analogy in ε respect ⊢: cultivation ↗ taste in painting ↗ r'↗: fine arts. They learn ℓ q'2 ⊢, ⊢ admired, & ↗: mod ↗ objects ↗ study,,

⌐ Bad — "He rightly writes"

THE HOME OF CHARLOTTE BRONTE

J. GREENWOOD, STATIONER, &c., HAWORTH.
(By permission of the Proprietors of the London Journal)

England

At Mrs Gaskell's, Manchester,
Monday Morning, Nov. 11. 1861

Dear Mother — I have been to Haworth,
"the home of Charlotte Brontë" as
you see by this sheet of paper
which I got there. — I had a

15 John Greenwood told Elizabeth Gaskell of Charlotte Brontë's death on 31 March 1855. The biography made her dead friend famous and Haworth a place of pilgrimage.

16 One of the last portraits of Mrs Gaskell, about 1864, from a photograph in the John Rylands University Library, Manchester.

up to London, Florence was at school in Knutsford, 'Julia at her day school nearly all day; and Mr Gaskell always constantly away' – at last Mrs Gaskell had the chance to write a full-scale book again. She tackled *Sylvia's Lovers,* her historical novel set at Whitby on the Yorkshire coast over half a century before, in good earnest :

To Charles Eliot Norton, 27 August 1860 (476)
I got on splendidly too with my new book, that-is-to-be – ; I had nearly finished the first vol; and was full of it all when one morng – 6th of June, I had a letter from Marianne, written in pencil & in bed from London, saying she was very ill, – supposed to be going to be small-pox. Mr Gaskell was in town, but Agnes Ewart went to ask his leave, & met me with it, at the railway Station, and off I went. Of course, with a suspicion of such a complaint I could not go to any friend's house, as I meant to see Marianne that night, – and it was Cup Day at Ascot, a thing which in my ignorance, I did not know would fill up every possible & hirable bed in London. I did not get there till $\frac{1}{2}$ p. 7, & then began my search for a bed, – at last I got a garret in a back St, & then went to Marianne; who had been left by the family, (female portion of,) to the care of the physician. It was *not* however small only *bad* chicken-pox.

Robberies and illnesses could be coped with. There remained, gently aching, one unsolved problem for a mother :

To Charles Eliot Norton, 19 January 1860 (453)
My girls, my darlings, *are* such comforts – such happiness! Every one so good & healthy & bright. I don't know what I should do if any one of them married; & yet it is constantly a wonder to me that no one ever gives them a chance. I suspect it is that here (in Manchester) the Unitarian young men are either good *and* uncultivated, or else rich *and* regardless of those higher qualities the 'spiritual' qualities as it were, which those *must* appreciate who would think of my girls. The new school of enlightened & liberal young men, of high cultivation & still higher moral and religious standard with whom we associate occasionally, are all held back by the more bigotted fathers of the last generation from too much intimacy with Unitarians. I think an unmarried life may be to the full as happy, *in process of time* but I think there is a time of trial to be gone through with *women*, who naturally yearn after children.

It is hard to know what her husband thought. Perhaps the only letter to his wife that survives,[2] written on 25 July 1860 when she had taken Marianne abroad to recuperate in a German spa, suggests that he might have been able to take a humorously philosophical view:

> I shan't be sorry when you are all on English ground again. Can you give me any idea when it is likely to be? I ought to fix when I am to go to Scotland, as the Potters are getting their beds filled, and my holidays are slipping away. What I said to Mr. P. was that I would be with them at the beginning of August, but I hear of a great number who are going up then. I don't see how you can be here by that time, if Kreuznach is to be taken properly.
>
> Another thing is – to see that you don't knock *yourself* up, with scientific pursuits, and soaring too high, and trying to make out what the sun is made of. (Tell Polly, it is stron*t*ium, not *s*ium). With respect to your *gout*, I never knew you wished it to be a secret – though it might shew a want of *goût* in me to mention it – but Polly's pimples shall be sacred. Thank the children all for their notes and good wishes – (but, BETWEEN YOU AND ME, their spelling is a trifle too phonetic, and we must try to reform it.) And now can *you* keep a secret? Mr. Greenwood is going to be married! Who to? Why, Miss Taylor – sister of the one whom his brother married. Of course, you mustn't let out to Dr. Roscoe that you have heard this – though, perhaps, Mr. G. may inform his friends before long.

The letter is a long one, unusually varied in tone and content, but such passages are very much in the ironical vein of Mr Bennet in *Pride and Prejudice*.

In those days, however, Unitarians needed a sense of humour and a spirit of patient resignation. William was able to tell his wife that he had been 'to Dukinfield on Sunday, and dined at Mr. David Harrison's, with Mr. Bass, who, though a Churchman, always comes to hear me when I am in his neighborhood'. Yet against the liberal Mr Bass one could set the young Anglican Charles Bosanquet, who spoke a great deal about religion but 'always on the supposition' that the Gaskells were Church people. Mrs Gaskell was forced to disillusion him:

To Charles Eliot Norton, 16 April 1861 (485)
> At first he could hardly understand it, – he had evidently had some unknown horror of Unitarians, – & gravely & seriously asked me 'if we believed in the Bible' – However I told him what *I* did believe – (more I suppose what would be called Arian than Humanitarian,) – and among other things said I had only one antipathy – and that was to the Calvinistic or Low Church creed, – to which he replied he was sorry[,] for his father & all his friends were what was called Low or Evangelical Church, – &

gave me quite a different (& most beautiful) account of what he considered their belief; – he said if the Bible taught him anything different from what he believed to be the doctrines of the Church he should immediately become a Dissenter. That 'Love & Truth' were the two qualities that formed the Essence of the Xtian religion, & that the *Spirit* in which actions were performed was of far higher consequence than the actions themselves. Much more was said, – he all the time getting over the 'shock' of coming in contact for the first time with Unitarians.

By degrees they became friends, 'to Meta, in an especial way bringing back some of the faith in *man*kind she had at the time lost so entirely in consequence of Capt Hill's character &c. Mind! there was no suspicion of "love" on either side' (485). Just as well perhaps, for his parents utterly refused to meet the Gaskells. They, in comparison, seemed admirably liberal and unprejudiced.

Victorian sectarianism was a complex matter, however. Catherine Winkworth tells us that when Mrs Gaskell and her two eldest daughters were in Rome in the spring of 1857, 'the most tremendous set' was made at them by some notable English converts to Roman Catholicism, 'prayers being offered in one of the churches on their behalf, &c., &c., so far very unavailingly'. It all remained on a social plane: the Gaskells were 'all the fashion', constantly invited out, asked to dine at all the embassies and called upon by a succession of Roman Catholic dignitaries. The future Cardinal Manning, whose own list of converts eventually amounted to several hundreds, failed for once to exert his magnetic power. The 'fair-haired, rather would-be-genius-like' Aubrey de Vere, who never said a word not meant to benefit the soul and lead to Catholicism, left her Unitarianism untouched. But, in the winter of 1861, Marianne was taken to Rome for five months by some friends and this time Manning almost succeeded in making a convert:[3]

To Marianne Gaskell, Early 1862 (500a)
I was taken ill that Tuesday & now I am glad the letter did not go, as the quieter all is done & the less that is said the better. I leave all at your end to the decision of *you and Mrs Dicey* whatever you two think best had better be done; only do avoid Dr Manning. I concentrate all my wish on that for the present, till I know more, I *wish* your letter would come, tho' it would only be a letter after the telegrams; not after the letters Meta wrote. I have not been out yet. I come down before lunch & go up to bed early (last night between 6 & 7) & am very good for nothing – but oh! if I do but hear good accounts of you my child – good accounts in every way – that you are pretty strong, that you are not led off by excitement to go a few steps (as you think *only*) on a wrong & terrible way – that you are

avoiding temptation & referring doubtful cases to Mrs Dicey who, you know love, is at present in the place of a parent to you, I shall get all right. Only tell me the truth. There is no news – or there seems to me none, compared with what I want to hear from you. *Don't go to the Storys' Friday afternoons* if it is there you meet Dr Manning because it will be awkward to have to so change your manner to him as to provoke questions & explanations. Oh! I am so sorry I ever let you go to Rome – we have so missed you at home & if it is all to end in this way, but I know it won't. Only you see I am not well & am so stupid & do so want your letter. Louy Jackson is coming (did I tell you?), at least she offered & Meta accepted when I was ill & we have not heard from her & think she must be coming. Godfrey Wedgwood is engaged to Mary Jane Hawkshaw & they are to be married in June. Mr Bosanquet is engaged to a Miss Eliza Carr of Northumberland & they are to be married in August. God bless you & *have you in His holy keeping* my dearest darling.

> Your ever most affectionate mother
> E. C. Gaskell.

Marianne was back in England by 19 March,[4] safe from Roman witchery:

To Charles Eliot Norton, 22 April 1862 (504)
About Marianne; I know her letter goes in the same sheet as this but I do not know what she has said in it; all I know is that – firstly Dr Manning strongly impressed her in Rome; but I hope that evil influence is done away with now. She says she never has been a Unitarian in belief; but she has never inquired; nor has she a logical mind; so that now that she is reading with her Papa very carefully, – she only seems to feel that all that he says 'is very *clear*', without being convinced, – i.e. seeing the force of the Unitarian arguments. Nor yet can she define her own belief, nor speak about it, nor give her reasons for it. All this is stating the very worst side for her, if you understand what I mean by 'worst side'. *Arguments* never did seem to have much force for her in *abstract* things. She is one of the clearest people I know about *practical* things; in consequence of this intellectual – what shall I call it? of her's, it becomes very difficult either for herself or others to exactly understand where she stands with regard to doctrine. However she is really *trying*; and she is also trying to be so good and humble that I feel as if the grace of God would be given her to perceive what to her may be saving truth.

To William Wetmore Story, 9 May 1862 (507)
I think you have mistaken my last letter – Please read it again, & see if I

say a word about not valuing, or thanking you for, your frankness as I ought. I know I wrote warmly about Meta; *not* angrily but only wishing to disabuse you of the notion that *she* had 'proclivities' towards R. C.ism. As long as I hoped & thought it was only that MA had frightened Mrs Dicey without cause, I was anxious to keep it from Mr Gaskell. When I learnt from your letter how serious it was, I was thankful to you for telling us, and for telling it to him, sorry as I was (*of course*) to have the *extreme* pain of learning such things. I think you are misjudging me, *a little*, dear Mr Story; but I don't mind – for *I* can love *you* all the same; I think you have been a true kind friend. Why Meta named Mr Norton Mr Martineau & Mr Kingsley is this. (I write in *great* haste, so I may not measure my words *fully*.) Marianne has all her life been influenced by people, *out of her own family* – & seldom by the members of it, in anything like the same degree, in all matters of opinion. She is now reading with her father; but I fear his *extreme* dislike & abhorrence of R. C-ism; & thinking all the arguments adduced by its professors 'utterly absurd', makes *her* more inclined to take up it's defence thinking it unjustly treated.

This awkward episode shows that liberal Unitarian sympathies in Manchester had very definite limits. His fellow minister J. R. Beard, for example, had tried to believe 'that Romanism had partaken of the general improvement of the age' but by 1860 was solemnly declaring in print 'that Rome morally, spiritually and politically is THE ABOMINATION OF DESOLATION'.[5] Such theological and religious odium in relatively unprejudiced men can be matched by Elizabeth Gaskell's spasm of irritated xenophobia in a letter of this time : 'the pure-bred Lancashire man is a right down fine fellow, – it is the admixture with Irish &c that pulls them down' (503). Certain fundamental values, however, were probably quite unaffected :

To Miss Leo, no date (619)
The bearer of this note is Anne Daly (an Irish girl very delicate poor thing, with a bad cough,) who has come over to be with her sister, Rebecca Daly, well known to me. They are orphans; very nice girls, – Anne Daly has been brought up in an Irish Sewing School, & can 'flower' i.e. embroider, *very* well; she can crotchet a little.

Like Marianne, Elizabeth Gaskell seems to have been perfectly clear about *practical* things, but perhaps under her husband's influence she modified the tolerance of Roman Catholicism expressed in *North and South* (1855).
However, it was not long before the hapless Marianne was again in hot water. Her relation Edward Holland, by now Liberal M.P. for Evesham and a

major figure in his county,[6] had a son called Thurstan, who seems to have been entirely delightful – 'very good, very intelligent, very gentlemanly, & very full of fun; aged 22, Eton & Trin. Coll. Cam.' (388), Mrs Gaskell told Richard Monckton Milnes in 1858. At one time, mysteriously, she was 'silently & quietly much displeased' with Thurstan, even though he and five rich young men were planning to build a model lodging house for the poor in London and she liked 'to see that their previous luxurious (so to speak) education has not unfitted them for strong feeling & prompt acting in behalf of those less fortunate' (461). But his brother came as a curate to Manchester, Marianne went to stay at Dumbleton Hall the summer after her escape from Manning's silken snares and 'the old Thurstan breach' was healed:

To Catherine Winkworth, 23 July 1862 (509b)

We had no dinner, but lunched at the boy's old tutors, lounged in the lovely 'playing-fields' meeting no end of friends (for every one in the least connected with the place goes to it on that day –) and then went with all the rest of the world to the river and embarked in Thurstan's boat, & rowed a great way up the river, & then walked to the field, where the different Eton boat crews were having their supper, under tents, band playing &c. Then it began to rain, so we ran back thro' the long wet grass to our boats, muffled ourselves in cloaks & plaids, & were rowed back to the island in the river to be illuminated by the fireworks. We sate in our boat among a thick crowd of other boats in pelting rain till the pretty Eton racing-boats came down the river from their supper; every minute the rain coming on more & more steadily, which delayed the boats. Then they came with shout & song & music down the dark river, into the bright coloured gleam of the fire works & coloured light coming smoothly down with the current out of the darkness into the shining water, – into the darkness again, – all the crews standing up motionless as they passed the brilliant illuminated 'Floreat Etona'. The thing reminded *me* of the Saxon Kings comparison of human life to the swallows flying thro' the tent, out of darkness coming, – into darkness going. Meta said she thought of the verse in the Ancient Mariner 'A Seraph band' &c, – for each figure was motionless and bright, & the smooth current bore them past so noiselessly & still. The fireworks were of course a failure in the pouring rain.

Though Thurstan was the son of a rich man, he had eleven brothers and sisters. Naturally enough perhaps, his family expected him to 'marry money' – Miss Darwin was mentioned at one stage – and make his own way in his profession of Chancery law. Then he announced his engagement to Marianne:

To George Smith, 25 July 1864 (553)

His father objects strongly – has forbidden both me & Minnie to reply to his letters; & I fear will with draw his present allowance to his son when he marries, – which is far enough off, (though WE none of us here object to long engagements,) as Thurstan's 'professional income' on which his father says he is to rely, is at present less than nothing. The *only* objections are the relationship (Edward constantly speaks of Minnie with great affection) *second* cousins – & Minnie's being older. – However we are in the middle of a pretty little family 'tiff', – ; which will, I suppose, die out in time, but is unpleasant in the interval. . . .

The couple, who had in fact been attached to each other for about six years, did not manage to get married until 1866.

All this stands in strong contrast to Florence's simple story. Her mother had thought she was a child still needing protection; she got engaged to a Charles Crompton in the summer of 1863. He was thirty to her twenty, the eldest of seven children but a Fellow of Trinity doing well in his profession :

To Charles Eliot Norton, 13 July 1863 (526)

I suppose he has those solid intellectual qualities which tell in *action*, though not in *conversation*. But his goodness is what gives me the thankfullest feeling of confidence in him. They will have to live in London – (probably Harewood Sq. off the New Road, Regent's-Park-wards) and will have to begin œconomically – (one of his nice feelings is his thorough hearty approval of his father's plan of dividing his property among his 7 children equally, instead of making an eldest son, à la mode Anglaise –) Florence is very œconomical and managing. We tell her she will *starve* her husband she is so full of œconomical plans. Mr Crompton's eldest sister (a year younger than he) is married to Mr Llewellyn Davis, a clergyman whose writings in Macmillan &c. – he is one of Mr Maurice's school, are very likely known to you – he signs J. Ll. D. He has also published sermons on the Atonement – true meaning of Sacrifice &c. Mr Crompton is not exactly a Unitarian, nor exactly broad Church, – but perhaps rather more of the latter than the former. He is so good-principled he may be called a religious man; for I am sure the root of his life is in religion. But he has not imagination enough to be what one calls *spiritual*. It is just the same want that makes him not care for music or painting, – nor much for poetry. In these tastes Florence is his superior, although *she* is not 'artistic'. Then he cares for science, – in which she is at present ignorant. His strong good, *un*sensitive character is just what will, I trust, prove very grateful to her anxious, conscientious little heart. They are to be married *here* – (the

Cromptons all wished for a *country* wedding, – and he had a particular friend, a clergyman, who he particularly wished to marry them –) but, after some discussion it is settled that they are to be married in Brook Street Chapel – where Mr John James Tayler used to preach, – by Mr Gaskell. No one but the two families are to be at the wedding, – and it is to take place some day in the first week of September, – *day* not fixed yet. They go into Scotland; return here to pay us a little visit before settling down for the lawyer's year in London, – about Octr 20. He will come the Northern Circuit, and bring her here to stay with us, as often as he can during those times. So much for *that*.

She was 'kindly received' by her new family and positively 'doated on' by her husband:

To Charles Eliot Norton, 1 February 1864 (546)
He is so truly humble; & so exquisitely sweet-tempered; so desirous of being a *son* to us; and a brother to the girls! My only fear is literally that he should spoil Florence; he is pretty strict & self-denying towards himself but if he could dress her in diamonds and feed her on gold, and give her the moon to play with, and *she wished for them* I don't think he would question the wisdom of indulging her. I hope by and bye he will lift her up into the standard of high goodness of which she is thoroughly capable. But she is very young for her age, & as yet requires the daily elevation of her thoughts & aims. But again she is so loving & generous, – her new affluence of money makes her remember all the little wishes we have ever expressed & she is like a fairy godmother to us. He is prospering exceedingly as a special pleader; & only wants us all to come & make his house our home.

It begins to look as if the growing pains of the family are almost over. Given the contrast in temperament – 'but frost which suits me never suits him' (558) – husband and wife were happy and settled. She continued to conspire with his colleagues in Manchester to get him off on holiday, 'en garçon, for I dare say that he would feel more independent in an hotel without me, and with no tie to bring him back from his Forums, or the old book-stalls of the Piazza Navona' (535). Two of their daughters had found partners; the other two had in fact found the pattern of their future lives: [7]

To Charles Eliot Norton, 4 July 1864 (551)
Meta & Julia (who left school 'for good' a fortnight ago, & is full of promise, – the merriest grig, the most unselfish girl by *nature*, that I ever

knew; with a deep sense of religion in her unusual, I think, at so early an age), – Meta & Julia are alone – such happy friends, keeping house for Mr Gaskell; who has been to Rome & come back, and is a different creature in consequence, showing the advantage of change & travel. Marianne is in London, seeing her friend's with Florence's for her home house. Dear little Florence is curiously unchanged by marriage in many ways; takes her place as *third* daughter at home, runs errands &c. but is a little bit tyran-nical over her sweet-tempered husband in her own house.

But Meta's health was precarious. After her broken engagement, Marianne's religious difficulties and neurotically intense work in the Lancashire Cotton Famine of the early 1860s, she suffered constantly from headaches and fainting. She was taken to Switzerland in autumn 1864, but it did not really serve:

To Anne Robson, 2 January 1865 (558)
She is bodily strong excepting for the violent pain in two places in her spine, which the least worry still brings on; and it is almost impossible to keep her from worry. For instance the other day, when I was unable to be with her; three people came in unexpectedly to lunch; we have a new cook and Meta did(n't) think we had enough meat for lunch etc. *so* her pain in her back came on and then, unless she exercises very great self-control crying that is almost hysterical succeeds. She does not like to have all this spoken about, so don't allude to it, as she has a horror of being thought hysterical but I think these fits of crying are of that nature, though accom-panied with this pain in the spine. Mr Erichsen is still prescribing for her – a great deal of open air, 6 hours a day – but no fatigue early hours, a *great deal of meat* to eat, bitter beer, a little society, but not large assemb-lies, as much change as possible and tonics. He has already greatly im-proved her health; which had never been strong since the sewing days.

This letter, one might note, was written from a house that Charles Cromp-ton's father had taken for two years in Worcestershire. 'They wanted us all to come', she told William's sister, 'but Wm did not fancy a journey in cold weather and for so short a time.' William, after all, was perfectly happy in Manchester, 'as usual at this time of the year, dining out almost every day and is besides engaged in preparing a set of lectures on the Lancashire dialect to be delivered at the Royal Institution' (558). After twenty-two years Hearn was still with them and part of the family. There might be problems with the other servants. Some might pretend they wished to stay, simultaneously applying elsewhere; others might leave, in which case there would be a daughter at home who could be told to deal with her : 'She has copies (& so have I, in the pocket of the dining-room portfolio, *or* in my chiffonier drawer, *or* (unlikely) in the 'My book' box, *or* some other box in the *dining*-room, –) of the *kitchen linen in her charge*, which should be looked over: and ask her ...' (567). One doubts if William was much bothered:

To Anne Robson, 10 May 1865 (570)

He goes up to his University Examinations on the 18th or 19th, and has been very much inclined to declare that he will & *must* come back at the end of that week; but I think now he is beginning to find out he can stay a little longer, and wait in & about London till after the Handel Festival, going home on Saturday July 1st. Mind, it is not *quite* fixed, but I *think* he is relenting. Everybody *here* wants him to take more holidays, and every body *there* (away from home) wants him to come to them; but it is almost impossible to push, pull, or stir him from home. I never know what makes him so busy; as if we any of us ask him he always says 'it's only so much extra fatigue going over all I have got to do.' I *fancy* a great many people refer to him on business or family difficulties; and besides the necessary thinking this requires, he writes letters *very* slowly and very neatly and correctly, so that replying to these letters takes up a great deal of time. He has his 3 days (of 4 hours each,) at the Home Mission-Board, – and that is in a very close room which (*I* should say) added to the fatigue. However the Memorial Hall will be opened in August, where he will have a good-sized, and well-ventilated room. Once a week he goes down to lecture at the Owens' College – (for the six *winter* & *bad-weather* months of the year). That takes up two long hours; and on a Monday too which is often a hard day with committees &c, but you might as well ask St Pauls to tumble down, as entreat him to give up this piece of work; which *does* interest him very much, & which no one could do so well certainly; only it comes at such an unlucky time. Then, there is the plaguing Unitarian Herald; which takes up six or seven hours a week, (*at the office*) & a great deal of odd time at home; and which we, his family, *wish* he would draw out of, & leave to be conducted by younger men. I think he really *likes* all these things; he meets with people he likes; and all the subjects he is engaged upon interest him very much. And when he *is* at home, we only see him at meal-times; so that it is not the giving-up of the *family* life to him, that it would be to many men. He seems very well, & very happy; and says he is never so well as in Manchester; but one wishes that at his age he could have a little more repose of mind. He does not like any of us to go with him when he goes from home, saying it does not give him so much change; & with us he does not make so many acquaintances certainly, as he did at Rome for instance, where he made so many pleasant friends. I had got money enough (from my writing) both to pay for *his* going, & for Meta's *or* mine, *or* both of us, *with him* but he quite declined it, giving the reason as above, – 'being more independent, & getting more complete change.' I wish he was not so thin; but that he has been for years now. For these last few winters he has always had a cold *during the cold weather*; but it goes off in the warm weather. He has a capital appetite, & generally sleeps like a top at nights. He keeps his study *terribly* hot; but then he likes it; and I sometimes fancy it is because he can't regulate the warmth of *other* houses that he dislikes so much leaving home. He *always* goes to the Edmund Potters in his holidays; wherever they take a house, generally in Scotland; this year I believe it will be in Wales. Mrs Potter says she has often asked me (in her letters to him,) to accompany him; but if she has, he has never told me of it; preferring the entire change, & independence. In East wind, or *very* cold weather his liver gets out of order, & then he is depressed & generally uncomfortable & easily annoyed; but in general I should say he is *much* more cheerful & happy in his mind, than he used to be, when younger. He is *very* fond of Charlie Crompton & his & Florence's 'coming circuit' 3 times a year is a great pleasure to us all. But Wm trots off to his study, whoever is here all the same.

In comparison, his wife was a social heroine : 'Then I cabbed, (coughing) to Lady Coltman's . . .' (455). William no longer sounds like Mr Bennet, more like Dickens's Wemmick in his 'castle'. As ever, Nancy Robson is told the most private items of family news :

Thurstan *is* getting on at the Bar; but it must be very slowly; and the 100£ a year we could allow (*at first* at any rate) and the 300£ a year his father allows will not keep house in London, and pay law-expenses too. But they are very cheerful, correspond daily; and contrive to see each other very often; he is coming down here next Tuesday, & will very likely take Julia & MA back with him; as if so, & all 3 go, they will travel 2nd class. . . .

I have been to ask Wm if he has any message – 'Tell Nancy I shall be writing in a day or two', was all he said. *I* think your account of Sam sounds anxious; but I don't think Wm does. But then he does rather hate *facing* anxiety; he is so *very* anxious when he *is* anxious, that I think he always dislikes being made to acknowledge there is cause.

There is just one matter she did not mention. All this summer of 1865, quite without her husband's knowledge, she was searching for a house in the south of England. Charles Norton was far enough away in America to be told when the search succeeded :

To Charles Eliot Norton, 8 September 1865 (583)

And then I did a terribly grand thing! and a secret thing too! only you are in America and can't tell. I bought a house and 4 acres of land in Hampshire, – near Alton, – for Mr Gaskell to retire to & for a home for my unmarried daughters. That's to say I had not money enough to pay the whole 2,600£; but my publisher (*Smith* & Elder) advanced the 1,000£ on an 'equitable mortgage.' And I hope to pay him off by degrees. Mr Gaskell is *not to know till then*, unless his health breaks down before. He *is* very well and very strong thank God; but he is sixty, & has to work very hard here, his work *increasing* with his years, and his experience; & in the winters he feels this. The house is large – (not quite so large as this;) in a very pretty garden (kitchen flower-gardens & paddock between 3 & 4 acres,) and in the middle of a pretty rural village, so that it won't be a lonely place for the unmarried daughters who will inherit. In the mean time we are furnishing it (500£ more) & hoping to let it for 3 years; after which we hope to induce Mr Gaskell to take possession himself.

CHAPTER SEVEN

Travels

After the delight of the softest of climates,
of indolence, of the most hospitable of
friends, we return to – BOSTON.
(Charles Norton to T. G. Appleton,
7 May 1855[1])

IN FINDING AND PURCHASING the house at Alton Elizabeth Gaskell had the help of all four daughters, her publisher George Smith and no less than three lawyers, Thurstan Holland, Charles Crompton and William Shaen. It would be hard to imagine a more formidable and persuasive combination. The house itself was a fine one, in a healthy situation, but the man they were to work upon as his retirement came near really loved his work and claimed that he was never so well as he was when in Manchester. Husband and wife had very different sensibilities. Both had definitely committed themselves to smoky, hard-working Manchester, but more and more Elizabeth Gaskell came to see *holidays* from the city in the north as the type of the life she wished to lead when duty had been done. Heaven had once seemed to be 'a place where we shan't have any consciences' (69). Towards the end it became more concretely accessible: 'a place where all books & newspapers will be prohibited by St Peter: and the amusement will be driving in an open carriage to Harrow, and eating strawberries & cream for ever' (561). There is always truth in jest.

Just after her triumphant London visit in the spring following the publication of *Mary Barton*, she wrote of a diversion:

To Eliza Fox, 29 May 1849 (48)
I did not come home straight as you thought I did. Your mesmeric clair-

voyance ought to have carried you that same Wednesday night, to a very pretty, really old fashioned cottage, at Shottery, the village where Shakespeare's wife lived in her maiden days, near S. on Avon; a cottage where one's head was literally in danger of being bumped by the low doors, and where the windows were casements: where the rooms were all entered by a step up, or a step down: where the scents through the open hall door were all of sweet briar and lilac and lilies of the valley: where we slept with our windows open to hear the nightingales' jug-jug, and where the very shadows in the drawing room had a green tinge from the leafy trees which over hung the windows. Cd. there be a greater contrast to dear charming, dingy dirty Panton Square? Anne Holland had preceded me a day as you know, and did not we pour out the treasures of our London campaign to the rural inhabitants staying in the house, who believed in ghosts, and told some capital stories thereupon; and another cousin; and we had rainy days for rest; when we sat with open windows, revelling in the sound of the raindrops pattering among the trees; and we had brilliantly fine days when we went long drives; in one of which (to a place where I believed the Sleeping Beauty lived, it was so over-grown and hidden up by woods) I SAW a ghost! Yes I did; though in such a matter of fact place as Charlotte St I should not wonder if you are sceptical; and had my fortune told by a gypsy; curiously true as to the past, at any rate, and I did my duty as a meek submissive lion, fresh imported from the desert (i.e. London), at a party; and then I rushed home; turning regularly home sick, all on a sudden; leaving Anne at Shottery, so it was on Tuesday evening last, this day week you should have been clair-voyant to the extent of seeing me arrive at the Manchester station, Mr Gaskell meeting me ...

She had, eventually, become homesick, but her delight in the country is very obvious and, as we know, of long standing. The family used to go on annual migrations to the seaside during the summer, 'keeping holiday in most rural farm-house lodgings,' she told Lady Kay-Shuttleworth, 'so that our children learn country interests, and ways of living and thinking' (72a). In 1850 we find her away during the autumn as well, this time for her health. She was at Poulton-le-Sands for a few weeks, but by November she had not really returned to Manchester: she and Marianne were 'again exiles from home' (83), near Warwick. Even as Christmas approached she was still away, at Boughton House near Worcester:

To Lady Kay-Shuttleworth, 12 December 1850 (86)

I

I am in great hopes that my husband may be able to come up in Xmas

week, as I am yet forbidden to return to Manchester – and it would be very
desolate to be thrown on the wide world, – even a wide world of friends,
– without anything of home about one, that very week so sacred to homes
& families and made so by the Birth of a Child. From thence I go to a
friend's in Essex, in whose warm sheltered house I spend January; and
then I leave Marianne at school, and return home. And I must try and
make up by hard work for all this laziness. My husband may be detained
in Manchester by his co-pastor's indisposition, – that is all I am afraid of;
but if he comes, he will bring our second girl with him, and as the two
sisters have never been separated so long before, and have neither of them
ever been in London I fancy they will have a very merry pleasant Christmas week, if – they come. . . .

I am summoned, and I must go away while I had yet a great deal to say.
I want you to thank Sir James for me for all his kind advice about my
health; advice which I feel to be good, and yet which I cannot follow; for
the work appointed both for my husband & me lies in Manchester. I would
fain be in the country, – & this last experience of country air has done me
so much good – I am a different creature to what I am in Manchester.
However I have written enough about myself, and my own concerns.

Perhaps life in London, too, made her a different creature to what she was
in Manchester:

To Marianne Gaskell, 9 February 1851 (100)[2]
Wednesday I did not go to Richmond, it was too bad a day for him to draw
but I went with Mrs Wedgwood and Miss Doyle to Bermondsey to see the
Convent of Sisters of Mercy. Bermondsey is a very bad part of London;
and these Sisters have been established about 11 years, and have done a
good deal of good and established a great large school. We went all over
the Convent heard all their plans and altogether I think I liked it even
better than the Convent of the Good Shepherd. I rested all evening. Tuesday a long piece of Richmond again. I think it is like me; I hope Papa will
think so but I am almost doubtful. In the afternoon I shopped and got
presents for all the home people and went to dine at Mrs Wedgwood to
keep Snow's birthday – Mr Darwin his two sisters all the children Mr
Furnival and Mr Clough, Lady Alderson and 2 of the girls made a great
large party and very pleasant it was. The Bunsens had asked me to dine
there but I had planned to go and breakfast with them the next day
(Friday) which I accordingly did; and very agreeable it was. Chevalier
Bunsen gave me his book of devotions with a long writing *in German
character* at the beginning to 'his well beloved friend' etc.

Amongst all these people she had come across a new social phenomenon, 'two handsome young girls, living in lodgings by themselves, writing books, and going about in society in the most independent manner, with their latch-key' – Dinah Mulock and Frances Martin.[3] Her motherly instincts were aroused: 'I wish she had some other means of support besides writing', she exclaimed to a friend about the former; 'I think it bad in it's effect upon her writing, which must be pumped up instead of bubbling out; and very bad for her health, poor girl' (105). But she must have been made much more sharply aware of her own very conventional style of life. She had met, of course, what sociologists call 'female role innovators'.

In the next few years, whilst the Gaskells were sowing thunbergias and planting gladioli, friends and relations went even further afield: 'Frederick & Annie Holland are gone to Rome', she told Marianne, 'only to stay 2 months however; & the Charles Buxton's are gone to Sicily which is, they say, carpeted & fragrant with flowers' (91b). Holidays in England must have seemed rather second-best. Susanna Winkworth, for instance, went to live and study with Professor Brandis at Bonn in late 1850, a time when Manchester was 'a behind-hand place for books' (79). She became the focus of a little humorous envy in the following year as she kept William Gaskell busy correcting the proofs of her translation of B. Niebuhr's *Life and Letters*, whilst a mere novel like *Mary Barton* seems to have been slighted in comparison. 'When I gave up Bonn with many sighs because W. was so against it,' she wrote in May 1852 to Tottie Fox, 'I made a paction 'twixt us twa that you *should* come to Silverdale . . .' (124). This was the last year in which she held back. Almost every year thereafter she went abroad or to Scotland, sometimes for months on end, though she did not give up the usual round of visits and trips into the country. Invitations abounded. 'If people have once got into the cycle of invitations', she explained to Marianne, 'they will most likely go on; & we can go from home for bits as we see fit' (582b).

She inevitably gained quantities of information about other life-styles and many insights into the workings of different societies. During the fifties she visited her relations at Dumbleton near Evesham (the Edward Hollands) and Boughton near Worcester (the J. Whitmore Isaacs). She went to Ashbourne Hall in Derbyshire, which Captain Frederick Holland had bought in 1852. (He intended 'to add to it considerably' (120), which seems quite characteristic of the Hollands. Meta wrote in 1859 that it was 'an old rambling house; standing at the end of *the* street of the little town' and 'haunted: by a Madam Cockaine, who every night drives up the avenue in a coach and six – the spectral coachman and horses all *headless*'.) She stayed with old friends like Lady Hatherton at Teddesley in Staffordshire, formerly Mrs Davenport of Capesthorne in nearby Cheshire. (Her 'Goodbye to Capesthorne and the tenantry', Mrs Gaskell reported, 'was quite like the Arabian Nights; six beautiful Indian shawls, endless jewellery . . .'.[4]) She stayed with newer friends like Mrs Davy of Lesketh How near Ambleside and was thus able to take a fondly retrospective look at one of her earliest sources of inspiration :

To John Forster, 28 October 1852 (*139*)
We dined quietly and early with Mrs Wordsworth on Monday. She is charming. She told us some homely tender details of her early married days, how Miss Wordsworth made the bread, and got dinner ready, and Mrs W. nursed all the morning, and, leaving the servant to wash up after dinner, the three set out on their long walks, carrying all the babes amongst them; and certain spots are memorial places to Mrs W. in her old age, because there she sat, and nursed this or that darling. The walks they took were something surprising to our degenerate minds. To get news of the French Revolution they used to walk up the Raise for miles, in stormy winter evenings to meet the mail. One day when they were living at Grasmere (no post-office there) Wordsworth walked over to Ambleside (more than four miles) to post some poem that was to be included in a volume just being printed. After dinner as he sat meditating, he became dissatisfied with one line, and grew so restless over the thought that towards bedtime he declared he must go to Ambleside and alter it; for 'in those days postage was very heavy, and we were obliged to be very prudent.' So he and Miss Wordsworth set off after nine o'clock, walked to Ambleside, knocked up the post-office people, asked for a candle, got the letter out of the box, sent the good people to bed again, and sat in the little parlour, 'puzzling and puzzling till they got the line right'; when they replaced the letter, put out the candle, and softly stole forth, and walked home in the winter midnight.

It is curious the loving reverence she retains for Coleridge, in spite of his rousing the house about one in the morning, after her confinement, when quiet was particularly enjoined, to ask for eggs and bacon! and similar vagaries.

She got to know the tight but diverse society of the Lake District pretty well. She visited Matthew Arnold's mother at Fox How near Ambleside, stayed with Mrs Fletcher of Lancrigg near Grasmere, knew all about the scandal caused by Harriet Martineau and mesmerism in 1851 and generally developed a real feeling for the way of life there :[5]

To Charles Bosanquet, 29 August 1859 (*439a*)
The Arnolds & Wordsworths long ago took lodgings for us at Skelwith

at the house of a 'Stateswoman' a Mrs Preston of Mill Brow; to whom I give you a note, as she is worth knowing, as a fine true friendly sensible woman; if you liked to lodge there and she would take you in I am sure you would be comfortable, & well cared for – N.B. She would *make* you change your stockings if you got your feet wet, and such like motherly and imperative cares; – at any rate go & see her if you go to Skelwith. . . . Wordsworth said once of the Prestons that they were a 'Homeric family'. I am sorry to say the father sometimes drinks. I say it because you perhaps ought to be told or else when sober he is a fine simple fellow. Mrs Preston's family have lived in that house and on that land for more than 200 years, as I have heard. They have no ambition but much dignity, – and look at that family of stately sons & daughters!

Go to Coniston, if only to row on the Lake, & look *back* on the solemn purple Old Man. And here is a note to Miss Mary Beaver of Coniston, if you care for another introduction to a woman, – but really the residents at the Lakes *are* all women I think; and once upon a time we thought of buying land & building a house there as a future home for our girls, because there is a kind of old-fashioned chivalrous respect paid to women in all that country, which we thought would be a pleasant surrounding for brother-less women; but the damp air of the place does not agree with Mr Gaskell, who is liable to spasmodic asthma, for which, curiously enough, no air does so well as Manchester smoke. But to return to Miss Beaver. She is a sweet tempered singularly intelligent, kindhearted lady, who has lived long at Coniston – knows the dialect, the botany, the character of her district remarkably well; and altogether I think you might like to know her.

Homeric country families and retired ladies living in the Lake District make a queer contrast with academic Oxford in the late fifties and early sixties, where the Gaskells made great friends with Benjamin Brodie, Professor of Chemistry, and his wife. She was introduced there by her old friends Lord and Lady Hatherton and, if the account of her first visit is not too highly coloured, almost frantically entertained :

To Charles Eliot Norton, 7 December 1857 (384)
So we went. (Star Hotel.) (We travelled 2nd class train to squeeze in Hotel expences, – it was like Old China in the Essays of Elia,) as soon as we had arrived there came Dr Wellesley, Principal New-Inn Hall, & owner of those beautiful drawings from the old Masters in our Exhibition, – prodded up to civility by a letter from his brother-in-law Lord Hather-ton, & he took us a race up past X where Ridley & Latimer were burnt, –

thro' the Radcliffe Quad into All Souls Quads, into High St – back to his own house to lunch; donned a scarlet robe himself, having to attend convocation, & rushed off (with scarlet wings flying all abroad,) with me on his arm, to deposit us at the Theatre to hear A. Stanley's lecture. The lecture was not (to me) so *very* interesting, being a sort of recapitulation of what he was *going* to say (if that's not Irish.) I saw Matt Arnold – who was in Oxford, getting ready for his inaugural poetry lecture, which came off the next Saturday, – and we were invited by the Cradocks to Brazennose in the evening, & by A Stanley to breakfast with him the next morng. Then Dr Wellesley picked us up again, rushed us up to the roof of the Radcliffe – (what a splendid view of towers & pinnacles) – to Maudlin to Chapel, & New College Ante Chapel, & up & down & round about so that I got quite bewildered. When we got back to our inn, I had one of my bad headaches, so we went to bed, instead of going to the Cradocks – Breakfast at A Stanleys was *very* pleasant. Your friends, – whom we do so like – Dr & Mrs Acland – (or are they Mr Ruskin's friends – & was it *he* that was speaking to us so much about them?) Mr & Mrs Brodie (known to us before) – Mr Conington, (another old friend, Prof. of Latin,) Matt Arnold. We were so jolly & happy. I do so like A. Stanley. He told me something I liked to hear, & so I shall tell it you. In Moscow he had seen a good deal of a priest of the Greek Church, – a pure Muscovite – but a very intelligent man. Speaking of forms of religion in England this priest was so well acquainted with the position of dissenting ministers with regard to their congregations that A S was surprized, & enquired where & how he got his knowledge. 'From an English novel. Ruth.'

To Lord Hatherton, 3 December 1857 (383)

After dinner we went all over New College with one of the Fellows, a nephew of Dr Moberley, of Winchester. First into the kitchen, where I was relieved to see, – that if the Founders attended to the *mental* wants, there were Cooks and Scullions at least equally attentive to the Corporal wants of William of Wykeham's 'poor scholars'. Such good luncheons as were going up into Collegiate cells! A certain Mr Holland was having, – all to himself, – stewed eels, minced chicken, beef steak with oyster-sauce, and College Puddings! I am afraid he requires one of the colds, of which you say 'they are sent to teach us temperance'. Then we went into the College cellar, and tasted the Ale; we were warned *only* to taste it, as our heads not being sufficiently strengthened by learning, might not be able to stand it.

She was no fanatic about the cause of Temperance. When a Mr Bowman operated on Meta's tonsils in 1861, she told Marianne, 'I have a note from him this morning recommending that "Miss Gaskell should have a glass of sherry at one o'clock on Monday". I think Mrs Gaskell will have one too' (484b)!

Many of her trips and visits were associated with periods of research or writing. She wrote much of *North and South* at the home of the Nightingales near Matlock. When preparing the *Life of Charlotte Brontë* in 1856 she went as far afield as Brussels. She visited Whitby, where *Sylvia's Lovers* is set, in 1859; then rushed to Eastbourne to get it finished in late 1862. Similarly, she crossed the channel to Dieppe in late 1865 when she was struggling to keep up with the monthly instalments of *Wives and Daughters*. Other visits approximated more closely to a fantasy life of ease and freedom, the grandest of all coming about accidentally:

To Marianne Gaskell, 13 and 14 September 1857 (372)

Chatsworth

You will wonder how we come to be here (with no clothes at all, in particular to start with, – Meta's brown silk, & brown muslin; my grey carmelite, & black moiré, high, & next to no collars &c –) Hearn packed us up a box for Rowsley in a great hurry on Friday morning. We went to the end of Shakspeare St in pouring rain, Joseph carrying our box, and found to our dismay that there was no inside places. However we got tilted up to the top of the coach behind by the eager & impatient coachman and were whirled off, hoping every moment that it would clear, but it would not & came down heavier & heavier to the great detriment of our clothes – (which however are all right again now.) I had no idea it was so long a journey, . . .

They had just come to see the house, but were invited to stay by one of the Duke of Devonshire's gentlemen:

Well! we thought it was a pity to miss seeing & doing many agreeable things for the sake of no gowns, – so we bravely consented to stay, after sending an apologetic message to the Duke, and saying we were only in our travelling-dresses. So a maid was sent back to Rowsley for what scanty clothes we had, and here we are established in two grand rooms (& a private W.C.) the curtains to my bed being of thick white satin stamped with silken rosebuds. Meta proposed that we should dress ourselves up in them. Presently the Duke came to us wheeled in his bath chair. He is very deaf; Meta made him hear better than I did. Then we went into the Sketch Gallery (not usually shown –) until luncheon time. At luncheon we were only ladies till Sir Joseph Paxton came in; he is quite the master of the place as it were; and was deputed by the Duke to arrange drives &c for the afternoon, – there were carriages and riding horses ad libitum. Meta, Mrs Norton, Sir Joseph & I went in a little low poney carriage, and four lovely (circus-like) ponies, postillions &c and felt like Cinderella. We went first to call on Lady Paxton, who lives in the grounds; a sort of fat pleasant looking Mrs Fairbairn, – then we drove through the kitchen gardens &c up to a point where the Duke & Lady Louisa were awaiting us, – there we talked and admired things, & then drove off again, up & down seeing views and improvements, & all the fountains playing, and all the water-works going, and ending by driving *through* the conservatory home, to *dress* for dinner. . . . After dinner the Statue Gallery and Orangery were lighted up, and then the Duke's private band (of 7 performers) played a collection of pieces, for which we had programmes given us; and then the County Member & his wife departed, Lady Louisa complaining that they had stayed so late. I sate next the Duke all the time of the Concert, as he can hear talking whenever music is going on, so he talked pretty incessantly.

This must have been about the social summit, though in 1859 only 'absolute home duty' prevented her from 'joining the P. of Wales incognito party to the Trosachs'. 'But it sounds grand – as I try to comfort Meta, who won't be comforted – to have *declined*' (438), she joked with George Smith.

Her visits to Paris are much more characteristic. She went on a number of occasions (in 1853, 1854, 1855, 1857, 1858, 1862, 1863 and 1865) and usually stayed with the delightful, detestable Madame Mohl. Scottish by birth but long settled in Paris, she had married an Orientalist of German birth, the scholar Julius Mohl. Her salon was in a great French tradition, but by all accounts quite inimitable :

To Emily Shaen, 27 March 1865 (564)[6]

120 Rue du Bac
Sunday

My dearest Emily,

I think you will like to hear how I am going on in Paris. It is a very amusing life; and I'll try and describe a day to you. Mme Mohl lives on the fourth and fifth stories of a great large hotel built about 150 years ago, entre cour et jardin, – 'cour' opening into the narrow busy rue du Bac, 'jardin' being a very large (10 acres) plot of ground given by Cardinal Richelieu to the Missions Etrangères, – and so not built upon, but surrounded by great houses like this. It is as stiffly laid out in kitchen gardens square walks &c as possible; but there are great trees in it, and altogether it is really very pretty. That's at the *back* of the house, and some of the rooms look on to it. On the *fourth* story are four lowish sitting rooms & Mme Mohl's bedroom. On the *fifth*, sloping in the roof, kitchen grénier, servants' bedrooms, my bedroom, wood-room &c; all brick floors, which is cold to the feet. My bedroom is very funny & picturesque, – I like sloping roofs, & plenty of windows stuffed into the roof any how; and in every corner of this room (& it's the same all over the house) french & English books are *crammed*. I have no watch, there is no clock in the house, & so I have to guess the time by the monk's singing & bells ringing, (all night long but especially in the morning). So I get up, & come down into the smallest & shabbiest of the sitting rooms, in which we live & eat all day long, and find that M. Mohl has had his breakfast of chocolate in *his* room (library) at $\frac{1}{2}$ past 6, & Mme Mohl hers of tea at 7, and I am late having not come down (to coffee) at a little past eight. However I take it coolly, and M. & Mme come in and talk to me; she in dressing gown & curlpapers; very very amusing he, very sensible & agreeable, & full of humour too. . . .

Then after my breakfast – which lingers long because of all this talk I get my writing 'Wives & Daughters', and write, as well as I can, for Mme Mohl's talking till 'second breakfast', about 11. – Cold meat, bread, wine & water, & sometimes an omelette, – what we should call lunch in fact, – only it comes too soon after my breakfast, & too long before dinner for my English habits. After breakfast no 2 I *try* to write again; and very often callers come; *always* on Wednesdays on which day Mme Mohl receives. I go out a walk by myself in the afternoons; & when we dine at home it is at six *sharp*. No dressing required. Soup, meat, one dish of vegetables, & roasted apples are what we have in general. After dinner M. & Mme Mohl go to sleep : & I have fallen into their habit; and at eight exactly M. Mohl wakens up, and makes a cup of *very* weak tea for Mme Mohl & me – nothing to eat after dinner, ever; not even if we have been to the Play. Then Mme Mohl rouses herself up, & is very amusing & brilliant; stops up till one, & would stop up later, if encouraged by her listeners. She has not been well, but for all that she has seen a good number of people since I came; she has generally a dinner party of 10 or 12 every Friday, when we spread out into all the rooms (& I am so glad; for continual living & eating in this room, & no open windows makes it very stuffy,) and 'receive' in the evening.

Guizot has dined here, & Mignet, & Montalembert since I came; & many other notabilities of less fame. But every body stays up the first half of the night, as I should call it. When we go out for the evening we go to dress directly after our after dinner nap & tea; and first cross the court-yard in snow or slop, to the Porter's lodge opening into the Rue du Bac, & send him for a coach. We jigget to some *very* smart house (for all Mme Mohl's friends are very smart people & live in very grand houses,) curtsey as low as we possibly can to the Master of the house, & shake hands with the Missus; sit down, & in general, have a great deal of very beautiful music from the Masters of the Conservatoire, quartetts & quintetts; make a buzz of talk, look at the fine dresses, & come home as hungry as a hawk about one A M. *I* am going out a great deal to dinner; last night I dined at a Russian house, a real Russian dinner.

She liked 'the society in Paris *very* best of all; & then Oxford, and then comes London', she wrote in 1860.[7] But these visits to France involved much more than a pleasurable immersion in Parisian literary and political life. They inspired some fine journalism, such as the articles on 'French Life' for *Fraser's Magazine*, and a project that centred on the life of Madame de Sévigné:

To Catherine Winkworth, 23 July 1862 (509b)
Sunday afternoon we went on to Vitré, just in Brittany the town near which les Rochers is. It is a *most* picturesque half inhabited town; we went to the Hotel de Sévigné, her old town house, which in her days was called La Tour de Sévigné, – an immense barrack of an old half-fortified house; only half furnished, & never cleaned since her days; a more filthy place I never saw; but the people were very civil, & the town extremely sketchable, with old walls covered with snap dragon, valerian, wallflowers &c, – with wooden colonnades supporting the first floors of the houses; and tourelles here, there & everywhere. Monday we took a little market cart, & drove, shaking & laughing to Les Rochers. No one has ever said half enough of its beauty – you go up rising ground, through grassy high hedged lanes, – suddenly turn to yr left into a sort of park-like field, up thro' a field very like a Silverdale field near Arnside Tower, with little rocks cropping out, & all sorts of delicate flowers carpeting the ground, see a vast picturesque pile before you with 13, (that I *counted*) towers, of all sorts of sizes & shapes, a great walled in garden, – walled, & pillared and balled with grey stone, whh is half tumbling down, showing old avenues, & heaps of roses, and sparkling fountains within, – a long range of grey, rich-coloured farm buildings at a little distance from the house with a space like a village green between, with cocks & hens, & donkeys, and turkeys &c all flourishing about, and here and there a blazing peacock, cows in the farm yard beyond, – opposite (you have the house itself at the farthest part of the left hand, the old garden coming from it towards you, – the farm-buildings on yr right, the green right before you & *opposite*,) a great grove

of high dark-coloured old trees – older than Mme de S. by a great deal, – then we dismissed our market cart to the stables & turned round & lo & behold we were high up on a plateau of ground with 30 miles of sunny champaign country lying below us [here a sketch is inserted] that sort of way, only not *such* a steep descent. It was a most charming day. . . .

She had previously told Catherine Winkworth about the way in which she had seen Louis Hachette, asked for access to collections of manuscripts, been 'to every old house in Paris that she lived in, & got a list of books "pour servir", & a splendid collection of all the portraits of herself, family & contemporaries'. Though this memoir of Madame de Sévigné was never published, we can have no doubt how hard she worked. It is thrown into relief by her obvious pity for a Stockport family she knew:

On by rail to Caen, where we stopped all night in a clean hotel, kept by a very cockney ci-devant London butler, of the name of Humby – ('Umby's 'Otel) recommended by the Healds, who had stayed there for 4 months last winter. It is not down in Murray, but ought to be for its cleanliness, civility, and moderate charges; but it was funnily cockney: and one felt how English people might live abroad without coming in contact with the picturesqueness & variety of foreign life. The poor Heald girls were utterly weary of their foreign life, & so was Mrs Heald I think. Of course they had to go abroad to œconomize. They went in November & took rooms (en pension) at Humby's. The Hotel looks on to a great common stretching down to the narrow river, – no distant view (Saturday morng) and the Healds lived there at a foggy time of the year in 3 small clean rooms, knowing no one, and *very* dismal, the sea (*flat* part of coast of Normandy,) 8 or 9 miles off, to which, along sandy fields, with sandy turf banks for fences all flat and foggy the Healds used to walk, 'by way of an object.' They got dingy novels from the Caen Circg Library, & had no other books, I fancy. No wonder they 'hate living abroad!'

Genteel *ennui* was utterly foreign to Elizabeth Gaskell, at home or abroad.

Her trips to Italy in 1857 and 1863 were more like holidays, but holidays taken after periods of severe strain. The former *might* be thought the most important of her entire life. It followed immediately upon the completion of her *Life of Charlotte Brontë*, by which time she had in a sense fought three great campaigns – for the Manchester poor and conscientious manufacturers, for 'fallen women', and for her dead friend. As she thought of the reviews that the *Life* was likely to receive, 'supercilious, or personal ones, or impertinently flattering ones' (314), she determined to leave them behind.

'Now give us lands where the olives grow',
  Cried the North to the South,
'Where the sun with a golden mouth can blow
Blue bubbles of grapes down a vineyard row!'
  Cried the North to the South.

Elizabeth Barrett Browning's poem must substitute for the letters that do not seem to exist for the spring and early summer of 1857. Perhaps Mrs Gaskell did not write many, 'overwhelmed with acquaintance and parties' as she was, going to churches and galleries, catacombs and Campagna. Staying with the American sculptor William Wetmore Story and his wife brought them into touch with other Americans in Rome – Hamilton Wild, James W. Field and Charles Eliot Norton.[8] We know that Mrs Gaskell was won as completely as Ruskin and his family had been the year before by 'the bright eyes, the melodious voice, the perfect manner, the simple, but acutely flattering, words' of the young Charles Norton. His Bostonian interests (Unitarian Sunday school, evening school, model housing for the poor and a School of Design for Women) matched those of Elizabeth Gaskell, when doing her duty in and to Manchester. In Italy he became their scholar and tutor in painting and sculpture, quite earnest enough fundamentally with his theories of the moral degeneration of Catholicism in the Eternal City of 1857 but also a wonderful distraction from the realities of life in Manchester and her fears about the reception of the *Life*. At the time he was preparing his *Notes on Travel and Study in Italy* and translating Dante; he was a true member of the artists' colony, 'a sort of poetic or fairy precinct, where actualities would not be so terribly insisted upon . . .'.[9]

Mrs Gaskell's long return via Florence, Venice and Paris eventually brought her back into the turmoil of Meta's engagement and the necessary revision of the *Life* demanded by the lawyers. Memories of Italy were almost swamped at first:

To Charles Eliot Norton, 28 September 1857 (374)
How far apart we, breakfast-party at Venice, 4 months ago have drifted! One is in Asia, – one in America, – and we Gaskells all now so stationary at home that Italy & everything seems like a dream! Last night the Indian telegraph came in; Lucknow *not* relieved, & one shrinks & prays when one thinks of the news the next mail may bring of the poor people there; and a *Madras* Regiment has refused to march and has consequently been disarmed.

But 'cold dim grey Manchester' could not obliterate her feelings. To the

Storys she confessed, 'It was in those charming Roman days that my life, at any rate, culminated. I shall never be so happy again. I don't think I was ever so happy before. My eyes fill with tears when I think of those days, and it is the same with all of us. They were the tip-top point of our lives.' And then, in a feeble attempt to recover emotional balance, 'The girls may see happier ones – I never shall' (375). Even her perceptions of England were affected:

To Charles Eliot Norton, 25 July 1858 (401)
I think, – and it is pleasant to think, – that one never is disappointed in coming back to Silverdale. The secret is I think in the expanse of view, – something like what gives it's charm to the Campagna – such wide plains of golden sands with purple hill shadows, – or fainter wandering filmy cloud-shadows, & the great dome of sky. – (We have not sate up all night on our tower this time, partly because there have been no *tranquil* nights, & partly because Julia (who is like Meta in her love of experiences & adventures) has been promised to sit up with us, the *next* time, & she is growing tall, & not quite strong enough for experiments.)

She undoubtedly believed she had discovered 'that Italy which is the home of the imagination, and which becomes the Italy of memory', as Norton had put it in his *Notes of Travel and Study*:

To the Storys, 1860 (482)
I think Rome grows almost more vivid in recollection as the time recedes. Only the other night I dreamed of a breakfast – not a past breakfast, but some mysterious breakfast which neither had been nor, alas! would be – in the Via Sant' Isidoro dining-room, with the amber sunlight streaming on the gold-grey Roman roofs and the Sabine hills on one side and the Vatican on the other. I sometimes think that I would almost rather never have been there than have this ache of yearning for the great witch who sits with you upon her seven hills.

Curiously, Italy exerted little direct influence upon her fiction, if we ignore some passages in 'A Dark Night's Work', especially one that evokes her very first meeting with Norton as he smiled up at her from amidst a turbulent carnival crowd. Curiously again, the letters about her second visit to Italy (three months in 1863) are very disappointing. 'We do so delight in Lady Charlotte', she cries to Marianne from Florence. 'She is so funny and good-natured & witty, & between her & the Stanleys we hear no end about the Prince of Wales' ménage' (523a). No details follow. Her next letter to Norton actually ends with an apology for not having told him anything about the

Italian visit. However, we notice that much of this letter is about the engagement of Florence; also, how deeply the Gaskells had been affected by 'the Distress' of the previous autumn and winter in Manchester. They came back every day 'too worn out to eat or do anything but go to bed' (526). Memories of all this had defeated those of the Italian holiday. There remains still a suspicion that although Elizabeth Gaskell's imagination was intensely kindled by Italy, it was for her a dream only partially anchored in reality, a cry and a constant yearning from the North to the South.

Letters about German life are more solid; they manifest the same delight in social phenomena and human variety as those on French or English life. Meta's broken engagement in 1858 took them to Heidelberg after their usual visit to Silverdale. Just before she went Elizabeth Gaskell reminded a correspondent 'how good & well it would be if every Parish priest would write down what he hears and learns about his own Parish, as traits of customs & manners & character might thus be preserved as Memoires pour servir' (395). Since she was writing to the Manchester antiquarian James Crossley,[10] an editor for the Chetham Society and the possessor of 100,000 volumes, she must have been preaching to the converted – or reminding herself. She has recorded some piquant contrasts :

To Charles Eliot Norton, 25 July 1858 (*401*)
Oh! we are getting so sorry to leave Silverdale. . . . Last Tuesday we had a party of boys & birds & girls. Mr Childs should have been here! We had a tame magpie, and a tame jack-daw (the latter belonging to a sweet little dwarf-child we picked up on a wild common one night –) said dwarf – and three children of a drowned fisherman &c – The birds fought for precedence but the children were very good & nice, – not flippantly clever like town children, but solidly-thinking with slow dignity. The birds sate at tea on the heads of their respective owners, occasionally giving a plug or a dig with their beaks into the thick curly hair, in a manner which *I* should not have liked, but it did not seem to disturb the appetites of the owners. It was very funny, & picturesque in the old quaint kitchen here.

To Marianne Gaskell, 1 October 1858 (*404a*)
Flossie & I were left in our bedroom counting up our money and doing our accounts; when loe & behold Mr Mohl was shewn in in a swallow tail coat & primrose coloured gloves. Flossie made a rush for the next room when she was caught by the German washerwoman, & sent back to have the bill paid. Mr Mohl had been calling on Sir Harry & Lady Verney on the floor below. He offered to get me any books out of the University library or to lend me any of his own – told me he was a Master of Arts of Cambridge when Prince Albert was appointed Chancellor.

The link between a dwarf-child picked up on a wild common and Julius Mohl's brother Robert in primrose-coloured gloves is Elizabeth Gaskell, ever sensitive to 'traits of customs & manners & character' :

To Marianne Gaskell, 19 October 1858 (405)
We set off 2 class railway to Mannheim, ½ an hour off. We walked about the town, & looked at shops, and saw the palace (rooms inside) & the Rhine – & altogether Flossy was highly pleased; but the heat & sun gave me a headache; and our first train back to Heidelberg was not till 7; so at 6, we went into a confectioner's shop and I gave Flossy her choice of a cake & asked myself for tea or coffee; neither were to be had. I said I had a 'migraine affreuse', and the girl brightened up, & said she had something good for the migraine, poured something into a liqueur glass, gave it me, I drank it, – and lo! if it was not *rum* pure, it was *rum* & *peppermint*!! However it *was* wonderful for the headache, but Flossy backed away from me, saying it was such a horrid smell. However my headache was better, and Flossy said she could keep away from me but that 'I was like a mixture of a public house & an apothecary's shop; she was *sure* it was *rum*, for it was what all the cakes and puddings Minnie disliked smelt of.' We went to the Railway waiting-room, which was all quiet and nicely-lighted up; so Flossy began to read a book she had brought with her; and I got Hendschel's Telegraph (the German Bradshaw) off the table, and began to puzzle out my train to Strasbourg to meet Louy, – when lo & behold, Flossy whispered to me, me, smelling of rum – that Mr Bosanquet had come in! I tucked my head down over my book, & told F E. to take no notice; but he drew nearer & nearer, pretending to look at the affiches on the walls, till at last he came close, & said 'Mrs G. can I assist you in making out yr train' – so I had to look up, & be civil, & let him take my (second) class tickets (whereupon he said it was thoroughly sensible, & I said nothing, because of the rum, –) & he went with us, & managed everything for us.

She had been away since early September and did not return to Manchester until 20 December, via Paris.[11] Once home in England her ever-active imagination began to work its transformations upon the simple documentary record :

To Charles Eliot Norton, 9 March 1859 (418)
And then came the most lovely poetical *wintry* November; clear deep blue sky, – white snow not very deep, except where it had drifted into glittering heaps, – icicles, a foot long, hanging on fountain & well, – trees encased in glittering ice, – & weighed down with their own beauty, – streets

— walks — clear & clean — and the high peaked house tops so beautiful. But it was not weather for travelling, being 18 degrees below something in Reaumur. Unknown cold — However we went to see Spire & Worms & Strasburg Cathedral, — & the girls worked away at German; and we 'marketted' for ourselves; and dined at one, — & walked till the early November night came on; I hired a piano & music, and laughed harder than I ever laughed before or ever shall again, the air, clear delicious dry air, put one in such health and spirits. And we knew nearly every body in Heidelberg — from the man-milliner, who offered to drive us to his 'Chasse' in the Black Forest, to Bunsen, — from Hormuth the old Ferryman to the two English clergymen &c &c, such a good-bying as we had!

She had a mind of winter as well as a mind of summer. The latter burned with insubstantial desires; the former seems more full of 'life, then : things as they are'. Her creative powers were roused by this German experience, as two substantial stories, 'They Grey Woman' and 'Six Weeks at Heppenheim', prove. We are closer to the absolute centre of her genius as a writer, in fact : her vital sense of laughing, earnest middle-class life in all its forms, at home and abroad. Arthur Pollard was absolutely right to stress 'her preference for the world she sees', which 'helps to give her novels their vivid sense of actuality'.[12]

In 1860 she went to Heidelberg again, when Marianne was ordered abroad for her health. It is noticeable on this occasion that her active social conscience was still at work. Over in Boston her friend Charles Norton had discovered that 'benevolence is dictated by the most refined selfishness, as well as by virtue'.[13] His practical philanthropy had caused him to build two five-story houses, each for twenty poor families, and in the June of 1860 he announced the success of his experiment in the *Atlantic Monthly* :

To Charles Eliot Norton, 27 August 1860 (476)
Thank you *very* much for all your very valuable information about model lodging houses, the beautiful little plan, and the details. A great many of these last have been of much use in several parts of England. It is curious how the conscience of Europe seems awakening to the duty of employing the better wisdom of the educated in this direction. Niettermeyer, the old *Juris Consult* (is not that the grandly correct word?) of Heidelberg, has bought what was the old barrack for the Elector Palatine's soldiers, and is at his own sole expense in his old age turning it into what Germans consider the best style of dwelling for working people. Again there is a little town (name forgotten, but easily to be got at,) on the verge of the Black Forest, where the 'industries' lately cultivated among the Blk Foresters have taken root in the shape of the manufacture of cheap jewellery; gold

with a greater acknowledged proportion of adulteration – (the name has come to me now, it is called *Porchheim*, or *Forchheim*, and the jewellery is called *P.* or *Forchheim* jewellery, – it is near Carlsruhe.) Well! these men who have learnt to be jewellers in the last ten years, and are thriving, and clustering together in this new little town, have been in want of dwellings, and the pastor, the physician (a Dr Otto) and one or two others, have bought land, on which they are building houses on the best & most sanatory Germans ideas; not great blocks, but separate dwellings, which they have the oppy of doing before Porchheim swells out into a large town. They have a remunerative fixed rent; and also a fixed weekly sum, which, if a tenant pays, in *addition* to his rent, his house becomes his, in so many years. However this letter is going to be gossipy, not philanthropic, only, you see, you led me astray, by having sent me those useful & valuable letters.

The frequency and diversity of Elizabeth Gaskell's travels can come as something of a surprise. She never saw herself as 'the minister's wife', with her spare energies at the plain disposal of the Cross Street congregation. Her responses to this much wider experience often suggest that she had a passionate desire to escape from Manchester and all its problems, to involve herself in lives that were more open and free. Her visits and travels were a solid advantage to her as a writer; she gained innumerable perspectives upon the phases of English life and character that were her principal concern as well as material she could use. At the same time, this letter about model lodging houses indicates that her voyaging self never lost its moral bearings. Her philanthropy, mainly but not exclusively exercised in Manchester, is so important that it deserves the same degree of attention as her travelling. Together the two came to compose perhaps the main dialectic of her existence as a social being. This would eventually resolve in favour of the easy, comfortable life led by middle-class people in the south of England, but not until she had – in her own eyes at least – thoroughly deserved such a reward.

CHAPTER EIGHT

Charities

> The working class districts are most
> sharply separated from the parts of the
> city reserved for the middle class. Or if this
> does not succeed, they are concealed with
> the cloak of charity.
>
> (F. Engels,
> *The Condition of the Working Class*[1])

ON 25 MARCH 1838 Elizabeth Gaskell wrote in her diary that Marianne, then three years old, 'would give rather too freely to the poor'. If this seems a little odd, we soon understand when one of Marianne's childish rigmaroles is quoted: 'I love you, and Papa, and Meta, and Elizabeth, and Fanny, and poor people.' The little girl was being taught to love the poor as well as her family and the servants. William Gaskell, we learn from this part of the diary, thought that her sensibilities were being excited too much, but however cool and practical acts of benevolence should be in his opinion, the basic religious duty was inescapable. So the letters are full of references to Sunday School girls, bazaars, visiting and a bewildering variety of charitable activities.

As we might expect, some spring from her literary connections. In March 1849 she asked her publisher if he could put her 'in the way of obtaining employment for a friend as a translator from either french, german or latin', especially on 'solid & thoughtful subjects' (41). Later that year she begged John Forster to persuade Tennyson himself to send an autographed copy of his poems to the old weaver Samuel Bamford (author of *Passages in the Life of a*

Radical), then 'living in that state which is exactly "decent poverty" ' (50). Other acts of charity depend upon her position in Manchester:

To David Grundy, 4 December 1858 (609)[2]
My dear Mr Grundy,
I wonder if you would be so kind as to give us a little help in this matter, – my two elder girls wanted to visit at the workhouse, & I applied to Mr Rickards who did not think it desirable; but made out a list of 10 old women, receiving parish relief, whom they might visit, &c, – and Mr Somerset the relieving officer called here and told me all these old women had borne a good character, – and they are all above 70. Now both Marianne & Meta are so sorry to see the thin poor clothing they go out in, to receive the parish money, (2s. *in* money 2s. *worth* in food so you see they cannot *save* to buy clothing,) & we think if you would kindly let us have a few fents & scraps of cloth we could manage a cape or cloak apiece for Xmas day. You perhaps are aware of that 'wisdom of the ancients', that says 'Much would have more', and 'Give them an inch & they'll take an ell', so doubtless you will see the applicability of the argument that you *once* gave us a grand and beautiful bundle of wollen shag, and *therefore* we ask you to give us some more. But I know two or three poor women to whom I should be glad to give the employment of making up even such small scraps of woollen stuff, – and poor old women shivering to the Union in a worn bombazine petticoat, & calico gown & shawl equally worn, won't be particular if they have a covering of many colours, so that it is warm.

It is disarmingly straightforward.
Hers are the conventional methods of the time, as we see in the case of Thomas Wright, a foundry worker who used to spend his free hours striving to rehabilitate prisoners. She welcomed him in Plymouth Grove, where he 'said "*By Jingo*" with great unction, when very much animated, much to William's amusement, not to say delight' (69). In 1849 she went 'to Tot-hill fields prison to see the silent associated system, of which our dear Mr Wright thinks so highly' (47). In the following year she joined in a scheme to honour Wright:

To Eliza Fox, 24 January 1850 (63)
On Saturday I heard from Mr Tom Taylor to this effect. A Mr Watts (*who is he*, answer me *that* Master Brook) an artist inspired by the record of Mr Wright's (whom Mr Taylor will call Mr *Hill*) good deeds, has painted a picture for the Academy Exhibition of the Good Samaritan, under which is to be an inscription relating to Mr Wright, – now Mr T. Taylor says

some people in London desirous of honouring Mr W. and encouraging the application of art to such high purposes are desirous of purchasing this picture and presenting it to some Manchester charity and he wants some detailed acct of Mr W. and to know if there would be any response in Manchester to this plan. I have got Mr Schwabe, the Bishop, and Dr Bell all pretty well interested, and have copied out prison reports, by way of statistical information as to Mr Wright.

Early in 1852 Wright was forced to give up his foundry work for health reasons and Mrs Gaskell wrote 'without end, till my wrist actually swelled with it – for the subscription to Mr Wright in the first place' (116a). The very concrete results of all this effort are tossed into the customary maelstrom of a letter to Marianne:

To Marianne Gaskell, 2 March 1852 (117)
I know that Voyage en lOrient, and I like it as much as I do anything of Lamartine's. Will you thank Mr Lalor for speaking to the Edit Inquirer about Mr Wright. We have got up to 2236£, and have more in hand. And I have had a letter from Mr Walpole (brother to the Home Secy) saying his brother will help on the Government pension, and the Hornbys (cousins of Lord Derby) are stirring *him* up; so we are in good hopes. I should think any air of Mendelsohn's must be beautiful. *Don't* call Shifts Chemises. Take the pretty simple *English* word whenever you can. As Mrs Davenport said the other day 'It is only washerwomen who call Shifts *"chemises"* now.' But independently of the word we shall be most glad of the *thing*. Flossie is at her last shifts in two senses of the word. The old red Camellia has seven flowers all out on it. Meta's that A A gave her, has two – variegated *single*. I don't think there is much home news.

Charities and shifts and camellias were all natural to her.
Dickens was one of those she approached and the result was an article on Wright in his weekly, *Household Words*, called 'An Unpaid Servant of the State'. It was not her first contact. During the mid-forties Dickens's sister and her husband, Henry Burnett, were fervent Evangelicals living in Manchester: [3]

To Charles Dickens, 8 January 1850 (61)
My dear Sir,
    In the first place I am going to give you some trouble, and I must make an apology for it; for I am very sorry to intrude upon you in your busy life. But I want some help, and I cannot think of any one who can give it to me

so well as you. Some years since I asked Mr Burnett to apply to you for a prospectus of Miss Coutt's refuge for Female prisoners, and the answer I received was something to the effect that you did not think such an establishment could be carried out successfully anywhere, *unless connected with a scheme of emigration, as Miss Coutts was*. (as I have written it it seems like a cross question & crooked answer, but I believe Mr Burnett told you the report was required by people desirous of establishing a similar refuge in Manchester.)

I am just now very much interested in a young girl, who is in our New Bayley prison. She is the daughter of an Irish clergyman who died when she was two years old; but even before that her mother had shown most complete indifference to her; and soon after the husband's death, she married again, keeping her child out at nurse. The girl's uncle had her placed at 6 years old in the Dublin school for orphan daughters of the clergy; and when she was about 14, she was apprenticed to an Irish dress-maker here, of very great reputation for fashion. Last September but one this dress-maker failed, and had to dismiss all her apprentices; she placed this girl with a woman who occasionally worked for her, and who has since succeeded to her business; this woman was very profligate and connived at the girl's seduction by a surgeon in the neighbourhood who was called in when the poor creature was ill. Then she was in despair, & wrote to her mother, (*who had never corresponded with her all the time she was at school and an apprentice*;) and while awaiting the answer went into the penitentiary; she wrote 3 times but no answer came, and in desperation she listened to a woman, who had obtained admittance to the penitentiary solely as it turned out to decoy girls into her mode of life, and left with her; & for four months she has led the most miserable life! in the hopes, as she tells me, of killing herself, for 'no one had ever cared for her in this world,' – she drank, 'wishing it might be poison', pawned every article of clothing – and at last stole. I have been to see her in prison at Mr Wright's request, and she looks quite a young child (she is but 16,) with a wild wistful look in her eyes, as if searching for the kindness she has never known, – and she pines to redeem herself . . . How soon will a *creditable* ship sail; for she comes out of prison on Wednesday, & there are two of the worst women in the town who have been in prison with her, intending to way-lay her, and I want to keep her out of all temptation, and even chance of recognition. Please, will you help me? I think you know Miss Coutts. I can manage all except the voyage. She is a good reader, writer, and a beautiful needlewoman; and we can pay all her expenses &c.

Such letters reveal the extraordinary network of Victorian philanthropy:

To Eliza Fox, 24 January 1850 (63)

My and your girl is going on well *as yet* in the Refuge where Agnes Ewart and I go to see her, and my letter to Dickens induced a very wise suggestion one from Miss Coutts to him, on which I acted, and have found a man and his wife going to the Cape, who will take loving charge of her; and sail in February. I have got Mr Nash the ragged school master to take care of her up to London when the ship is ready to sail and have found out a whole *nest* of good ladies in London, who say they will at any time help me in similar cases.

The very first serial to run in *Household Words*, between 30 March and 13 April 1850, was Elizabeth Gaskell's story of a fallen woman called 'Lizzie Leigh'. For this story she received £20 and – here, as we know, the wheel came full circle – some of it went to the Refuge. *Ruth* was completed by the end of 1852 and there is later evidence that she had not dropped her interest in the subject:

To Grace Schwabe, 19 June 1853 (162)

Then I wanted to tell you I have still got your two guineas. I should have sent or given them to Lieutenant Blackmore, but for two or three things which I heard and which I thought it would be right for you to know before giving the money. I met a Mr Allen at dinner at Mr Wedgwood's one Sunday; he is a relation of her's, and a *very* good active energetic young man; visiting at hospitals, and much among the very class whom Lieut Blackmore[4] had tried to aid. We talked (apropos of Ruth) a good deal about the difficulty of reclaiming this class, *after they had once taken to the street life*, and as he knew Lieutenant Blackmore's place pretty well, I asked him about it, as I had before heard, through Lady Buxton, of things going on at it that were very far from right – he said there might be some exaggeration in what I had heard – (of men being concealed in the house,) but that Lieutenant Blackmore although sincere in desiring the attainment of a good object was neither scrupulous nor wise in his means; that he was the best 'touter' in all London, & that some of 'his statements were a tissue of lies.' I give the exact words.

Charity is not always easy. The motives may be mixed: Mrs Gaskell was very aware that conscientious manufacturers were anxious to show that 'benevolent theories, which were so beautiful in their origin, might be carried into effect with good and *just* practical results of benefit to both master and man' (72a). Her novel *North and South* points in this direction for the benefit of non-conscientious manufacturers, though she knew that Samuel Greg's 'Utopian schemes' had been a failure. Others may have been more successful in a broad way, but then she worried about their individual souls:

To Mary Cowden Clarke, 23 May 1852 (127)

I think I *do* quite understand YOU, but I don't think *you* quite understand *me*! There's conceit for you! What I mean is you don't understand how in Manchester when you or I want a little good hearty personal individual exertion from any one they are apt to say in deeds if not in words 'Spare my time, but take my money' – a sort of 'leave me, leave me to repose' way, handing you their purse in order to be spared any trouble themselves, although by taking a little trouble they may benefit any person in a far more wholesome & durable way than by lazy handing over the money they don't want. It is the fault *of the place*; and our dear good Mr Darbishire has caught a little of it, dear friend, & noble fellow as he is. . . .

The numbers of people who steadily refuse Mr Gaskell's entreaties that they will give their time to anything, but will give him or me tens & hundreds, that don't do half the good that individual intercourse, & earnest conscientious thought for others would do! I dare say you think I am going off on a rhapsody, but I have real cases in view, both of this kind, & of the kind where, having given money largely & from a really generous feeling at the time, a most bitter sense of ingratitude has been felt & expressed by the donor, if any difference of opinion, or resistance to what the donee thought wrong afterwards occurred.

But it was only in her most dejected moods that she felt anything like Friedrich Engels, who had lodgings in Manchester during the 1850s and charitably supported Karl Marx out of the proceeds of his family firm, Ermen and Engels:[5]

To Eliza Fox, 26 November 1849 (55)

Our girl (yours and mine) sails in the Royal Albert on March 4, and her outfit is ready all except the sheets, which I must see about today; but except that, all is ready and right; and I like the girl much, poor creature. I have been to see her twice a week, and Agnes Ewart says she does so brighten up at the sight of me and seems so affectionate to everyone. Well I suppose it won't do to pull this world to pieces, and make up a better, but sometimes it seems the only way of effectually puryfying it.

Years of experience made her surprisingly professional in her attitudes, as a letter to one of her husband's fellow ministers makes clear:[6]

To S. A. Steinthal, Late October 1859 (630)
My dear Mr Steinthal,
    I have got a much clearer idea of what Miss Hibberd wants, and her reasons for wanting it from your letter just received; perhaps I was stupid before. But it is difficult to give help in such a case. A *great* deal must depend on Miss Hibberd herself. I will tell you how. I can give her one or two introductions (for instance,) to people who can give good information, if, in the one case the questioner has the art of *extracting*, – in the other if she has the art of *rejecting* rubbish. I am not choosing my words, but I consider that I am writing in confidence. Miss Jane Alcock to whom I am enclosing a note, has visited for years & years; and has really valuable information to give; but she does not talk much, or express herself easily, and is very shy and reserved; would almost be frightened at the notion of any thing she said being of value, or that it would be re-produced in speech or action. I should however rely very much both on her *facts* and on her *opinions*, (two very different things, & to be kept carefully separate in an enquiry of this sort.) Then there is Agnes Ewart to whom I will also enclose a note; she talks a *great deal*, she does really know a great deal, and her facts would be good & accurate; her opinions (I think) crude & unformed, but expressed without the least shyness or reserve. I think these two are the best women I can think of. Stay! there is Miss Winkworth, who comes to Manchester tomorrow; but who is ill & out of health, so I don't know if she could see any one. Or else at one time, & for years she visited very constantly & has an enlarged enough mind to form just opinions & to classify them into theories, fit to be worked upon. All these people however can but bring a grain of corn each to form the loaf of bread. A person *must* live in Manchester to make this loaf. Does – but she is sure to – Miss Hibberd know Mary Merryweather, – (M. M. as she is often called); because her management of Mr Courtauld's girls is *the* most successful I ever heard of – & she had just that feeling of *independence* (for want of a better word, writing in a great hurry,) to encounter; a feeling, call it what you will, stronger in Lancashire & Yorkshire, (from race perhaps,) than any where else in England.

She must have been a fount of practical, untheoretical knowledge – the very reverse of George Eliot's latter-day saint, Dorothea Brooke in *Middlemarch* :

To Eliza Holland, Early April 1859 (424)
    It is hard work making one's idea of life dear and I am more and more convinced that where every possible individual circumstance varies so completely all one can do is to *judge* for oneself and take especial care *not* to

judge others or for others. Else, I think a sewing club is an error – good for the people whh sew, as it is self denying on their part, but not doing half or a quarter so much good to others as might be done by the same amount of self denial. The best mode of administering material charity seems to me to be by giving employment and taking thought in adapting the kind of employment and in helping to find out who can do it. If you *cut out* the work, *gave it to poor women to do for a moderate payment* and then either gave the ready made clothing yourselves or sold it at cost price to be given by others to the poor who needed it. I should say it was far better wiser and more noiseless.

The breadth of her interest is very wide. To Lady Kay-Shuttleworth she writes about Charlotte Brontë's hard life, the problems of single women, a community of sisters of mercy just established by Miss Sellon, F. D. Maurice's 'striking and curious sermon' called 'Religion versus God' and the Institution for the Care of Sick Gentlewomen (72). The next letter to her is about benevolent manufacturers; a short note announces that she is 'very full of public nurseries just now', and so on. She felt herself to be part of a national enterprise that transcended sectarian boundaries:

To F. J. Furnivall, 3 December 1853 (172)
I am constantly hearing, & consequently often repeating instances of people who have owed more than they can well speak of without breaking down to Mr Maurice's writings or Mr Maurice's self. – 'Influence' is such a difficult thing to trace and define; the most powerful is so like the great powers of nature, so imperceptible in its working that it almost seems to me as if too much talking about it vulgarized it. There is no doubt whatever it seems to me of the *fact* – that Mr Maurice has more influence over the more thoughtful portion of the English people than any one else I know of, – but almost the deeper the influence is the less people can put it into a clear cold expression, so as to logically convince those who have never felt what it is.

Maurice, an ex-Unitarian, was then being attacked for theological unorthodoxy, but Elizabeth Gaskell was not particularly interested in *doctrines*:

To William Robson, 20 February 1850 (67)
I hope you will not think I have taken too great a liberty in having requested a pamphlet and two papers, (which will explain themselves,) to be forwarded to you. The pamphlet is the first of a series 'on Christian Socialism' proposed to be issued by the writers of 'Politics for the People':

those writers were as you probably know, the revd Frederick Maurice, the author of No 1, of the Present tracts; the revd Charles Kingsley, (who will soon publish No 2, of tracts on Christian Socialism,) Mr Ludlow, a barrister writing under the pseudonym of 'John Townsend', Mr Scott the Prof. of English literature at the University College, &c. They are anxious to obtain a circulation among the working-classes for these tracts, and it is they who have instituted the Co-operative Tailors Society; and who hope to form a similar Society for Needlewomen. Even if you differ considerably from them, by helping them to circulate their views, and have their plans discussed, you will be helping them in their earnest loving search after the Kingdom of God, which they hold far above any plans of their own.

She asked her brother-in-law to circulate the tracts amongst working men because the editors 'want their advice, & thoughts, & practical sense'. This last item must have been intensely congenial to the creator of Nicholas Higgins in *North and South*.

During the 1850s, despite occasional crises, Manchester was becoming more prosperous, so Elizabeth Gaskell had less need to work hard at her charities. Much of her time, passion and energy must have been given to her daughters in their emotional and religious difficulties. She was also becoming a little warier as she gained experience. When she read that 'Bible-women' were being encouraged to keep journals, she had strong reservations:

To Charles Bosanquet, 7 November 1859 (446a)
Do you know I think they will find that it will destroy the simplicity and *unconscious* goodness of the women, if they encourage them to keep journals (Clause 7, page 292) of more than mere statistics? I see a little of the danger of this in the conversations recorded, whh are thrown into dramas, as it were – with a little account of looks, & gestures which seem 'touched up' as it were. For instance the blind Staly-bridge & Dukinfield man, page 209, speaks better language than he was likely to speak, – & what is more, nearly all the people, whose words are given, say much the same sort of things, without distinction of individual character. . . . A *very* good man in Manchester was a few years ago brought into much notice for his philanthropy, and many people were only too glad to learn something of the peculiar methods by which he certainly *had* reclaimed the erring. So he was asked about his 'experiences', and told many *true* interesting histories. Lately I have observed that it was difficult to 'bring him to book' as it were about his cases. He would tell one of a story that made one's heart bleed, – tell it dramatically too, whh faculty is always a temptation,

117

& when, unwilling to let emotion die without passing into action one asked for the address &c, – it always became vague, – in different ways. For some time I have suspected that he told *old* true stories, as if they were happening *now*, or had happened *yesterday*. And just lately I have found that this temptation to excite his hearers strongly, has led to *pure invention*. So do you wonder that I am afraid lest 'godly simplicity' may be injured by journal-keeping, & extracts from journals being printed. So ends my lecture. Julia is deep in the evenings illuminating texts & mottos.

Can she be referring to the prison-visitor, her good Mr Wright? Did the novelist in her recognise the fiction, the conversion of real life into texts and mottoes – suitable for his kind of book but not for hers!

To Samuel A. Steinthal, Late October 1859 (630)
Who wrote that paper on the factory system that Ld Brougham read? Mr Thomas Wright, beautiful as he is in many ways, is not to be *quite* relied on for his facts, – and not at all for his opinions, – which he generalizes into two great theories, – one that good mothers are all important – true, – and another that we are going to the dogs because 'people think so much about recreation now a days.'

The dulcet tones do not dull the critical edge. We are more conscious of her power than her charm for once.

The Gaskell family's benevolence was now to undergo its sternest test since the 1840s. With the outbreak of the American Civil War in 1861, exports of raw cotton were prevented by the Northern blockades. For a while Lancashire survived on its stocks, but by November 1862 hundreds of thousands were unemployed or on short time. Lady Kay-Shuttleworth's Deaf and Dumb Memorial Annuities were neglected; charity had to begin at home. 'We are overwhelmed by poor people', she wrote to Marianne in Rome, 'who I do think tell each other, till we really are preyed upon. We made no great ado about presents this year. Julia a *scarlet* Connemara Cloak. Nothing to poor Meta but a waltz of Chopin's. Florence a remnant of silk for a gown' (496). To the social reformer Vernon Lushington, a London barrister, she sent a letter outlining three ways of contributing to the relief of distress:[7] to Mr Gaskell for the South Lancashire collection, to C. J. Herford for Manchester proper ('educated men are working hard at distributing relief after enquiry') or to Travers Madge if he wished to contribute 'to any particular class of cases . . . factory girls, able-bodied men seeking work & getting none, – or to whomsoever you liked in fact; and in a thoroughly wise & conscientious spirit'. He seems to have sent a cheque with no strings attached:

To Vernon Lushington, Early April 1862

I do not think you know how much good it will do, – at least I hope so; and we will do our best to make it do so. We have been talking over how to make it go the farthest . . . We think of using part of it in allowing 6d or 8d a week to the poor old women, whom my daughters know *well*, – & who at present have only the workhouse allowance; barely enough for the cheapest, poorest food, – only just enough to keep life in. They have worked hard all their working-yrs, poor old friendless women, and now often crave and sicken after a 'taste of bacon' or something different to the perpetual oat-meal. . . . there are many ways surging up in my mind in which I know that at this time, i.e. of slackness of employment *men* can benefit by money or money's worth (without having their just sense of independence injured) by help which comes as from friend to friend. . . .

As I hope you know you are always welcome, if it is only for the pleasure of 'bullying you', – and playing Chopin *at* you, – which is called 'educating your taste' by some people.

The second winter of distress was worst of all:

To George Smith, Late September 1862 (517)

I wish North & South would make friends, & let us have cotton, & then our poor people would get work, and then you should have as many novels as you liked to take, and we should not be killed with 'Poor on the Brain', as I expect we shall before the winter is over. We were really glad before leaving home to check each other in talking of the one absorbing topic, which was literally haunting us in our sleep, as well as being the first thoughts on wakening and the last at night.

To Charles Eliot Norton, 13 July 1863 (526)

Last autumn & winter was *such* hard work – we were often off at nine, – not to come home till 7, or 1/2 past, too worn out to eat or do anything but go to bed. The one thought ran thro' all our talk almost like a disease. Marianne worked quite as hard, if not harder than Meta, – (tho' we all gave our lives to 'the Distress' –) but Marianne did not think so deeply about it all as Meta, – nothing like it. She decided quicker in individual cases; and shook them off sooner, – out of her mind I mean, – but Meta laboured day and night in weighing and planning and thinking, – and going out again, after a hard hard day if she thought one little scrap of duty or kindness or enquiry had been omitted. And oh! I was so sorry to see her fade away under it all – the over-pressure on the brain telling on the spine, & necessitating rest, while yet the very brain made her refuse by it's activity. I cannot tell you what a nightmare last winter was – and at the last we seemed to have done more harm than good – not 'we' alone – perhaps 'we' less than most; but the imposition, the deterioration in character &c &c were so great. It is of no use dwelling on it now – i.e. going into details, – but if you were here I should so have liked to consult you about what *really does good* among the poor. We fear next winter will be as bad; but at present there is a great lull. To go back to the kind of disheartening things – people who were good & hardworking before, & at the beginning of the 'relief', people we knew & had respected, were found paying a man 6d a week to answer to their name, & claim relief for them in different districts. Our charwoman, – a widow, who had brought up her children well & without help from the parish, – declined coming to wash here (which she had done for 7 years,) because she could get more by *not* working, & applying to the Relief Board. One *local* Relief committee – consisting of small shop-keepers, were found to have supplied themselves with great-coats out of the Funds intrusted to them &c &c &c &c.

She sounds disillusioned and weary, but the practice of benevolence continued. Edward Holland was told that Mr Gaskell would 'most gladly contribute the 5 per cent requested to the distress around us, as desired by the Manchester, Sheffield, & Lincolnshire railway Cy' (510). They 'paid for the passage of a Mrs Regan & child' (520) to Australia – emigration was still the universal panacea. They spent most of their days 'from 9 AM to 7–30 P.M. in the Sewing-Schools', but by March of 1863, 'as soon as the great strain of the Distress was lessened by the organization in the distribution of Relief, and by the increased amount of mill-work for our girls', she told Charles Bosanquet, 'we resolved to have some entire change before this next winter, by going abroad for a time' (535a). In fact, the winter of 1863–4 was to see some very odd juxtapositions: John Pender's wife, with whom the Gaskells were to dine on Christmas day, wore £10,000 of diamonds and £400 of lace at a ball (540); Charles Bosanquet and a friend gave a modest sum to buy 'grey linsey enough for 6 good comfortable *shirts*, – which have been distributed & caused great thankfulness' (540a). Manchester was still a town of contrasts and the Gaskells always lived in both worlds.

The Cotton Famine eventually ended. The machines were turning once more in the factories:

To an unknown correspondent, 9 March 1864 (549)
    I also enclose some of my cards. If you have time they will enable you to
    see the things best worth in Manchester; viz
    '*Murray's* FINE spinning – mills', in *Union* St (I think) just off Ancoats

Lane, every body there knows 'Murrays'. You would there see the whole process of preparing & spinning cotton, with the *latest* improvements in the machinery required : the more questions you ask the better they will be pleased, as they will evince interest. . . .

'*Whitworth's*' Machine Works, *Canal St, Brook St* or very near there. (The rifle works which have made Mr Whitworth so famous, are out of Manchester, and not easily shown). But these works are very interesting, if you do not get a stupid *fine* young man to show you over – try rather for one of the *working* men.

Sylvia's Lovers, started about December 1859, had at last appeared in print and her greatest creative phase was beginning with the serialisation of *Cousin Phillis* in the *Cornhill Magazine* between November 1863 and February 1864. But one human engine had broken down. Meta had proved in her own person that it was possible to 'give rather too freely to the poor' :

To Charles Eliot Norton, 5 February 1865 (560)
Meta's health is, I am sorry to say, not satisfactory; though we hope better than it was. For more than a year she has been suffering from extreme nervous debility & pain in the spine; brought on by any worry or distress. I think this was originally brought on by her anxiety about Marianne, during the last visit of the latter to Rome when she became so intimate with Dr Manning; and partly it came from her devotion to the sewing-schools in that first winter of the Cotton Famine; the air in the rooms was so terribly bad, & the stories of individual distress which she heard preyed so much upon her. She fought against feelings of languor, headache, & backache as long as she could, when she had much better have yielded to them; and has had to pay a long penalty for this. We took her, – did I tell you? – to Switzerland as a bracing place this last autumn. I, my 4 daughters, Charlie Crompton and Thurstan Holland went to Pontresina in the Grisons, 6,000 feet above the level of the sea – primitive, cheap & bracing; There she had a very bad attack of headache, – (bewildering whirling headache is the kind –) and a Mr Erichsen a great famous London surgeon was staying in the hotel, & prescribed for her with such good effect that she has continued under his care; & by his advice she went to Brighton in November, & stayed there till Xmas, living out of doors, and having warm seawater douches on her spine with very good effect. But he says it will be a year or more yet before she will have regained her usual health – and all that time, & probably longer she is to follow a certain régime, of frequent change of air, very good living, early hours, – to be perpetually in the open air &c &c &c. She is *not* to read deep books, she is

not to visit the poor, she is *not* to be worried &c. So she, to whom we all went for sympathy and advice leads a life as apart from ours as we can make it; but the old habit of going to her still survives and we have continually to check ourselves to keep her in peace. And this she knows & grieves over. But just now she seems very much better.

For one member of the family at least the cloak of charity was more like a hair-shirt than anything else.

CHAPTER NINE

The lives of authors

nothing matters but the quality
of the affection –
in the end – that has carved the trace in the mind
(Ezra Pound, Canto LXXVI)

WE MAY READ ELIZABETH GASKELL today because she was an author, but in her lifetime she lived in anything but a palace of art. She knew little about some things, such as those private fantasies of self and sex the Brontë sisters were so expert in projecting; she wrote with poise and assurance about social relationships. It was from her standing as wife and mother that she derived her considerable authority in matters of ordinary conduct and uncomplicated belief. Two letters about the author's life can be profitably read together in this context. One concerns what a writer owes to others :

To an unknown correspondent, 25 September 1862 (515)
Your MSS has not been forwarded to me along with your letter; so at present I have no opportunity of judging of it's merits; when I have read it I will give you the best & truest opinion I can. I feel very sorry for you, for I think I can see that, at present, at least you are rather overwhelmed with all you have to do; and I think it possible that the birth of two children, – one so close upon another may have weakened you bodily, and made you more unfit to cope with your many household duties. Try – even while waiting for my next letter, to strengthen yourself by every means in

your power; by being very careful as to your diet; by cold-bathing, by resolute dwelling on the cheerful side of everything; and by learning to œconomize strength as much as possible in all your household labours; for I dare say you already know how much time may be saved, by beginning any kind of work in good time, and not driving all in a hurry to the last moment. I hope (for instance,) you soap & soak your dirty clothes well for some hours before beginning to wash; and that you understand the comfort of preparing a dinner & putting it on to cook *slowly*, early in the morning, as well as having *always* some kind of sewing ready arranged to your hand, so that you can take it up at any odd minute and do a few stitches. I dare say at present it might be difficult for you to procure the sum that is necessary to purchase a sewing machine; and indeed, unless you are a good workwoman to begin with, you will find a machine difficult to manage. But *try*, my dear, to conquer your 'clumsiness' in sewing; there are thousand little bits of work, which no sempstress ever does so well as the wife or mother who knows how the comfort of those she loves depends on little peculiarities which no one but she cares enough for the wearers to attend to.

My first piece of advice to you would be *Get strong* – I am almost sure you are out of bodily health and that, if I were you, I would make it my first object to attain. Did you ever try a tea-cup full of *hop-tea* the first thing in the morning? It is a very simple tonic, and could do no harm. Then again try *hard* to arrange your work well. That is a regular piece of head-work and taxes a woman's powers of organization; but the reward is immediate and great. I have known well what it is to be both wanting money, & feeling weak in body and entirely disheartened. I do not think I ever cared for literary fame; nor do I think it *is* a thing that ought to be cared for. It comes and it goes. The exercise of a talent or power *is* always a great pleasure; but one should weigh well whether this pleasure may not be obtained by the sacrifice of some duty. When I had *little* children I do not think I could have written stories, because I should have become too much absorbed in my *fictitious* people to attend to my *real* ones. I think you would be sorry if you began to feel that your desire to earn money, even for so laudable an object as to help your husband, made you unable to give your tender sympathy to your little ones in their small joys & sorrows; and yet, don't you know how you, – how every one, who tries to write stories *must* become absorbed in them, (fictitious though they be,) if they are to interest their readers in them. Besides viewing the subject from a solely artistic point of view a good writer of fiction must have *lived* an active & sympathetic life if she wishes her books to have strength & vitality in them. When you are forty, and if you have a gift for being an authoress you will write ten times as good a novel as you could do now, just because you will have gone through so much more of the interests of a wife and a mother.

All this does not help you over present difficulties, does it? Well then let us try what will – How much have you in your own power? How much must you submit to because it is God's appointment? You have it in your own power to arrange your day's work to the very best of your ability, making the various household arts into real studies (& there is plenty of poetry and association about them – remember how the Greek princesses in Homer washed the clothes &c &c &c &c.) You would perhaps find a little book called The Finchley Manual of Needlework of real use to you in sewing; it gives patterns and directions &c. Your want of strength may be remedied *possibly* by care & attention; if not, you must submit to what is God's ordinance; only remember that the very hardest day's bodily work I have ever done has never produced anything like the intense exhaustion I have felt after writing the 'best' parts of my books.

All this letter is I fear disheartening enough: you must remember I have not seen your MSS as yet; & I can only judge of it from such a number of MSS sent me from time to time; and only *one* of these writers has ever succeeded in getting her writings published, though in several instances I have used my best endeavours on their behalf.

Have you no sister or relation who could come & help you for a little while till you get stronger, – no older friend at hand who would help you to plan your work so that it should oppress you as little as possible? If this letter has been of *any* use to you, do not scruple to write to me again, if I can give you help.

Her heart went out to her unknown correspondent – to the extent of disingenuousness: she must have been writing *Mary Barton* when Julia was a baby. But her professed view is very typical of her age. A woman's first duty was to her family and only dire necessity (the need to support an invalid mother or a bankrupt father, a tubercular husband or an errant son) could possibly justify joining the ranks of those 'demure authoresses in whose downcast eyes we can detect the glint of steely purpose'. If we find this preposterous, we should not forget the advantages to a woman in those days. As George Eliot remarked when Harriet Martineau's niece and companion died, 'She was a person whose office in life seemed so thoroughly defined and so valuable'.[1]

The other letter, once again a work of charity, is about the actual craft of writing. It is pleasant enough, but hardly sophisticated:

To Marianne Gaskell, Late March 1859 (420)

Letter to "Herbert Grey" – see his note: nice, kind, *'graceful'* civilities – beginning Dear Sir & ending Yrs truly.

As you ask me for my opinion I shall try and give it as truly as I can; otherwise it will be of no use; as it is I think that it may be of use, as the experience of any one who has gone before on the path you are following must always have some value in it. In the first place you say you do not call The 3 paths a novel; but the work is in the form which always assumes that name, nor do I think it is one to be quarrelled with. . . .

But I believe in spite of yr objection to the term 'novel' you do wish to 'narrate,' – and I believe you can do it if you try, – but I think you must observe what is *out* of you, instead of examining what is *in* you. It is always an unhealthy sign when we are too conscious of any of the physical processes that go on within us; & I believe in like manner that we ought not to be too cognizant of our mental proceedings, only taking note of the results. But certainly – whether introspection be morbid or not, – it is not a safe training for a novelist. It is a weakening of the art which has crept in of late years. Just read a few pages of De Foe &c – and you will see the healthy way in which he sets *objects* not *feelings* before you. I am sure the right way is this. You are an Electric telegraph something or other, –

Well! every day your life brings you into contact with live men & women, – of whom yr reader, knows nothing about: (and I, Mrs Gaskell for instance, do know nothing about the regular work & daily experience of people working for their bread with head-labour, – & that not professional, – in London.) Think if you can not imagine a complication of events in their life which would form a good plot. . . .

Then set to & imagine yourself a spectator & auditor of every scene & event! Work hard at this till it become a reality to you, – a thing you have to recollect & describe & report fully & accurately as it struck you, in order that your reader may have it equally before him. Don't intrude yourself into your description. If you but think eagerly of your story till *you see it in action*, words, good simple strong words, will come, – just as if you saw an accident in the street that impressed you strongly you would describe it forcibly. . . .

You see I am very frank-spoken. But I believe you are worth it. I judge from yr letter which I like –

Please don't thank me. But try & follow my advice for I am pretty sure it is good. You know everybody can preach better than they can practise.

All my morning's precious time taken up in letter writing!! Dearest Polly,

I pity the man don't you? But it is good advice after all, & I wd not have written it for every body. Show it to Mr H A B — as a 'specimen of *reviewing*'.

The last sentence brings Susanna Winkworth's description of her irresistibly to mind: 'She was a noble-looking woman, with a queenly presence, and her high, broad, serene brow, and finely-cut mobile features, were lighted up by a constantly-varying play of expression as she poured forth her wonderful talk. It was like the gleaming ripple and rush of a clear deep stream in sunshine.'[2] She kept her balance on the borderline by refusing to become at all obsessive about the writer's role. Mr H. A. B., a lively, eloquent young Unitarian from Liverpool, would not have been surprised:

To Henry Arthur Bright, no date (593)
My dear Mr Bright,
I *did* 'feel like reading' your article, and like it very much, as I knew I should from what you told me of it. But then you know I am not (*Unitarianly*) orthodox! So you may be 'anile' and 'senile' and all the rest of it in spite of my opinion to the contrary. However if you are ever so mischievous we shall be glad to see you here. Harriet says our dear ugly bleak Silverdale would please you. You can hear from her *what* it — and what our life is. — And if you would like to come to us on Friday or Saturday next, — (*do*, if you can, & especially if you will promise to like Silverdale, and stay over Sunday as long as you like,) we have Harriet's room at liberty, & a warm welcome ready for you. Mind! I won't talk theology — Unitarian or otherwise, — and you are to be carnal & *hungry* not spiritual and regardless of food. We never talk sense — but we are very happy. Now write & say you will come.

Yours very truly
E C Gaskell

Elizabeth Gaskell may have been a shade disingenuous, or even self-deceived, but her conscious priorities were clear and consistently developed:

To Eliza Fox, February 1850 (68)
One thing is pretty clear, *Women*, must give up living an artist's life, if home duties are to be paramount. It is different with men, whose home duties are so small a part of their life. However we are talking of women. I am sure it is healthy for them to have the refuge of the hidden world of Art to shelter themselves in when too much pressed upon by daily small Lilliputian arrows of peddling cares; it keeps them from being morbid as you say; and takes them into the land where King Arthur lies hidden, and

soothes them with its peace. I have felt this in writing, I see others feel it in music, you in painting, so assuredly a blending of the two is desirable. (Home duties and the development of the Individual I mean), which you will say it takes no Solomon to tell you but the difficulty is where and when to make one set of duties subserve and give place to the other. I have no doubt that the cultivation of each tends to keep the other in a healthy state, – my grammar is all at sixes and sevens I have no doubt but never mind if you can pick out my meaning. I think a great deal of what you have said.

As she became aware of her full powers in her late thirties, the intelligent younger women she had befriended formed the perfect sounding board. They were made aware of her developing sense of personal independence that others, her sisters-in-law for instance, were not:

To Catherine Winkworth, 21 August 1849 (49)
The Darbishires are all at Rivington today. They've got into a very helter-skelter way of spending Sundays ever since they read the 'Nemesis'; to-morrow they've a dance; we're asked but I'm going to have a headache, and Sukey is going to 'quite accidentally' come in on her way from her District and sit with me. . . .

Mr Froude is domesticated at the Darbishires' till October, when he is to be married and go to the Satterfields' old house in Green Heys. If any one under the sun has a magical, magnetic, glamour-like influence, that man has. He's '*aut Mephistophiles aut nihil*', that's what he is. The D. D.'s all bend and bow to his will, like reeds before the wind, blow whichever way it listeth. He smokes cigars constantly; Père, Robert, Arthur, Vernon (nay, once even little Francis), smoke constantly. He disbelieves, they disbelieve; he wears shabby garments, they wear shabby garments; in short, it's the most complete taking away their own wills and informing them with his own that ever was. . . . I stand just without the circle of his influence; resisting with all my might, but feeling and seeing the attraction.

J. A. Froude's novel, *The Nemesis of Faith* (1849), had made public such religious doubts that he had given up his fellowship at Oxford and was temporarily a tutor to the children of S. D. Darbishire, a local Unitarian. She seems to have taken his measure easily enough, but it was a complicated world she had to live in:

To Eliza Fox, 17 November 1851 (108a)
What do you think of Kossuth? Is he not a WONDERFUL man for clever-

ness. His speech was real eloquence, I never heard anyone speak before that I could analyze as it went along, and *think* what caused the effect but when he spoke I could only feel; — and yet I am not quite *sure* about him, that's to say I am *quite* sure about his end being a noble one, but I think it has so possessed him that I am not quite *out and out* sure that he would stick at *any* means, it's not for me to be poking into and judging him. . . . I wish you could see Lucy Holland's water colour drawings; I wonder if you would think them *good*. They are *very* pretty at any rate and Meta has been copying some. . . . And oh! Fanny and I have had a split about Libbie Marsh, which that wretched man at Liverpool was going on republishing ad infinitum and I stepped in and objected as gently as I cd, and I am afraid Fanny is hurt. I am *very* sorry; but I showed my letter to Wm, and he says it was quite a gentle proper letter. Do *you* hear any of her plans from any one? Susanna W. keeps Wm busy at work correcting her proofs, for my dear! Niebuhr is on the point of appearing before the public! and poor Mary Barton gets more snubbed than ever as a 'light and transitory' work. I have offered myself to the 'Critic' as a writer. I did it in a state of rage at that Marples man at Liverpool, and Chapman and I swore I would penny-a-line and have nothing to do with publishers never no more; so my critics generously offered me 7*s*. a column. (I never saw the paper but I heard it was a respectable dullard) and I counted up and think its about 3*d* a line, so I think I shall do well, — Wm is very mad about it, and calls me names which are not pretty for a husband to call a wife 'great goose' etc. . . . Tell me some literary gossip, for though I've turned farmer, I've a little sympathy yet left for 'book sellers hacks'. . . . How are the Dickens? wretch that he is to go and write MY story of the lady haunted by the face; I shall have nothing to talk about now at dull parties.

Her own influence must have been as magical, magnetic and glamour-like as Froude's, but was she the feminine, feminist or female equivalent?

Dickens thought he knew the answer on one occasion : 'Mrs Gaskell, fearful — fearful. If I were Mr. G. O Heaven how I would beat her!' Yet Dickens was acutely aware of one very important fact indeed to an editor, that she was a born story-teller, his 'dear Scheherazade'. Whatever the difficulties and ex- asperations of dealing with her, he wanted her stories for his periodicals. *North and South* proved a particularly difficult serial to run :

To Charles Dickens, 17 December 1854 (220)
I was very much gratified by your note the other day; *very* much indeed. I dare say I shall like my story, when I am a little further from it; at present I can only feel depressed about it, I meant it to have been so much better.

I send what I am afraid you will think too large a batch of it by this post. What Mr Wills has got already *fills up* the No for January 13, leaving me only two more numbers, Janry 20, & Janry 27th so what I send today is meant to be crammed & stuffed into Janry 20th; & I'm afraid I've nearly as much more for Jany 27.

It is 33 pages of my writing that I send today. I have tried to shorten & compress it, both because it was a dull piece, & to get it into reasonable length, but there were a whole catalogue of events to be got over: and what I want to tell you now is this, – Mr Gaskell has looked this piece well over, so I don't think there will be any carelessnesses left in it, & so there ought not to be any misprints; therefore I never wish to see it's face again; but, *if you will keep the MS for me, & shorten it as you think best for H W*. I shall be very glad. Shortened I see it must be.

'She is writing furiously, thirty pages a week; expects to finish in ten days', Catherine Winkworth reported about this time. 'Mr. Dickens writes to her praisingly, but he does not please me, and I hope she won't be "wiled by his fause flattering tongue" into thinking him true and trustworthy, like Mr. Forster.'[3] Under such stress, with friends warning her, tensions are inevitable:

To Anna Jameson, Late January 1855 (225)
You can't think what pleasure your kind note of appreciation gave, and gives me. I made a half-promise (as perhaps I told you,) to Mr Dickens, which he understood as a whole one; and though I had the plot and characters in my head long ago, I have often been in despair about the working of them out; because of course, in this way of publishing it, I had to write pretty hard without waiting for the happy leisure hours. And then 20 numbers was, I found my allowance; instead of the too scant 22, which I had fancied were included in 'five months'; and at last the story is huddled & hurried up; especially in the rapidity with which the sudden death of Mr Bell, succeeds to the sudden death of Mr Hale. But what could I do? Every page was grudged me, just at last, when I did certainly infringe all the bounds & limits they set me as to quantity. Just at the very last I was compelled to desperate compression. But now I am not sure if, when the barrier gives way between 2 such characters as Mr Thornton and Margaret it would not go all smash in a moment, – and I don't feel quite certain that I dislike the end as it now stands. But, it is being republished as a whole, in two vols; – and the question is shall I alter & enlarge what is already written, bad & hurried-up though it be? I can not insert small pieces here & there – I feel as if I must throw myself back a certain distance in the story, & re-write it from there; retaining the present incidents, but

filling up intervals of time &c &c. Would you give me your *very* valuable opinion as to this?

Such a relationship could never be simple, even if the editor was one of the most famous novelists in England :

To Marianne and Meta Gaskell, Late 1855 (273)
I am very sorry I did not write yesterday, but I was so much tired, & people were here, Mary Worthington (staying) & Miss Brandreth calling &c, – so it slipped through. I got SAFELY! to Altringham, then in the 'bus I sate next to somebody, whose face I thought I knew, & then I made out it was only that he was very like Mr Hensleigh Wedgwood; however he read 'Little-Dorrit' & I read it over his shoulder. Oh *Polly*! he was such a slow reader, *you*'ll sympathize, Meta won't, my impatience at his *never* getting to the bottom of the page so we only got to the end of the page. *We* only read the first two chapters, so I never found out who 'Little Dorrit' is, . . .

This author was also a man, which becomes very evident when he was ill-advised enough to make his marital problems public; his contributor was a woman with problems of her own :

To Charles Eliot Norton, 9 March 1859 (418)
You know about our going abroad; and that I got money for it &c, by selling Lady Ludlow &c; but when at Heidelberg we wished to go on to Dresden (alas! we never went, – for the weather became so *intensely* cold, I was afraid to venture the girls' health in travelling, –) but I wrote two stories for Household Words, & asked for immediate payment, in order to obtain money to gratify this wish. And they, Household Words, (very kindly) sent me 40£, saying that it was more than the stories would come to they believed, but I could wait my own time for sending them a *third* story, which would make all straight. So I *fancy* (I cannot get them to *tell* me), that I am indebted to them about 18£.
But I was extremely annoyed & hurt by their conduct in Janry – They published a 'Chip', called '*Character-Murder*' alluding to & quoting from a paper of mine called 'Disappearances' – published long ago in H W, & since with my leave republished along with Lizzie Leigh &c. They quoted *from it* up to a certain point; but then added more of their own *as a quotation*, which made the '*Character-Murder*', & went on to regret that the aspersion (of which I had never even heard,) had appeared in their pages. I thought that it was a mistake of theirs; & wrote to Mr Wills (the manager) sending him my paper 'Disappearances', & begging him to read

Character Murder over again, to see how little I had said, in comparison with what I was there made to say by implication. He only returned for answer that 'he was sorry I fancied that I had any reason for annoyance.' And you know I have particular reasons for shrinking from any accusation of Character Murder. So I did feel both sorry and hurt. All this time I was writing my third story, – to pay off my debt to them, – whatever it is; – but instead of it's stopping itself, as it ought to have done at about 40 pages of MS, which I suppose would have brought in about 18£ in H W, & so set me clear, I very soon saw that I could not compress it into less than 200 pages, – upwards of 100 of which are already written. *Now Mr Dickens objected (in the* case of North & South) *to any sending sheets in advance to America.* He said the end of the story would come back to England before it was all published here, & in fact he quite refused to allow me to do so with regard to North & South; nor should I like to ask him now. But I wanted to revert to the old proposal of publishing *entire* in America. I don't *think* my present story would bear weekly splitting up into numbers. I am sure it would do much better published as a whole. But it is not very good; too melodramatic a plot; only I have grown interested in it, and cannot put it aside. I should much *much* prefer it's being published in America, either as a whole or by the Atlantic. (Mind it is not really good. I am quite aware of that. The fault is in the plot.)

But now comes in the complication. I have within this week received an additional motive for wishing it *not* to be published in H. W. in the fact that last Thursday I received a circular, saying that (on account of matters connected with Mr & Mrs Dickens' separation), Mr Dickens was giving up Household Words, and starting a new periodical with different publishers &c. I wrote directly to Mr Wills, to ask again how much I was indebted to Household Words, & who was the real personal creditor to whom I owed the money, which I shd be very glad to repay with interest &c, as the story I was writing was unfortunately of such length that, (as the new periodical announces 'a new story by Mr Dickens in weekly numbers',) they would not be able to publish it for a longer time than I should choose to be indebted to them. Mr Wills has not yet replied to this. I am afraid he is making some arrangement by which they *can* take my story; as Mr Dickens happens to be extremely unpopular just now, – (owing to the well-grounded feeling of dislike to the publicity he has given to his domestic affairs,) & I think they would be glad to announce my name on the list of their contributors. And I would *much* rather they did *not*.

'I *know*', she wailed later in this letter, 'it is fated to go to this new Dickensy periodical, & I did so hope to escape it.' She was right. 'A Dark Night's Work' came out in *All the Year Round* between January and March 1863.

Her relations with writers like Thackeray and J. S. Mill were far from easy, though at one time she thought the former the greatest living novelist.[4] The world of masculine authorship may have been safer at a distance, or so the intricacies of her connection with Nathaniel Hawthorne appear to show.[5] As early as 1851 she knew of *The Scarlet Letter*, a work causing a literary sensation just while she was composing her own story of a child made the instrument of its mother's rehabilitation, *Ruth*. In the years to come, Hawthorne only just missed meeting her. He became a close friend of Henry Arthur Bright in Liverpool and knew the Martineaus, but attempted introductions fell through. Through Bright, perhaps, Mrs Gaskell heard the famous anecdote of Hawthorne's meeting with Martin Tupper, author of *Proverbial Philosophy*, one of Queen Victoria's favourite books:

To Marianne Gaskell, Early summer 1856 (292)
Apropos of your friend, M. F. Tupper – he said he (M F T) had got hold of Hawthorne when he was in London, & invited him down to Albury, – where he met him & greeted him *All Hail Great Scarlet Letter*! Mr H was dreadfully puzzled how to answer, – but at last settled down on Good morning Mr Tupper.

It is a pity she never seems to have heard the replies he thought of making: 'O wondrous Man of proverbs!' or 'O wiser Solomon!' Sadly, they never quite managed to meet face-to-face.

The year after her Roman trip of 1857, Hawthorne arrived there and renewed his acquaintance with her old friend, William Wetmore Story. The savage repose of one of Story's works in progress, a sitting statue of Cleopatra, so impressed him that he brought it into an important chapter of his novel *The Marble Faun*. Then he went to Redcar on the Yorkshire coast, about twenty miles from Whitby, where Elizabeth Gaskell came just a few weeks after his departure seeking impressions for her own *Sylvia's Lovers*. Probably through Bright again she got to know something of Hawthorne's Italian romance, and was even able to ask George Smith playfully, 'Do *you* know what Hawthorne's tale is about? *I* do; and I think it will perplex the English public pretty considerably' (441) – which must have given its future English publisher at least a moment's twinge. When the work came out in 1860, she was able to boast that she had known the Cleopatra statue from the first:

To William and Emelyn Story, 1860 (498)
I feel funnily like Quin, who, when George III. made his first speech be-

fore Parliament after his accession, said, 'I taught the boy to read!' – for I come in crowing over my having seen the thing even in the clay and describing more fully what every one is asking about. I can't say, unluckily, 'I taught the boy to imagine beauty.'

In such matters she was very straightforward. When a friend complained that he could not find a good life of Zoroaster and a popular history of the religion of ancient Egypt, Meta was simply deputised to write to the savant Julius Mohl in Paris:[6] 'Mama said at once – triumphantly – "Oh we can find out for you; we know the first Orientalist in the world, the kindest person too ..." ' Perhaps he felt flattered and kindly sent the names of two suitable books in his wife's next letter, as he was asked, but the request is a little artless. Elizabeth Gaskell's preferred literary life was a complex of friendship and open, free talk: 'I could *tell* the stories quite easily', she confessed once when she felt disinclined to write them down. 'How I should like to do it to you and Mr Story and Edith, sitting over a wood-fire and knowing that the Vatican was in sight of the windows behind!' (498). By a coincidence that is only too explicable in a world of this kind, her story of 'the lady haunted by the face', which Dickens had appropriated in earlier years, was also remembered by Emelyn Story and recounted to Hawthorne. Down it went in his notebook as 'a marvellous tale, on the authority of Mrs Gaskell, to whom the personages were known' and later its key incident was utilised in *The Marble Faun*. This happy life with congenial friends could be dangerously relaxing, Ruskin had found when he met Norton and his circle in Italy, but Elizabeth Gaskell thrived artistically. One of her best stories, 'Lois the Witch', is the proof; it sprang from both English and American connections.

If art and life are so close, strange dilemmas can arise. Some are easily soluble, as when she introduced an author with a work in manuscript to her publisher. Hamilton Aïdé, she told him, was the son of a Scottish heiress and 'a Greek exile, of *good* character'. With his lovely eyes and neat little moustachios and whiskers he must have been a charmer: 'he acts beautifully in either French or English private theatricals,' she wrote to George Smith, 'sings enchantingly (you could not transact your business with him in a duett, could you? Without any disparagement to your possible musical talents I think you would be a gainer by any mode of hearing him sing,) draws passably – and is altogether full of *tastes* – about the *talents* I am not so sure' (407). He had in fact published a novel called *Rita, an Autobiography* already, but the Manchester circulating libraries could not produce it for her to read. George Smith sent her a copy:

To George Smith, 14 February 1859 (413)

My opinion of you is that you are very wicked and naughty; depriving me
– by an action which appears on the surface most kind and generous, till
I begin to examine into the motives that prompted it, – of all excuse to
Mr Aidé for not sending him word what I think of 'Rita'. You are quite
aware that I must agree with you. I tell him my 'honest opinion' of his *first*
volume at any rate: It introduces one just exactly into the kind of dis-
reputable society one keeps clear of with such scrupulous care in real life,
– it is not merely *one* character that is none of the best, – but every one
we get a glimpse of is the same description of person. I don't think it is
'corrupting', but it is disagreeable, – a sort of dragging one's petticoats
through mud. I wish the little gentleman, – who really seems more than
commonly good (for a man, – begging your & your son's pardon,) had not
written this book; because it gives one a sort of distrust of his previous life.

Her tone is light – George Smith's son, incidentally, was about two weeks old
– but at bottom she is serious. Moreover, what is moral in life is moral in art,
tout court.

An altogether plainer-looking person, with a far greater genius, was to test
her values more severely. Late in 1857 she had come across *Scenes of Clerical
Life* appearing in *Blackwood's Magazine*: 'They are a discovery of my own, &
I am so proud of them. *Do* read them. I have not a notion who wrote them', she
cried enthusiastically to Norton (384). When *Adam Bede* was published early
in 1859, again under a pen-name, she was bold enough to beg a copy from
Blackwood giving her delight and admiration as a pretext. Then, in an un-
guarded moment, she actually wrote to the new author:

To George Eliot, 3 June 1859 (431)

Dear Mr 'Gilbert Elliott',

Since I came up from Manchester to London I have had the greatest
compliment paid me I ever had in my life, I have been suspected of having
written 'Adam Bede'. I have hitherto denied it; but really I think, that as
you want to keep your real name a secret, it would be very pleasant for me
to blush acquiescence. Will you give me leave?

Well! if I had written Amos Barton, Janet's Repentance & Adam Bede
I should neither be to have nor to hold with pride & delight in myself –
so I think it is very well I have not. And please to take notice I knew what
was coming up above the horizon from the dawn of the first number of
Amos Barton in Blackwood. – After all it is a pity so much hearty admiration should go unappropriated through the world. So, although to my
friends I am known under the name of Mrs Gaskell, to you I will confess

that I *am* the author of Adam Bede, and remain very respectfully & gratefully

Yours,
Gilbert Elliot.

Smith, however, insisted that the wonderful new author was not the respectable
academic she had guessed but a certain Miss Evans, who had defied convention
by going to live with a married man, the writer and critic G. H. Lewes. The
horns of this dilemma had a Trollopian sharpness: 'Do *you* really believe it?
Please say', she begged Smith. 'I do not think you do. It is a noble grand book,
whoever wrote it, – but Miss Evans' life taken at the best construction, does so
jar against the beautiful book that one cannot help hoping against hope' (438).
She now began to make distinctions, in both life and art. To Norton she wrote,
'All this is miserable enough; – but I believe there are many excuses – the
worst is Mr Lewes' character & opinions were (formerly *at least*) so bad' (444).
As far as art was concerned, she discovered that its critics could not stay
healthily unconcerned with psychic depths; morbid or not, it was essential to
speculate about the inner being of the author if responses to art and life were to
make sufficient sense:

To Harriet Martineau, Late October 1859 (444b)
> And after all one gets into a desponding state of mind about writing at all,
> after 'Adam Bede', and 'Janet's Repentance' choose (as the Lancashire
> people say,) whoever wrote them. You heard truly that I have stuck out
> that I believed that a *man* wrote them. I am shaken now, and should like
> much to receive your evidence. I would rather they had not been written
> by Miss Evans, it is true; but justice should be done to all; & after all the
> writing such a book should raise her in every one's opinion, because no
> dramatic power would, I think enable her to think & say such *noble* things,
> unless her own character – perhaps somewhere hidden away from our
> sight at present, – has such possibilities of greatness & goodness in it. I
> never can express myself metaphysically; and I have been interrupted
> many times while trying to make this sentence clear.

Many years before Harriet Martineau had been very reserved towards 'Tottie'
Fox's father when he had separated from his wife and set up an establishment
with Eliza Flower. She remained consistent: she could not bring herself to
approve of George Eliot's liaison with Lewes despite what she was prepared to
call 'the *impayable* benefit of a great book'.[7] Elizabeth Gaskell could not ultimately take so severe a view. From Whitby, always associated with her own
historical novel *Sylvia's Lovers*, she had the grace to write again to the author
of *Adam Bede*:

To George Eliot, 10 November 1859 (449)
My dear Madam,
  Since I heard, from authority, that you were the author of Scenes from 'Clerical Life' & 'Adam Bede', I have read them again; and I must, once more, tell you how earnestly fully, and humbly I admire them. I never read anything so complete, and beautiful in fiction, in my whole life before. I said 'humbly' in speaking of my admiration, because I remembered Dr Johnson's words.
  Perhaps you may have heard that I upheld Mr Liggins as the author for long, – I did it on evidence, quite independent of, & unknown to the Bracebridges. He is a regular rascal. But I never was such a goose as to believe that such books as yours could be a mosaic of real & ideal. I should not be quite true in my ending, if I did not say before I concluded that I wish you *were* Mrs Lewes. However that can't be helped, as far as I can see, and one must not judge others. Once more, thanking you most gratefully for having written all – Janet's Repentance perhaps most especially of all, – (& may I tell you how I singled out the 2nd No of Amos Barton in Blackwood, & went plodging through our Manchester Sts to get every number, as soon as it was accessible from the Portico reading table –)
                                      Believe me to remain,
                                        Yours respectfully
                                          E C Gaskell.

There was an equally gracious and fascinating reply: [8]

  I had indulged the idea that if my books turned out to be worth much, you would be among my willing readers; for I was conscious, while the question of my power was still undecided for me, that my feeling towards Life & Art had some affinity with the feeling which had inspired 'Cranford' & the earlier chapters of 'Mary Barton'. That idea was brought the nearer to me, because I had the pleasure of reading 'Cranford' for the first time in 1857, when I was writing the 'Scenes of Clerical Life', & going up the Rhine one dim wet day in the spring of the next year, when I was writing 'Adam Bede', I satisfied myself for the lack of a prospect by reading over again those earlier chapters of 'Mary Barton'. .... I cannot believe such details are indifferent to you, even after you have been so long used to hear them: I fancy, as long as we live, we all need to know as much as we can of the good our life has been to others.

A strong bridge had been built between the two authors. Mrs Gaskell had 'tried to be moral, & dislike her & dislike her books – but it won't do. There is not a wrong word, or a wrong thought in them, I do believe' (451). But the bridge would not bear any regular traffic; there is no record of any personal connection later. *The Mill on the Floss* was given to her by Smith as soon as it was published, on 4 April 1860, and a first edition of *Romola* (1863) appeared in the final sale of the contents of the house in Plymouth Grove, but it looks as though her many private troubles in the early 1860s prevented Mrs Gaskell from continuing the friendship so splendidly begun.

The relationship with Charlotte Brontë was utterly different, resulting in one of the great biographies of the nineteenth century. We should always remember that others had cast a lurid light from the very beginning: the Kay-Shuttleworths gave the two authors a chance to meet in the rented house near Lake Windermere – but it was in what Ruskin would call a circle of stage fire:

To Catherine Winkworth, 25 August 1850 (75)

She is more like Miss Fox in character & ways than anyone, if you can fancy Miss Fox to have gone through suffering enough to have taken out every spark of merriment, and shy & silent from the habit of extreme intense solitude. Such a life as Miss B's I never heard of before Lady K S described her home to me as in a village of a few grey stone houses perched up on the north side of a bleak moor – looking over sweeps of bleak moors. There is a court of turf & a stone wall, – (no flowers or shrubs will grow there) a straight walk, & you come to the parsonage door with a window on each side of it. The parsonage has never had a touch of paint, or an article of new furniture for 30 years; never since Miss B's mother died. She was a 'pretty young creature' brought from Penzance in Cornwall by the Irish Curate, who got this moorland living. Her friends disowned her at her marriage. She had 6 children as fast as could be; & what with that, & the climate, & the strange half mad husband she had chosen she died at the end of 9 years. An old woman at Burnley who nursed her at last, says she used to lie crying in bed, and saying 'Oh God my poor children – oh God my poor children!' continually. Mr Brontë vented his anger against *things* not persons; for instance once in one of his wife's confinements something went wrong, so he got a saw, and went and sawed up all the chairs in her bedroom, never answering her remonstrances or minding her tears. Another time he was vexed and took the hearth-rug & tied it in a tight bundle & set it on fire in the grate; & sat before it with a leg on each hob, heaping on more coals till it was burnt, no one else being able to endure in the room because of the stifling smoke. All this Lady K S told me. The sitting room at the Parsonage looks into the Church-yard filled with graves. Mr B has never taken a meal with his children since his wife's death, unless he invites them to tea, – *never* to dinner.

When she went to Haworth, everything seemed to fit:

To John Forster, September 1853 (166)[9]
The sinuous hills seemed to girdle the world like the great Norse serpent,
& for my part I don't know if they don't stretch up to the North Pole. On
the Moors we met no one. – Here and there in the gloom of the distant
hollows she pointed out a dark grey dwelling – with Scotch firs growing
near them often, – & told me such wild tales of the ungovernable families,
who lived or had lived therein, that Wuthering Heights even seemed tame
comparatively. Such dare-devil people, – men especially, – & women so
stony & cruel in some of their feelings & so passionately fond in others.
They are a queer people up there. . . .

Charlotte Brontë's imagination was feeding Elizabeth Gaskell's, but life in the
parsonage *was* queer, with the wind 'piping & wailing and sobbing round the
square unsheltered house in a very strange unearthly way' and Mr Brontë still
dining alone though Charlotte was his last child left alive. No wonder she made
a story of it all to Forster:

In the evening Mr Brontë went to his room & smoked a pipe, – a regular
clay – & we sat over the fire & talked, – talked of long ago when that very
same room was full of children; & how one by one they had dropped off
into the church yard close to the windows. At $\frac{1}{2}$ past 8 we went in to prayers,
– soon after nine every one was in bed but we two; – in general there she
sits quite alone thinking over the past; for her eyesight prevents her reading or writing by candle-light, & knitting is but very mechanical, & does
not keep the thoughts from wandering. Each day – I was 4 there – was the
same in outward arrangement – breakfast at 9, in Mr Brontë's room, –
which we left immediately after. What he does with himself through the
day I cannot imagine! He is a tall fine looking old man, with silver bristles
all over his head; nearly blind; speaking with a strong Scotch accent (he
comes from the North of Ireland), raised himself from the rank of a poor
farmer's son, – & was rather intimate with Lord Palmerston at Cambridge,
a pleasant soothing recollection now, in his shut-out life. There was not a
sign of engraving map writing materials &c beyond a desk, no books but
those contained on two hanging shelves between the windows, – his two
pipes & a spittoon, if you know what that is. He was very polite & agreeable
to me; paying rather elaborate old-fashioned compliments, but I was sadly
afraid of him in my inmost soul; for I caught a glare of his stern eyes over

his spectacles at Miss Brontë once or twice which made me know my man; and he talked *at* her sometimes.

He is very fearless; has taken the part of the men against the masters, – or vice versa just as he thought fit & right; & is consequently much respected & to be respected. But he ought never to have married. He did not like children; & they had six in six years, & the consequent pinching & family disorder, – (which can't be helped), and noise &c made him shut himself up & want no companionship – nay be positively annoyed by it. He won't let Miss Brontë accompany him in his walks, although he is so nearly blind; goes out in defiance of her gentle attempts to restrain him, speaking as if she thought him in his second childhood; & comes home moaning & tired, – having lost his way. 'Where is my strength gone?' is his cry then. 'I used to walk 40 miles a-day &c.' There are little bits of picturesque affection about him, – for his old dogs for instance, – when very ill some years ago in Manchester, whither he had come to be operated upon for cataract, his wail was 'I shall never feel Keeper's paws on my knees again!' Moreover to account for my fear – rather an admiring fear after all – of Mr Brontë, please to take into account that though I like the beautiful glittering of bright flashing steel I don't fancy fire-arms at all, at all, – and Miss Brontë never remembers her father dressing himself in the morning without putting a loaded pistol in his pocket, just as regularly as he puts on his watch. There was this little deadly pistol sitting down to breakfast with us, kneeling down to prayers at night – to say nothing of a loaded gun hanging up on high ready to pop off on the slightest emergency. Mr Brontë has a great fancy for arms of all kinds.

The biography was already being written. It would be enormously expanded by deep draughts from the infinite world of talk and anecdote. It would, in particular, be filled with extracts from Charlotte's own letters, because 'her language, where it can be used, is so powerful & living, that it would be a shame not to express everything that can be, in her own words' (303). But ultimately it was Elizabeth Gaskell's creation, informed by her deepest sense of her heroine's suffering and endurance:

To Charles Kingsley, 6 June 1857 (351)
I can only say Respect & value the memory of Charlotte Brontë as she deserves. *No one* can know all she had to go through, but those who knew her well, and have seen her most intimate and confidential letters. The merciful judgment of all connected with that terrible life lies with God; and we may all be thankful that it does.

I tried hard to write the truth. Now Mr W. W. Carus Wilson threatens me with an action. I think I can stand it all patiently. Only do think of her, on, through all. *You do not know what she had to bear; and what she had to bear.*

CHAPTER TEN

Ars longa,
vita brevis

The heavens do not declare the glory of
the Lord; they only tell how long it will
be before the boy will come for the day's
article
(W. J. Fox to Eliza Flower, 1846[1])

IN HIS REVIEW OF *Wives and Daughters*, the last novel, Henry James was
prepared to use the word 'genius', but with the benignly strict qualification that
it was 'little else than a peculiar play of her personal character' – or so he was
'almost tempted to say'. He was, bluntly, right. To which we could add that the
genius capable of fashioning the world of a novel was just as capable of mould-
ing the world of real experience till we can hardly tell fact from fiction,
knowledge from speculation :

To John Forster, 17 May 1854 (195)
There is every chance you will have a long letter; but I'm afraid it will be
a very dull one. For in the first place it is what ought to be sleepy bed-time,
only I am not a bit sleepy; only so *very* sorry, that I could cry with a good
grace, that Mrs Shaen's visit has come & gone all in the brief space of one
day, – what I look forward to all through a long year cut short by this bad
fever that is all about. Do you know 'Jess Macfarlane'? You ought to
know it, it is so pretty; and the some of the words have run in my head all
evening

> When first she came to town
> They ca'éd her Jess Macfarlane
> But now she's come and gane
> They ca' her the *wandering darling.*

And then don't you remember the naïve verse

> I writ my luve a letter
> But alas! she canna read –
> And I like her a' the better.

I am rather afraid I've heard somebody say it is not a proper song; but I don't know why it should not be for all I know of it, and I am sure my two verses are charming & innocent.

Oh! I am afraid this letter is going to be what Dr Holland once called a letter of mine 'a heterogeneous mass of nonsense.' But that was before I wrote Mary B – he would not *say* so now.

Oh! Mr Forster don't you think Mr Chapman has behaved shabbily to me. Not *one* copy has he sent me, though I made it an express stipulation that I should have some to give away, partly because of Mr Gaskell's lectures. Mr Chapman agreed to it; and now I have had to buy those to send off where Mr Gaskell told me! After all you are not coming up to a certain Mr Hibbert who is now reading Mary Barton for the *fourteenth* time. You once took it down – (or *said* you did) to the Isle of Wight, & told me you would read it & tell me what you thought of it, just as you do now, – but the Fates dispersed your plan to empty air. But I *will* flatter myself, & think you *are* reading it over your breakfast. I keep going on – and on – & not coming to what is on my mind, & in my heart to say, – which is simply this. I don't believe one word of what you say about Mr Ruskin. It has given me *great* pain to have the idea, the diabolical idea, suggested, – but I think I do know enough of them to assure myself it is not true. I never *spoke* to him. All I had heard when I wrote was first – from Emily Buxton who knows them pretty well. She said 'you will be sorry to hear that Mrs R[uskin] has gone home to her father; they have had a violent quarrel; but there are shocking & groundless rumours in circulation. We (herself & her husband) were with them at Denmark Hill on the very day, but of course knew nothing of it.' Now I was asked by the Ruskins this very same day to go with the C. Buxtons & Wm Cowpers to see the Turners. Of course I should have liked to have gone but I was here in Manchester; & the message that came afterwards from Mr Ruskin was that if I came up to town *soon* after Easter I was to see them; if not, he & his wife would be abroad in Switzerland till August. You will wonder how he came to ask me – I have known Mrs Ruskin for some time, – she was at the same school as I was – though of course she was much younger. Still we had the bond of many mutual schoolfellows. Now don't think me hard upon her if I tell you what I have *known* of her. She is very pretty very clever, – and very vain. As a girl when she was staying in Manchester her delight was to add to the list of her offers (27 I think she was *at*, then;) but she never cared for any one of them. It was her boast to add to this list in every town she visited just like somebody in the Arabian Nights, who was making up her list of 1000 lovers. *Effie Grey was engaged at the very time she accepted Mr Ruskin* (he did not know of it till after their marriage). I don't think she has any more serious faults than vanity & coldheartedness – not to her own people, nor her father's house, but you know how much suffering they may cause. Four years ago her old schoolmistress prophecied to me the precise end of it all; – just what *I* believe it to have been; that she, with her high temper & love of admiration would not submit to the rather strict rules he insisted upon as to hours &c. This very same lady has been staying with the Ruskins this Xmas, and after spending *a week or 10 days in their house* said that Mr Ruskin was spoiling Effie because he could not bear to thwart her, yet disapproved of all her excess of visiting &c. She said he had a bad temper, & Mrs Ruskin had been spoilt from her childhood – (her next youngest brothers & sisters were swept off by scarlet fever & she was left the only one for some time &c &c) – and that some day she (the schoolmistress) was afraid there wd be an outbreak – Don't you see all the elements for just such an event as that which has taken place? Mrs Wedgwood I know had just the same ideas & the same fears. All I heard till your letter came, was the fact of her having left him & gone to her parents – bad & sad enough, but not *so* terribly bad. I don't mean to say she was ever wrong, but I *know* that he forgave her many scrapes at Venice, and so many stories were told falsely about them – One was that when abroad 2 years ago they travelled in separate carriages. Well! and the reason was this, for I saw some of the letters. He had to write a great deal, & had his carriage fitted up with desk &c, and he told her he should be but a dull companion, so if she liked, he would take another carriage, & she should choose whom she liked to go with her & he would pay all expenses. So she chose a Miss Kerr, a poor Scotch girl, the niece of some friends of mine; who speaks of Mr Ruskin's kindness & tenderness & generosity (of course allowing for his bad temper which every body knows.) & how Mrs Ruskin & she used to enjoy the evngs when they all scrambled into one carriage &c. Now I *know* all this. And while I seem to be throwing blame on Mrs Ruskin I remember her unusually trying position, – so very lovely, – no children, not caring very particularly

for any one but her home-people in Perthshire, & amused as well as flattered by the rapturous admiration she created. But she is gone to her
father's I suppose? I can not bear to think of the dreadful hypocrisy if the
man who wrote those books is a bad man. I almost hoped you might have
contradicted the rumour of the quarrel & her having left him at all.

There! I am afraid I have not been very courteous in my contradiction
of what you have said; but at any rate I have given you my grounds at some
length. Any how I am very very sorry for both of them; & all these
rumours make it so difficult for the simple & natural reconciliation to take
place; each conscious of past faults, & each going to do better. She really
is very close to a charming character; if she had had the small pox she
would have been so. I'm sure you will not repeat what I have said of her.
To make up for my dull letter I enclose you Miss Brontë's announcement
of her marriage-to-be – It is quiet, quaint, & a little formal; but like herself, & meaning the full force of every word she uses. She told me of Mr
Milnes interview with Mr Nicholls, – & of the latter's puzzle to account
for Mr Milnes interest in him. He never for an instant suspected anything;
or my head would not have been safe on my shoulders. To hear her description of the conversation with her father when she quietly insisted on
her right to see something more of Mr Nicholls was really fine. Her father
thought that she had a chance of some body higher or at least farther removed from poverty. She said 'Father I am not a young girl, not a young
woman even – I never was pretty. I now am ugly. At your death I shall
have 300£ besides the little I have earned myself – do you think there are
many men who would serve seven years for me?' And again when he renewed the conversation and asked her if she would marry a curate? – 'Yes
I must marry a curate if I marry at all; not merely a curate but *your* curate;
not merely *your* curate but he must live in the house with you, for I cannot
leave you.' The sightless old man stood up & said solemnly 'Never. I will
never have another man in this house', and stalked out of the room. For a
week he never spoke to her. She had not made up her mind to accept Mr
Nicholls & the worry on both sides made her ill – then the old servant
interfered, and asked him, sitting blind & alone, 'if he wished to kill his
daughter?;' and went up to her and abused Mr Nicholls for not having
'more brass.' And so it has ended where it has done. Since I have seen her
I am more content than this letter made me at first. You will return it to
me, please. I think by way of making my 3 sheets with your one, – which
was very 'nice' (ah! you see I have got to that word quite unconsciously
again,) very interesting, & very kind I must pop in 2 *clever* letters from an
old Parisian friend of mine Madame Mohl; an Orleanist to the back-bone
as you will see, – a friend of Mme Récamier's in days gone by. The

'Emma' she alludes to is a very charming American lady – & that I think is the only allusion that requires explanation. Don't you like reading letters? I do, so much. Not grand formal letters; but such as Mme Mohl's I mean. Is it not clever about Mr Senior & his way of reading books? Please to read my letters instead of Mary Barton one morning at breakfast, & then return all three to me. Oh! Mr Forster if you don't burn my own letters as you read them I will never forgive you! I am vexed with myself for having said that bad about Mrs Ruskin, but I wanted you to understand their position a little more than I thought you did. I have letters from my children daily; all brilliantly well. The panic among the servants still goes on, & will do I suppose till the fever has left the neighbourhood, – and I feel almost selfish to have got the children away, & to be keeping the servants here. Shall I tell you a Cranfordism. An old lady a Mrs Frances Wright said to one of my cousins 'I have never been able to spell since I lost my teeth'. Mr Gaskell is at Dumbleton; going by Oxford to London next week. Mrs Shaen wanted me to return with her on Saturday & give him a surprize; but I am not very sure that he would like it; and besides there's Margaret Hale! I have sent 76 pages to you by Mrs Shaen; all I have written except a very few lines. It is dull; & I have never had time to prune it. I have got the people well on, – but I think in too lengthy a way. But I can still make it good I am sure. I should like to see that French collection of pictures. I shd like to see the Francesca, – & M. Plassan, because you like them – & Rosa Bonheur's because I know her & like her. She is a spirited woman excessively fond of animals & out-door life. One of her pictures, – a man following a plough turning up rich brown ridges under a full shadowless noonday sun is in the Luxembourg, – another still more famous is of horses, – a gathering of wild horses – she thinks that all animals have separate *countenances*, as well as separate ways of expressing passion – & to paint this famous horse picture, she dressed herself as a young man, & went & painted it in the greatest livery stables in Paris. I should think it was one or two o'clock in the morning but one clock is dissolutely wrong, another gone to be cleaned, my watch ditto and I only know I promised you a long letter, & here it is! The house seems so lonely & empty without any of my girls. I am literally alone in it – not even a book to beguile the time – five fathoms deep they lie beneath dust-sheets &c – safe from me & the white washers. Have compassion upon me, sometime; but not to trouble yourself while you are writing about Lord Nugent, & be sure you tell us all you can about his mother. I have done at last.

Yours most truly (I don't like 'sincerely')
E C Gaskell

The flow is irresistible, down to that last dashing parenthesis. 'Reading her letters suggests, singularly, the charm of such a relation with her as would spring from having had occasion to contribute to her pleasure, her rest, her relief', Henry James decided in his book on Story and his friends. 'Clear echoes of a "good time" (as we have lived on to call it) break out in her full, close page; making us ask ourselves what could have been more delightful, in those days, than to be in any degree able to see that she had it.' To ask awkward questions seems in some degree uncouth, but did Ruskin really not know that Effie Gray was 'engaged' when she agreed to marry him? He knew a good deal about her affairs, none of which in any case amounted to a formal engagement. The full story is very odd. Not many marriages are annulled on grounds of non-consummation. Mrs Gaskell's ready sympathy for Ruskin made her rush to his defence, perhaps with a degree of justice but also in a way that allowed her to skirt unpleasant possibilities. At this time she probably did not even realise that Charlotte Brontë had once been passionately fond of a married man, her old teacher in Brussels, the Paul Emanuel of her novel *Villette*. Catherine Winkworth's account of the various conversations at Plymouth Grove about Mr Nicholls ends, 'But I *guess* the true love was Paul Emanuel after all, and is dead; but I don't know, and don't think that Lily knows . . .'[2] Lily suddenly seems a surprisingly apt diminutive for Elizabeth.

Authors who play god so easily in their fictions may go too far in human lives. Her intrigue with Monckton Milnes to obtain an extra stipend for the Reverend Mr Nicholls so that he could afford to marry Charlotte Brontë was successful in its way, but she ran into trouble when she introduced a French refugee to her friends in Manchester on Milnes' recommendation:

To Richard Monckton Milnes, 20 April 1858 (391)
Yesterday I met M. Hallé (the pianist) here. M. Meyer had been introduced to him by Mme Roche: and the Hallés had shown him great kindness on her account. Their house door opens from the outside, and to the left hand of the hall is M. Hallé's private study. He had been writing letters (to friends in Paris among the number,) and left them open in his portfolio when he was summoned to a pupil. No one except Mme Hallé goes into this room in a general way. When the hour of lesson giving was over M. Hallé returned to his letters and his room, & found M. Meyer sitting there writing; having opened the house door himself, walked in, without a person in the house knowing that he was there, turned M. Hallé's letters out of the portfolio – (M. Hallé fears he had read them, but of this there is no proof whatever beyond the general unscrupulousness of the whole action;) and written several letters himself, while waiting for the chance of M. Hallé's return.

Now this is only one instance – I heard it almost in the words I have given it from M. Hallé himself – of similar conduct. No one here knew why he had left Paris, any more than we now know why he returned. He told me that the physicians had recommended change of air for his wife: which was the sole approach to a reason for his coming here that he gave.

Nor can she ever have realised the full breadth and depth of Milnes' activities, which ranged from the openly philanthropic (campaigning with Henry Bright against shipboard floggings, for instance) to the secret and specialised collecting of erotic and sadistic literature. When she visited him at his country house in Yorkshire, Fryston Hall, she was staying at a place he jokingly called Aphrodisiopolis! It was, however, full of distractions:

To Marianne Gaskell, 22 August 1865 (575a)
There was a constant procession of people thro' the house at Fryston – Judges, Marshals, Mr FitzStephen, Mrs Borter & Edith, Mr & Mrs Lowe, Mr Cholmondeley, Sir John Lowther, Mr Kitson (brother to your old schoolfellow) Mr Wickham, Mr & Mrs Parker, Mr Swinburne ('Atlanta in Calydon') Mrs Blackburn & Miss Blackburn, Miss Newton (a cousin of my lords) Mr & Mrs Maurice (rev. F. D.) & all their men & maids. Oh! & School inspectors & three or four clergymen, Dr and Mrs Vaughan etc.

Even Algernon Swinburne, who had made the young American Henry Adams think of 'a tropical bird, high-crested, long-beaked, quick-moving, with rapid utterance and screams of humor, quite unlike any English lark or nightingale', would have seemed just another species amongst legal buzzards and clerical rooks. There would have been quite enough serious talk to counteract his more outrageous utterances. Maurice's pronouncement on this occasion that Lincoln's 'second inaugural was the grandest thing that had been written since the Bible' seems every bit as prophylactic as the Fryston butler's legendary cry of 'Prayers! my Lord!' that rescued an archbishop dying with embarrassment as Swinburne was reading his own poetry at another of these house parties.[3]

Monckton Milnes may have been a bird of paradox, but he assisted in the education of Elizabeth Gaskell as well as that of Henry Adams. His wonderful collection of Blake editions, woodcuts, engravings and original watercolours enabled her to recognise at least the broad kinship of two creative artists whose genius was so foreign to her own:

To George Smith, 25 July 1856 (297)
I have had a very successful visit to Haworth. . . . I came away with the 'Professor' the beginning of her new tale 'Emma' – about 10 pages written

in the finest pencil writing, – & by far the most extraordinary of all, a packet about the size of a lady's travelling writing case, full of paper books of different sizes, from the one I enclose upwards to the full $\frac{1}{2}$ sheet size, but all in this indescribably fine writing. – Mr Gaskell says they would make more than 50 vols of print, – but they are the wildest & most incoherent things, as far as we have examined them, *all* purporting to be written, or addressed to some member of the Wellesley family. They give one the idea of creative power carried to the verge of insanity. Just lately Mr M Milnes gave me some MS. of Blake's, the painter's to read, – & the two MSS (his & C. B's) are curiously alike. But what I want to know is if a photograph could be taken to give some idea of the fineness of writing, – for no words of mine could explain it . . .

Not much is made of all this, either here or in the *Life of Charlotte Brontë*, but at least the tiny writings are not ignored. She is aware that other worlds lie beyond the bounds of her own sensibilities. 'Emily impresses me as something terrific' (347a), she wrote after publication of the *Life*. The bald statement encapsulates the strange power of her account of Emily, opaque though it may be when compared with today's analyses.

Her basic tolerance and humanity combined with the enlargement of sympathies brought about by her travels and experiences :

To Charles Eliot Norton, 25 & 30 October 1859 (444)
I think we got to know Rossetti pretty well. I went three times to his studio, and met him at two evening parties – where I had a good deal of talk with him, always excepting the times when ladies with beautiful hair came in when he was like the cat turned into a lady, who jumped out of bed and ran after a mouse. It did not signify what we were talking about or how agreeable I was; if a particular kind of reddish brown, crêpe wavy hair came in, he was away in a moment struggling for an introduction to the owner of said head of hair. He is not as mad as a March hare, but hair-mad. Well! and then we saw Holman Hunt's picture, & Holman Hunt's self. I am not going to define & shape my feelings & thoughts at seeing either Rossetti's or Hunt's pictures into words; because I *did* feel them deeply, & after all words are coarse things.

She did not contract with age. She always had a welcome for the lively, progressive young and did her best for them :

To George Smith, 6 December 1864 (556)
Do you know two VERY clever people just made one? i.e. John Addington

Symonds, (only son of Dr Symonds of Clifton, whom some people know) who took no end of honours at Oxford, – is witty, clever *really* brilliant, – and Catherine North, daughter of the MP for Hastings even more full of genius, —— well – on their wedding journey they have been writing a paper on Christmas, – which looks to me *very* clever, & Mr Symonds wants to know if it can go into the Cornhill for January (he is a writer in the Saturday by the way, – a *regular* writer.) I have only got it by this *morning*'s post, & will send it on by this *evening*'s; only I knew it was the time for 'making up' the next months Cornhill, – & that not one hour was to be lost, so I write anyhow to catch the morning's post; and will write again on my *own* business in a day or two.

Yours most truly E C Gaskell

'Thoughts on Xmas. In Florence, 1863.'
by John Addington Symonds
110 words in a page
32 pages
3520 words in the whole paper
Mr Symonds took the Newdegate, & a double first. But he *might* be very dull for all that; only he *is* not.

We may again suspect that she did not guess what lay behind this particular marriage. If by any chance she did know, the theme of a man struggling to suppress his own homosexuality would undoubtedly have been 'an unfit subject for fiction'. Her deepest sympathies and profoundest knowledge lay in utterly different directions:

To John Ruskin, 24 February 1865 (562)[4]
And then again about 'Cranford'. I am so much pleased you like it. It is the only one of my own books that I can read again; but whenever I am ailing or ill, I take 'Cranford' and – I was going to say *'enjoy'* it, but that would not be pretty, – laugh over it afresh. And it is true too, for I have seen the cow that wore the grey flannel jacket, and I knew the cat that swallowed the lace, that belonged to the lady, that sent for the doctor, that gave the emetic &c &c.

I am so glad your mother likes it too. I will tell her a bit more of 'Cranford' that I did not dare to put in, because I thought people would say it was too ridiculous, and yet which really happened in Knutsford. Two good old ladies, friends of mine in my girlhood, had a niece who had made a grand marriage, as grand marriages went in those days & that place! (to Sir Ed. Cust.) The bride & bridegroom came to stay with the two Aunts – who had bought a new dining room carpet as a sort of wedding welcome to the young couple. But I am afraid it was rather lost upon them, for the first time they found it out was after dinner the day after they came. All dinner time they had noticed that the neat maid servant had performed a sort of 'pas-de-basque', hopping & sliding with more grace than security to the dishes she held. When she had left the room one lady said to the other, 'Sister! I think she'll do.' 'Yes!' said the other, 'she managed very nicely'.

And then they began to explain that she was a fresh servant, & they had just laid down a new carpet with white spots or spaces on it; and that they had been teaching this girl to vault or jump gracefully over these white places, for fear lest her feet might dirty them. The beginning of 'Cranford' was *one* paper in 'Household Words', – and I never meant to write more; so killed poor Capt Brown, – very much against my will. See what you have drawn down upon yourself, by gratifying me so much – I'll stop now, however.

'I do not know', Ruskin had written, 'when I have read a more finished little piece of study of human nature (a very great and good thing when it is not spoiled). Nor was I ever more sorry to come to a book's end. I can't think why you left it off!' He was even ready with an alternative ending: 'You might have killed Miss Matty, as you're fond of killing nice people, and then gone on with Jessie's children, or made yourself an old lady – in time – it would have been lovely.'

The unconscious irony is very sad. By now the narrator of *Cranford* was an ageing woman, turning back in times of illness to the memories of her youth in a little Cheshire town but bound to satisfy, month by month, the hundred thousand purchasers of the *Cornhill Magazine*. Publishing in the 1860s had become very big business; her own friend George Smith was in the forefront, a great entrepreneur, the 'prince' of nineteenth-century publishers.[5] She could control the course and endings of her stories; her life was subject to innumerable pressures:

To George Smith, 25 July 1864 (553)
Will you advance me 100£ of the payment of 'Wives & Daughters'. I want it to take Meta (& the others too) into Switzerland; but it is on *Meta's* especial account that we go. She has been having the old headaches, and tendency to fainting, – whh is called by the doctors 'nervous exhaustion', and 'utter want of bracing', – and her own and unvarying instinct leads her to wish, almost with yearning, for 'glacier-air'. She was once in that air with Miss Darwin, & was so much the better for it, that though she would quite *agree* to Scotland, yet Minnie & I came to the resolution yesterday, –

when Meta was ill all day long – that we would go to Switzerland, 'coute qui coute' pretty literally.

To George Smith, 6 December 1864 (557)
I accept the offer of 100£ for the copyright of North and South *with thanks*. Only please I don't want the money now; only to know how much I may reckon upon, for the purchase of the (impossible) house. Oh! What a fool I was to let the East Grinstead house slip through my fingers! This is a soliloquy. You see I have not the knack of getting interest for my money. Mr Shaen has 600£ towards the nest egg for the house; but as I *may* want it any day he says it is not worth investing. So will you please keep the 100£ for me?

The economic machine of the great metropolis was to help her protect her family's health. It would also allow her to realise her dream of a life of ease in the south once duty had been done in smoky Manchester. All she had to do was write away furiously, especially at *Wives and Daughters*, for which Smith was to give her £2000 cash, and find *the* house. Her letters record the stresses and strains. She told Norton that during the autumn of 1864 she was so ill that she could hardly leave Plymouth Grove for three months (560). She recovered in the spring but only relatively:

To George Smith, 20 February 1865 (561)
I *believe* about 870 pages of my writing; but it is very difficult to tell. I could make it longer I have so much to say yet; but oh! I am so tired of spinning my brain, when I am feeling so far from strong! However my brains are as nothing to yours! How do you manage! I hate intellect, and literature, and fine arts, and mathematics! I begin to think Heaven will be a place where all books & newspapers will be prohibited by St Peter: and the amusement will be driving in an open carriage to Harrow, and eating strawberries & cream for ever. I must say I expect to have that Roman Emperor with the very long throat (that he wished for on earth) for my companion.

A desperate truth, we now realise, lies within the jest.
In March 1865 she went to stay with Madame Mohl in Paris, where she hoped to have time to write. She found herself surrounded with chatter and besieged by callers. Not surprisingly, 'I broke down in Paris' is the opening of her next but one letter to Smith; and it ends, 'Oh for a house in the country' (565). Ill at Florence's house in London, presumably unable to get back to Manchester, she had to lean upon her eldest daughter:

To Marianne Gaskell, 24 April 1865 (566)

My dearest Polly,

Pray let Jane go as soon as you can get rid of her; even if there is no one to take her place. About Lizzie – I am vexed, for it does not seem as if she had given the true reason. Don't THINK of getting her a silk gown. I had thought of it when I fancied she had injured her health in our service – i.e. in our bad air – . Something from 5s to 10shillings – for a present for her: *not more.* I think your jackets *are* dear; especially as braiding is so out of fashion. But *pray* see that they *fit*; the brown Holland ones last year were *not* well cut – too low in the neck and too tight across shoulders &c. . . . I think Lizzie is leaving for *wages*, whh I would have increased.

Florence does *not* admire her Lamy trimming. *No* morning gowns are trimmed at the bottom in Paris. The *only* kind I saw was like a spiked VV *petticoat* of darker silk below; which was done (*I think*) with *lined* RIBBON – (& got dirty directly I should fancy.) Mme Lamy said she was not trimming any *morning* gowns skirts; and all the *walking* gowns here strike me as *very* long after Paris; tho' their *evening* gowns are longer than English. Florence says the cord wears out directly. *Pray* don't have your skirt trimmed, unless you put the ribbon vandykes – (a good way up –) *not* at the bottom so as to look *loose like a petticoat* do you understand? – *Pray* be careful about Lizzie's making. I did say she should never make a *new* dress again; her seams & sewing are so bad & careless; make her *almost* backstitch the seams, & iron them out flat. I am sorry she is making your gowns. I am so afraid she will spoil them. The green sounds *lovely.* But oh! *don't* let Lizzie spoil them!

To Marianne Gaskell, 25 April 1865 (567)

I think what I would do the most about is Sarah. *After* one Jane is gone, and before the other comes, will you speak to Sarah, before Jessie and tell her I wish her to mind what *Jessie* says to her, about *personal cleanliness, and tidiness in her bedroom*, & that I feel sure from what I know of Jessie that she will always speak kindly to her (*mind you say this* BEFORE JESSIE;) of course she is to receive all directions *about her work* DOWN-STAIRS from the cook; but she is to be willing & grateful for instructions about her *up*stairs work, (study schoolroom steps passage &c) from either Hearn, or Jessie. I hear *Sarah wants new &* LONGER *gowns.* Her large legs seem to have made a great impression; & her *rough manners*, on Florence. Please see after her always being respectful, and nice-mannered. *Her mother is*; & you might tell her how much I was struck with her mother's pretty ways, and gentle voice. And will you ask Hearn to see about her having longer *petticoats*, & *new* dark print gowns, *with frills round the* *neck*, and tidy sleeves &c; as well as some new *lighter* prints – (say lilacs) for Sundays. Will you say *at the very first* to the new Jane, that she is not to go out without letting us know & asking leave of the head of the house at home. That she is NEVER to send Sarah out *after* dark. I am so glad you are sending Amelia to Knutsford on May 1st. I mean (*at present*) to come home at the end of next week (May 6th) or beginning of week after. I always meant to be at home by the time of the change of cooks. But I am thankful never to see Jane again; & I am vexed with Lizzie too. I am so much better today – (owing to a good night, owing to Meta's b – y bottle!!) I am afraid I wrote a grumbling letter yesterday my darling, – I *was* so weak. I had to keep lying down in the midst, & I don't know what I said. I hope your jackets will be very pretty my darling. *Meta likes braiding*, better than beads, so I am very glad they are to be braided; & if she but makes them to fit they will look handsome to the end of the Chapter; a good thing always does.

It is evident that leaning on her daughters was in itself a very complicated operation. Problems were compounded when at length a house was found, at Alton in Hampshire:

To Marianne Gaskell, 22 August 1865 (575a)
I am so very sorry you had all the useless trouble & fatigue of going over to Alton yesterday. I was very ill when I wrote to you 3 weeks ago so I cannot remember if I said positively you were *to go on the 21st* but I *quite* agree that it is better in general to *keep blindly to the words of an agreement*. I am so behindhand with my writing W & D's that I had to write as hard as I could at Fryston (before breakfast & late at night) but I *fancied as I had distinctly said to Thurstan that I wished the Valuer to go down about the White's furniture & settle about that before I went down* & as he *repeated* that in his answer to me as 'most desirable' I suppose I thought that you would understand that as the lists were not forthcoming either to the Whites or to me – the whole thing was delayed *until the valuer had been.* I am sorry enough about it, as it makes me be every day in a state of uncertainty very unfavourable to my powers of writing. I wrote to Thurstan on the *10th* & fancied that all would have been arranged by the 21st. but you know as well as I do the delays which have arisen; first the lists, then Mr White away in York & Mrs White declining to act until his return. I am sick of the whole thing & very much regret that it has all to be settled just now, when I *must* save all my health & strength for writing & have no one to whom I can delegate the acting. I am very sorry indeed for your day yesterday & terribly disappointed that you have seen the house without me.

I was *very* much disappointed at there not being a line from you with the lists; for which thank you dear. I wish you had just asked the question in the envelope about whether – the element of valuation having been introduced into the concern, *after* I had planned to go down on the 21st – it did not make some difference. However it is spilt milk, spilt fatigue & disappointment & money. (By the way are the Kath. Dock dividends due yet? I want them sadly; *& you must want some more money I am afraid?*)

No use worrying you at a distance, & I *am* so badly behindhand in Wives & Daughters. All these worries about Alton do so incapacitate me from writing. Now I must do it all myself – I mean about Alton etc. Indeed I see Thurstan grudged me the time you could have given me & you would have had to return before much of the *work* was done. . . . To-day we have telegraphed to Mr Ewart to ask if Mr White has ever sent for the valuer; as the days are passing on & Papa may come home next week. It is very hot & distressing here. My old sleepless nights have begun again & Julia seems very much out of order; does not touch her breakfast & has constant feeling of sickness & headache. We are going to have the drains up in the yard & see if anything is wrong there. Julia won't hear of going from home but I think she must not be left alone again. She has worried her sweet little self about servants, Papa's letters etc. *As soon as ever* I hear that the valuer has been I shall go. *I shall want the list in Mr White's handwriting* sent to Thurstan because on it *I made my pencil memoranda of what furniture would be wanted.* Florence would come & help me any day & Charlie is only too anxious she should, but I feel that I ought not to take her away from Lady Crompton who has no *woman* but her just now, only all the boys. . . .

When are you coming home? Give us some idea please, you need not be tied to it you know, if any reason turns up etc. *And don't forget the Kath. Docks dividend.* I shall never write up the money for the house I'm afraid. However I'm going to take a tonic (by Meta's & Hearn's compulsion) & see what I can do. I am so sorry to think of your fatigue yesterday love. But *do* write & ask questions when you are not sure. You are doing nothing you know while I am writing hard at my book, & Meta doing the letters etc. of the family. Goodbye darling.

Your own affectionate Mammy

Not only was she writing *Wives and Daughters* this year, she was also contributing gossipy articles to Smith's newly founded *Pall Mall Gazette*. She had, astoundingly, taken up journalism. News and clever *mots* from Paris, a series of letters purporting to have been written by a Dissenting minister who had difficulty in escaping his flock and finding a retired spot where railways had not 'ploughed up the village mind' . . . She must have been able to compose them with hardly a pause for thought, turn life into art that would 'look handsome till the end of the Chapter; a good thing always does'. Her 'particularly well-formed hand' skimmed over the paper:

To Marianne Gaskell, 2 September 1865 (582)

Thursday, after *Meta* had had no letter, she went to Pall Mall, – *they* had had none, & advised us to continue the furnishing by way of having *every* thing made & ready as soon after Sep 29 as *possible*. So again a long *crazing* day of furnishing; going into the City, – far beyond St Paul's out of duty, being told carpets were cheaper there, – but they were coarse common things, not really cheaper, so we came back to Shoolbreds, Meta being rescued (in Wood St Cheapside,) from getting crushed between two immense lorries by a very kind man. Home at 8 – yr letter forwarded by Julia came soon after, – *also* one from Mr Smith (forwarded) to ask for another letter-article for Pall Mall Gaz. *by return* of post – simply impossible – but has to be written *today, before* we go to James Reiss's, ½ p 3 – Oh dear! I *am* nearly killed, but the *stress* of every thing is nearly over. Yesterday Friday mg – I planned to come home in time to go to ½ p. 6 tea at Miss Marslands with Julia, as engaged; & Meta & Hearn were to follow at night, doing kitchen things at Burton's &c first – when, just as I was starting came a note from Mr Enoch to Meta. He had heard from Mr Williams; anonymous ladies had been over the house, liked it, appointed to call on Mr Williams at 3 P M yesterday. I left Meta writing to Mr Enoch to ask whether (to save time, Mr Williams being so dilatory in writing) she had not better go down to Alton to be there *by 3*, see the lady at Mr Wms & get list of *her* furniture if she thought of taking house. You will see from the last letter (which I have just received along with yrs) what Mr Enoch said when he called. Mr Smith can get us 22½ discount on the things – furniture we get off *his* shops, – he ships off so much. I am the less scrupulous since I heard of Wilkie Collins' 5000£. I *must* go & write for the P. M. G. tho' Meta forgets we dine at the James Reiss – we are going that *she* (Meta) may see his unique collection of engravings; one of the rarest in England, that she did so want to see; & what I'm to say I don't know. . . .

Remember this has been our *busiest* week – this over, & I fancy there will be much less to be done; don't *hurry* home, darling. Do get strong in the quiet & good air of Dumbleton. – I *think* we cd spend 3 weeks *stationary* in Switzerland for 60£?? I must however write a great deal more at Wives & Daughters first – My illness (3 weeks from bed to sofa & vice versa – caused by drains I do believe –) threw me terribly behind hand. *Do* take care of yrself. My love to E T H – oh *how* dead I feel! –

E G

Both Hearn & Meta (*in the dusk*) thought the garden *out of order*, & carelessly kept outhouses very untidy.

Such letters are exhausting to read. We might fairly claim that the impression they convey of a fretful, discouraged woman is distorted and ephemeral. Yet wistful sentences surface in letters otherwise full of her usual charm and vivacity, as when she wrote to Charles Norton in the late summer of 1865 about some Americans they had been entertaining: 'We hope they were the forerunners of you all in your turns. But life never flows back, – we shall never again have the old happy days in Rome, shall we?' (583).

For a brief interval life brightened. Her longing for a breath of sea air took her first to Newhaven and then to Dieppe. From there she wrote to Marianne with most of her old gaiety, despite her subjects – a theory why the drains were smelling in Plymouth Grove, the possibility that letters had gone astray through a 'tipsy Crewe butler', Julia's wish to go to Switzerland and so on. She ends quite happily:

To Marianne Gaskell, 6 October 1865 (585)

We have a pleasant sitting room au premier, *two* double-bedded rooms, (one opening out of the sitting room, –) breakfast (coffee bread & butter in our room –) lunch any time we like – chocolate, cold meat, bread & butter Neufchatel Cheese & grapes – in the Salle à manger at a little table, & dinner at the table d'hote (10 persons only 1 gentleman which Julia finds dull –) soup, fish, 2 meats, pudding & desert –) for 9 francs a piece, *service* included. Bougies, wine & fire extras. We are 2 minutes from the sea, & the house is as sweet as a nut. For $\frac{1}{2}$ a franc we can go into the Establissement close at hand, hear a (shocking) out in air band) & read the news. Everything is shutting up for the winter – but the air & sky are splendid, & I feel like a different creature. Our passage here was as smooth as smooth cd be. I shall write to Papa next, – about the drains. No room in this letter.

Yr own dearly loving Mammy.

Such a delightful crossing. I was so sorry when it was over – 'like a lake'.

From Dieppe she went to Rouen so that Julia could see it,[6] and then on to Alton through Boulogne, sending a lilting invitation to Thurstan Holland: 'We can give you bread & cheese & cold meat, and "Alton Ale" & tea & bread & butter & "excellent milk" (Hearn says,) & a hearty welcome. Come sooner if you can. I want all sorts of advice about the garden &c &c – No time for more from your ever affectionate cousin' (587). Even the death of Charles Crompton's father fell into the pattern of country life and ordinary living:

To Marianne Gaskell, 31 October 1865 (588)

But we don't know who to leave in charge of the house when we go? &c &c &c, and you know I'm an old fidget, and if we *don't* let it! – It will be so nice, & so complete. We long for you to see it so much. Every day we like it better & better even in the midst of all the *half* furnished state, painters, & charwomen – Tomorrow, & not till then, these latter will have finished their 5 weeks' cleaning – & then I have engaged a very nice servant (out of place) to come in & cook & clean the rooms we live in. Oh I must tell you something. Last night the ringers rang the 3 church bells, and then came to say they had been ringing for our arrival (we had never heard the bells) & I had to give them 2s–6d. Hearn like it tho'. She seems very well now; I am giving her sherry every day, twice; Oh dear – Mrs Moray, I wonder what I ought to do? I had such a charming note from C[harles] C[rompton] this morning, which I have sent on to Papa. I do think her being of such help to Lady C. just now may draw them together very nicely. I am so sorry to think that we shall never see the dear kind judge again. Charlie proposes that F should come down here for a little time, as he says she is quite knocked up; but of course she could not come just yet. I am going to finish my story while here if I can – but I am constantly called off just now. Only I may as well make use of this waiting time. We have seen none of our neighbours as yet. I am going to sell all the apples we can't give away or eat at 1s–6d a bushel. We like the gardener & his wife very much. They have 7 children & each works very hard, and are very civil. Your most loving mother in the dark.

One problem remained. William Gaskell was still a Manchester man, not in the secret of the 'pretty home awaiting him' in the midst of a rural village down south. But his retirement was not far off and of course, she told Norton, 'in London every one says he will be welcomed as a co-labourer with many of his friends; so that he will not leave off work, tho' he will *lessen* it by the change. $1\frac{3}{4}$ hours will take him to London where his brothers and sister & Florence already are, & where we hope Marianne will be by that time' (583). It was certainly a well-laid plan. And even the poor of Manchester had less need of the Gaskells' many works of charity:

To an unknown correspondent, 1865 (590)

My dear Madam,

I received your fortnightly subscription of 6s. (in stamps), duly in course of post, and beg to return you my best thanks for your kind & continued subscription towards our poor operatives. At the same time I hope I may say that work has now a good deal increased; and, (though many fear that this improvement is only temporary,) that just at present no further contributions are required, as we hope the funds in hand will prove sufficient for some time. If the worst anticipations are realized, and work again becomes scarce, and the funds fall low, I will take the liberty of reminding you of the fact, that if you then like to recommence your kind subscription you may do so. Pray believe me to remain

Yours gratefully & truly

E C Gaskell

No grants had been made from the Cotton Relief Fund since 19 June. The final meeting of its Council was held on 4 December 1865; but by that time Elizabeth Gaskell was dead. She had recovered her good spirits, Thurstan Holland wrote to Norton, and was feeling as well as could be until the very last moment. She fell forward in the middle of a sentence whilst at tea in the drawing room of the new house on 12 November 1865. Her death was sudden and without pain.

To Lady Houghton, Milnes' wife, went a letter from Henry Arthur Bright:[7]

I was at her funeral on Friday. – It was at a quaint old Presbyterian meeting house at Knutsford, (her Cranford you remember), – a meeting house some two hundred years old, with curious outside stairs leading to the galleries; – on the slope of a hill, with a little graveyard round it. –

There were very few there, only Mr. Gaskell and his two brothers, his son-in-law, and future son-in-law young Holland; – and then some few friends from Manchester, – and Hamilton Aidè, who had walked across from Tatton.

'Was it not fit that she shd be buried there?' Thurstan had asked Norton. Retrospectively, it was. It was just as fit that two young people she had once helped, Bright and Aïdé, should appear. She had so often been a great force for life:

March 7th 1859

My dear Mrs Gaskell

If you please we want to be congratulated, told that we are charming people, quite sure to be happy, worthy of one another and as many other

159

pleasant truths as you can think of. Julia with a bit of cats tail and Meta have not half done us justice and we appeal confidently to you – tell us that our wedding cake is admirable, that our little country wedding is the beau ideal of weddings and we shall be so pleased and believe every word of it – and then we will tell you how pleased we are that mama's book should have been accepted just at the same time and that your kindness should have been the means of procuring this extra happiness and we will say how grateful Mama is to you and how proud of the cheque Mr Smith has already sent her and we shall all be happy and charming and your very affectionate friends

Annie
Fleeming $\Big\}$ Jenkin.

Elizabeth Gaskell's character can be discovered in the letters she received as well as in those she sent. Fleeming Jenkin and his bride were supremely confident that she would delight in their 'pretty *walking* country-wedding' (418) and rejoice to hear that George Smith had accepted Mrs Henrietta Jenkin's West Indian novel, *Cousin Stella*, for publication. Perhaps the reflection we see in this letter is too flattering, but it is not far from the truth and is a portrait that her contemporaries would have recognised without difficulty. Charlotte Brontë, just, kind and penetrating, can speak for them: [8]

Thank you for your letter; it was as pleasant as a quiet chat, as welcome as spring showers, as reviving as a friend's visit; in short, it was very like a page of 'Cranford.' . . .

A thought strikes me. Do you, who have so many friends, – so large a circle of acquaintance, – find it easy, when you sit down to write, to isolate yourself from all those ties, and their sweet associations, so as to be your *own woman*, uninfluenced or swayed by the consciousness of how your work may affect other minds; what blame or what sympathy it may call forth? Does no luminous cloud ever come between you and the severe Truth, as you know it in your own secret and clear-seeing soul? In a word, are you never tempted to make your characters more amiable than the Life, by the inclination to assimilate your thoughts to the thoughts of those who always *feel* kindly, but sometimes fail to *see* justly? Don't answer the question; it is not intended to be answered.

NOTES

Introduction

1 Numbers in parenthesis are those assigned to letters printed in *The Letters of Mrs Gaskell*, ed. J. A. V. Chapple and Arthur Pollard (Manchester 1966).
2 The text of Letter 217 has been emended from a more complete copy in the Symington Collection, Leeds City Archives Department.
3 See Ellen Moers, *Literary Women* (1977), 14, 22, 290.
4 Letter 13. Sam Gaskell struck others as being 'a thoroughly good, clever fellow' (H. S. Solly, *The Life of Henry Morley*, 1898, 215) and 'delightfully cracky' (*Letters and Memorials of Catherine Winkworth*, I. 183).

Chapter 1

1 Copies of letters from John Stevenson, William Stevenson and Jane Byerley are in the collection of J. G. Sharps, who also possesses the original of John Stevenson's letter of 30 July [1828].
2 See J. A. Sutherland, *Victorian Novelists and Publishers* (1976), 10–11, 43–4.
3 See F. W. Fetter, 'The economic articles in *Blackwood's Edinburgh Magazine*, and their authors, 1817–1853', *Scottish Journal of Political Economy* 7 (1960), 89, 103, 217; A. L. Strout, *A Bibliography of Articles in 'Blackwood's Magazine', 1817–1825* (Lubbock, Texas 1959), 179.
4 Item 425, Plymouth Grove Sale Catalogue, 1914 (Manchester Central Public Library copies), states that Gray's *Works* (1821) were presented to her by William Gaskell on 2 August 1825; but this is very early, only two years after a similar gift of Cowper's *Poems* by her father and step-mother (item 504).
5 William Gaskell's widowed mother married the Reverend E. R. Dimock, Unitarian minister in Warrington 1822–41.
6 Swinton Colthurst Holland's will, dated 17 November 1827, was proved at London on 28 February 1828 (P.R.O., PROB 11/1736 6485). He had purchased the Dumbleton estate in June 1823 (Hereford & Worcester R.O., Ref 705 : 139 BA 8397/109 and 107 i). See also Keele University Library, Wedgwood MS. E58–32354, for a visit Elizabeth made to Swinton in about 1822, when she met her Wedgwood connections, then undergraduates at Cambridge.

7   *A French Sociologist Looks at Britain: Gustave d'Eichthal and British Society in 1828*, ed. B. M. Ratcliffe and W. H. Chaloner (Manchester 1977), 66–9.

8   Unpublished letter in the Brontë Parsonage Museum, Haworth. We have not been able to consult a number of early letters sold at Sotheby's on 13 December 1977, but the earliest date given in the Sale Catalogue is 18 June 1831.

9   The records of the Church of the Divine Unity, Newcastle, contain a useful scrapbook devoted to this event and various Turner manuscripts, including his register of baptisms.

10 R. J. Morris, *Cholera 1832* (1976), 16, 60–1, 65–6.

11 See manuscript letters to William Turner in the Library of the Newcastle Literary and Philosophical Society: from J. A. Turner, 27 May 1834; from Ann Turner, 21 May [pre-1841].

12 H. McLachlan, *Records of a Family 1800–1933* (Manchester 1935), 119–20.

Chapter 2

1   Unpublished letter in the Newcastle Literary and Philosophical Society Library.

2   List of donors in *Transactions of the Unitarian Historical Society* 8 (1944), 57.

3   Item 205 in Plymouth Grove Sale Catalogue: *Works* of S[amuel] D[exter] Bradford. He was a graduate of Harvard.

4   It was perhaps submitted to J. R. Beard's magazine, *The Christian Teacher*, in the first instance, but not printed. See II (1836), 64.

5   Leon Faucher, *Manchester in 1844* (1844, facs. edn. 1969), 16, 21–2.

6   Robert Vaughan, *The Age of Great Cities* (2nd edn. 1843, facs. edn. 1969), 143.

7   Harold Perkin, *The Origins of Modern English Society 1780–1880* (1969), 252–70.

8   Unpublished letter in the Pierpont Morgan Library, New York.

9   The *Warrington Guardian* (30 November 1861) records his retirement.

10 Letter 16 now dated 1840. Harriet Martineau's *The Hour and the Man* was being reviewed in early December. See R. K. Webb, *Harriet Martineau: a Radical Victorian* (1960), 191, n.4.

11 H. Gaskell obituary in the *Liverpool Daily Post and Mercury*, [Early March 1909]; see also R. Dickinson, 'James Nasmyth and the Liverpool Iron Trade', *Transactions of the Historic Society of Lancashire and Cheshire* 108 (Liverpool 1957), 95–104.

Chapter 3

1 Quoted by F. E. Mineka, *The Dissidence of Dissent: 'The Monthly Repository'*, *1806–1838* (Chapel Hill 1944), 302.

2 Edmund Potter, *A Picture of a Manufacturing District* (London and Manchester 1856), 24; Perkin, *Origins*, 228.

3 See A. Prentice, *History of the Anti-Corn-Law League* (2 vols 1853), *passim*; Faucher, *Manchester*, 147–8; N. McCord, *The Anti-Corn Law League 1838–46* (2nd edn 1968), 99. (The *Manchester Times* for 5 June 1841 gives 2 June as the date of the Stevenson Square fracas.)

4 See E. G. Franz, 'Heidelberg und Heppenheim in Erzählungen und Briefen der englischen Schriftstellerin Elizabeth Gaskell', *Archiv für hessische Geschichte und Altertumskunde*, n.s. 32 (Darmstadt 1974), 487–9.

5 See Prentice, *History*, I.235 *et seq.*; *Manchester Times* 21 August, 4 and 11 December 1841, 5 February 1842.

6 See J. Drummond and C. B. Upton, *The Life and Letters of James Martineau* (1902), I.178–9.

7 *Letters and Memorials of Catherine Winkworth* [henceforth *L&M*], I.60, 62.

8 See J. Estlin Carpenter, *James Martineau* (1905), 157–64, 263–9, 281–2, 342 n.; Drummond and Upton, *Martineau*, I.117.

9 The early letters do not appear to have survived, but they are mentioned in the unpublished letter to Fanny Holland (Brotherton Collection, Leeds University Library) from which we quote on page 35.

10 *L&M*, I.107.

11 Carpenter, *Martineau*, 287; F. W. Newman, Preface (p. xiii) to translation of V. A. Huber, *The English Universities* (1843); *L&M*, II.391–2.

12 *L&M*, I.157; Jane Carlyle quoted by Carpenter, *Martineau*, 260.

13 See *L&M*, I.144, 113; R. L. Patten, *Charles Dickens and His Publishers* (Oxford 1978), 228–35. A number of nephews, including a William Rothwell Gaskell and a William Broadbent Gaskell, benefited directly under Holbrook Gaskell's will, dated 23 November 1838 and proved at London on 31 March 1842 (P.R.O., PROB 11/1959 6498). However, these were second cousins.

Chapter 4

1 *L&M*, I.203.

2 Drummond and Upton, *Martineau*, II.297.

3 *L&M*, I.275, 370.

4 *L&M*, I.146; *A History of the Family of Holland*, coll. E. S. Holland, ed. W. F. Irvine (privately printed, Edinburgh 1902), 79 *et seq.*
5 See Solly, *Morley*, 115, 119, 123 and 226. Morley, who became Professor at University College London, wrote *Palissy the Potter* (1852).

Chapter 5

1 Keele University Library, Wedgwood MSS., Mosley Collection.
2 Carpenter, *Martineau*, 158–60; *L&M*, I.139n.; *Grove's Dictionary* (5th edn), *sub* Zengheer, Jakob.
3 Keele University Library, Wedgwood MS. E58.32354, annotation.
4 *L&M*, II.109 *et seq.*, especially 137–40; 'Snow' Wedgwood to K. E. Wedgwood, 12 July 1857, and Mary Rich to K. E. Wedgwood, p.m. 6 August 1857 (Keele U.L., Wedgwood MSS., Mosley Collection).
5 Webb, *Harriet Martineau*, 200.

Chapter 6

1 R. and E. Garnett, *The Life of W. J. Fox: Public Teacher and Social Reformer 1786–1864* (1910), 311–12. Bridell died of consumption in August 1863.
2 The autograph letter is in Rutgers University Library, New Brunswick. See A. B. Hopkins, *Elizabeth Gaskell: her Life and Work* (1952), 368–9.
3 *L&M*, II.120, 126, 129, 132; J. R. S. Leslie, *Henry Edward Manning* (1921), 123. See also unpublished letters to Mrs Gaskell from Henry Bishop and Aubrey de Vere in the John Rylands University Library, Manchester.
4 'Miss Gaskell' brought a letter from one of the Storys to Browning. Henry James, *William Wetmore Story and His Friends* (1903, facs. edn. n.d.), II.115.
5 See J. R. Beard, *The Confessional; a View of Romanism in its Actual Principles, Aims and Workings* [1860], pp. iii–iv. In 1850 J. G. Robberds preached a sermon against Popery at Cross Street Chapel.
6 See the long obituary in the *Gloucester Journal*, 9 January 1875.
7 The Houghton Library at Harvard University contains a number of relevant letters from the Gaskell daughters to C. E. Norton and his family.

Chapter 7

1 Norton letter quoted by Kermit Vanderbilt, *Charles Eliot Norton: Apostle of Culture in a Democracy* (Cambridge, Mass. 1959), 49.

2 Letter 100 redated from George Richmond's *Diary* (photostat copy, National Portrait Gallery Archives).
3 *L&M*, I.272–3.
4 *L&M*, I.332.
5 Catherine Winkworth wrote on 22 November 1852 that Mrs Gaskell 'is much impressed with the calm, leisurely, thoughtful, refined life of the houses where she has been staying [in the Lakes], and is full of plans for introducing it at home' (*L&M*, I.369).
6 Letter 564 corrected against autograph original, now in Brontë Parsonage Museum, Haworth.
7 Unpublished letter to E. E. Hale, 14 December 1860, in the Sophia Smith Collection, Smith College, Northampton, Mass.
8 See *L&M*, II.120 *et seq.*
9 J. Ruskin, *Praeterita*, ed. K. Clark (1949), III.2.46; Vanderbilt, *Norton*, 37–42, 47, 58–64. Hawthorne writes of Italy as 'a sort of poetic or fairy precinct' in his preface to *The Marble Faun* (1860).
10 For Crossley see M. A. Smith, 'Autograph letters', *The Manchester Review* 11 (1967), 100–1.
11 See Franz, 'Heidelberg und Heppenheim', 500.
12 Wallace Stevens, 'The man with the blue guitar', IV. 9; Arthur Pollard, *Mrs Gaskell: Novelist and Biographer* (Manchester 1965), 254.
13 Quoted from Vanderbilt, *Norton*, 38.

Chapter 8

1 Quoted from Steven Marcus, *Engels, Manchester, and the Working Class* (1974), 169.
2 See M. A. Nickel, 'The dating of a Mrs. Gaskell letter', *Notes & Queries*, March 1975.
3 Norris Pope, *Dickens and Charity* (1978), 126, 33.
4 For John Blackmore see A. Easson, *Elizabeth Gaskell* (1979), 112–13.
5 W. O. Henderson, *The Life of Friedrich Engels* (1976), 201–6, 211, 216.
6 Letter 630 dated by reference to Letters 446a and 447, and *L&M*, II.233, 288, though the date is far from certain.
7 Henderson, *Engels*, 213–14. Eight letters to Lushington are printed for the first time by H. W. McCready in *Transactions of the Historic Society of Lancashire and Cheshire* 123 (Liverpool 1972), 144–50.

Chapter 9

1 Elaine Showalter, *A Literature of Their Own: British Women Novelists*

from Brontë to Lessing (Princeton, N.J. 1977), 55; V. Wheatley, *The Life and Work of Harriet Martineau* (1957), 376.

2 *L&M*, I.127.

3 *L&M*, I.472.

4 In 1852, when revising the last hundred pages of *Ruth* with Catherine Winkworth (*L&M*, I.370).

5 See the substantial article by Anne Henry Ehrenpreis, 'Elizabeth Gaskell and Nathaniel Hawthorne', *Nathaniel Hawthorne Journal* 1973.

6 Meta's letter is in the Bibliothèque de l'Institut de France, Paris.

7 Garnett, *Fox*, 167, 189–90; Wheatley, *Martineau*, 194–5, 370; Webb, *Harriet Martineau*, 99.

8 *The George Eliot Letters,* ed. G. S. Haight, III (1954), 198–9. Collated with the autograph original in the John Rylands University Library, Manchester.

9 Letter 166 corrected against incomplete autograph original in the Brotherton Collection, Leeds University Library.

Chapter 10

1 Garnett, *Fox*, 286.

2 Mary Lutyens, *The Ruskins and the Grays* (1972), 65–8; *L&M*, I.440.

3 See James Pope-Hennessy, *Monckton Milnes: the Years of Promise* (1949), 84; *Monckton Milnes: the Flight of Youth* (1951), 114, 139–45, 151, 194. Meta Gaskell reported Maurice's saying in an unpublished addition to Letter 583.

4 Letter 562 corrected against photostat of the original in the Houghton Library at Harvard.

5 Sutherland, *Victorian Novelists and Publishers*, 43.

6 Meta to C. E. Norton, 24 November [1865] (Houghton Library MS.)

7 Ehrenpreis, 'Elizabeth Gaskell and Nathaniel Hawthorne', 113–14, prints the Bright letter. The manuscript letter from Annie and Fleeming Jenkin is in The Houghton Library, Harvard University.

8 Charlotte Brontë to Elizabeth Gaskell, 9 July 1853, quoted in the *Life* (1857), II.295.

TABLE OF DATES

1797—1 Dec.   William Stevenson married Elizabeth Holland

1798—27 Nov.   John Stevenson born; died *c.* 1828

1805—24 July   William Gaskell born at Latchford near Warrington

1810—29 Sept.   ELIZABETH STEVENSON born at 12 Lindsey Row, Chelsea

1811—Oct.   Mother died; Elizabeth sent to her aunt, Mrs Hannah Lumb (*née* Holland), of The Heath, Knutsford

1814—   William Stevenson married Catherine Thomson; two children

1823–9—   William Stevenson had severe financial problems

1829—22 Mar.   Father died; stepmother and her children moved to Scotland in September

1829–32—   A round of visits: Knutsford, Dumbleton, Newcastle, Edinburgh, Woodside and Manchester

1832—30 Aug.   Married William Gaskell at Knutsford

1833—? 4 July   Daughter still-born

1834—12 Sept.   Marianne Gaskell born; diary of progress started 10 March 1835

1837—Jan.   'Sketches Among the Poor. No. 1' published in *Blackwood's Magazine*

—5 Feb.   Margaret Emily Gaskell born

1838—Summer   'Clopton Hall' sent to William Howitt; printed 1840

1842—7 Oct.   Florence Elizabeth Gaskell born

1844—23 Oct.   Son, William Gaskell, born; died 10 August 1845

1846—3 Sept.   Julia Bradford Gaskell born

1847—   *Mary Barton* sent to printer; published October 1848

—5 June   'Life in Manchester: Libbie Marsh's Three Eras' begun in *Howitt's Journal*

1850—31 Jan.   Dickens requested a story; 'Lizzie Leigh' begun in *Household Words* on 30 March

1850—20 Aug.   First met Charlotte Brontë

1850—Dec.   *The Moorland Cottage* published

1851—13 Dec.   *Cranford* begun in *Household Words*

1853—Jan.   *Ruth* published

1854—2 Sept.   *North and South* begun in *Household Words*

1855—16 June   Asked to write *Life of Charlotte Brontë*; published March 1857

1857—June   ME engaged to Captain Charles Hill

1858—19 June   *My Lady Ludlow* begun in *Household Words*

TABLE OF DATES

1859—*c.* Dec.   Began to write *Sylvia's Lovers*
1861—12 Apr.   Outbreak of American Civil War
1862—Autumn and Winter   Lancashire Cotton Famine at peak
1863—20 Feb.   *Sylvia's Lovers* published
1863—Mar.   FE engaged to Charles Crompton; married 8 September
  —Nov.   *Cousin Phillis* begun in *Cornhill Magazine*
1864—July   MA engaged to E. Thurstan Holland
  —Aug.   *Wives and Daughters* begun in *Cornhill Magazine*
1865—Apr.   Fell ill in Paris
  —*c.* July   Bought house called 'The Lawn' at Alton, Hampshire
  —12 Nov.   Died there
1866—14 Aug.   MA married E. Thurstan Holland
1884—11 June   William Gaskell died in Manchester

INDEX

This is a selective index. Relatively unimportant and very frequent references have been ignored; the many letter headings have not been indexed. A few details that supplement standard works have been inserted.